To Frank
from Nancy
— Christmas 2012

(You will know some of the
people mentioned herein.)

BISON
BOOKS

D1414027

RON HULL

BACKSTAGE

Stories from My Life in Public Television

University of Nebraska Press / Lincoln and London

Library of Congress
Cataloging-in-Publication Data
Hull, Ronald Eugene, 1930–
Backstage: stories from my life
in public television / Ron Hull.
p.   cm.
ISBN 978-0-8032-4066-7
(pbk.: alk. paper)
1. Hull, Ronald Eugene, 1930–
2. Television producers and directors—
United States—Biography. 3. Television
broadcasting—United States—Biography.
4. College teachers—United States—
Biography. 5. Television broadcasting—
United States—History—20th century.
6. Public television—United States—
History—20th century. I. Title. II. Title:
Stories from my life in public television.
PN1992.4.H77A3 2012
791.4302'32092—DC23
[B]
2012003448

Set in Sabon by Bob Reitz
Designed by A. Shahan.

To Naomi, who has been with me all the way

CONTENTS

ACKNOWLEDGMENTS

Several people deserve thanks: My wife, Naomi, and our children, Kevin, Brian, Brandon, and Kathryn. Four irreplaceable friends: Howard A. Dinsdale, MD, Robert E. Knoll, PHD, J. Michael Lawlor, and Jack G. McBride. Rod Bates, general manager of Nebraska Educational Telecommunications, who gave me a career after retirement. Virginia Faulkner, former University of Nebraska Press editor, who encouraged me to write this book. Heather Lundine, former University of Nebraska Press acquisitions editor, for her support and "green-lighting" this project. Bridget Barry, University of Nebraska Press associate acquisitions editor, for her encouragement and thoughtful suggestions throughout the editing process. The employees of Nebraska Educational Telecommunications for making NET the important Nebraska institution it has become in service to the people of our state.

1

Where the West Begins in the Middle of . . .

The plane, shakily lurching through the sky, was obviously landing. But where? The forbidding snow-covered mountains and frozen ground could only mean a crash landing in this unknown place. Riveted with fear, I clutched my mother's arm as I edged closer to her seat in the State Theatre of Rapid City, South Dakota, and witnessed the power of movie storytelling.

I was seven years old, and this, the first movie I can remember, was the 1937 Columbia Pictures film *Lost Horizon*, starring Ronald Coleman and Jane Wyatt. This motion picture magically opened the door to my imagination. Though some of the scenes reputedly were filmed in an ice-making plant in Los Angeles, I believed every detail of that story about the Valley of the Blue Moon somewhere in the mountains of Tibet, and I've been searching for Shangri-la ever since.

I was close in May 2006 when I boarded the Trans-Mongolian Railway in Beijing, China, and headed northwest past miles of the Great Wall, topping the mountains like the spikes on a dragon's back, on north through the Gobi desert to Ulaanbaatar, Mongolia, the first stop on the way to Moscow, Russia.

Vast expanses of blowing sands, herds of wild horses running zigzag through the dunes and valleys, sheep, deer, and camels wandering aimlessly not far from the compartment window, and scattered bones of animals that had not seen the trains during the night: all of it provided a continuing, fascinating show.

But this was not the best part of the trip. The best part was the people on the train. There is a short-lived, but nevertheless real, culture that begins to form as the train leaves the station. We were people of every size, shape, color, nationality, and ethnicity—a microcosm of the world—each with a fascinating life story we were eager to share over wine in the dining car with its elaborate wood-carved decorations .

This Trans-Mongolian train also afforded time to think, to read, to recall. The gentle swaying of the train, the low hum of the wheels smoothly skimming the rails, lulled me into a welcome, contented state of mind. Triggered by the fascinating world unfolding just outside my window, this, like Shangri-la, afforded a mental journey and a time for looking back.

I closed my eyes and the Trans-Missouri country came in view.

From the wide Missouri to the foothills of the Rockies there is a beautiful stretch of land called Nebraska. Willa Cather accurately described it: "To the east a cornfield that stretched to daybreak; to the west a corral that reached to sunset." Or as another writer put it, "Nebraska is the land where the west begins in the middle of." And it does. The farmers are to the east, the ranchers and cowboys to the west.

This land has nurtured a hardy, resourceful, independent people. The first flood of immigrants came in the 1870s as homesteaders, farmers, ranchers, cattlemen, Czechs, Germans, Jews, French, Poles, Swedes, and African Americans. Land was the magnet they came for—land of their own.

Over the years, and out of these ranks, came some highly individual people: Roscoe Pound, dean of the Harvard Law School,

George Norris, father of the Tennessee Valley Authority, Willa Cather, Marlon Brando, Fred Astaire, Sandy Dennis, Dick Cavett, Johnny Carson, Loren Eiseley, John Neihardt, William Jennings Bryan, and Mari Sandoz. These scientists, politicians, actors, comedians, and writers, each fiercely independent, creative people, brought the Midwest ethic of honesty and hard work to their careers.

Nebraska has always had a bad press. It started back in the nineteenth century when early explorers, military people, and even a Russian grand duke who came to hunt buffalo proclaimed that this land would never support agriculture. About that time, spread across the maps of the region, were the words "the great American desert." Hollywood used to portray Nebraskans as "hicks," and even today many Americans, particularly along the northeastern seaboard, still ask if we are afraid of the Indians. It takes a long time to change perceptions of a place. I was reminded of this when President Jimmy Carter appointed me to the "President's Advisory Committee on the Arts for the John F. Kennedy Center for the Performing Arts." Every president uses this presidential commission to create an advisory committee to the Kennedy Center.

One piece of correspondence concerning this appointment that reached my desk was, I feel sure, a clerical mistake from the White House. Accompanying the appointment letter was a second piece of paper and on it were listed four of the new members of the commission. We all understand that racial and ethnic considerations are important, but this added a new dimension to political correctness. The paper listed four names (for obvious reasons the first three names are fictitious):

Ms. Marvel Washington (Black)
Mr. Jose Guiterrez (Hispanic)
Ms. Kathleen Wu (Asian)
Mr. Ron Hull (Nebraska)

Apparently we Nebraskans are an ethnic group all our own.

We call ourselves Cornhuskers, and you will find us loyal to the state's history and culture passed down to us by the explorers, adventurers, Native Americans, pioneers, cowboys, and all the others who came here and made this a unique and special place. The people make it so; they have a sense of honesty and fair play that they learned the hard way. To survive in Nebraska, neighbors had to help each other through blizzards, drought, prairie fires, rattlesnakes, heat, cold, and wind—the harsh and sometimes cruel forces of nature. Nebraskans know how to work, expect to, and teach this to their children.

Nebraska and stories of its people are central to many of the pages that follow, and though I consider myself a Cornhusker, this is my adopted home. Life for me began in the much less sophisticated territory north of Nebraska, in the Black Hills of South Dakota.

2

The Mystery in Grandmother's Trunk

Calamity Jane, Wild Bill Hickok, Potato Creek Johnny, Deadwood, the gold rush, the magnificent scenic wonders of the Black Hills, and the legends and stories of the real West were all there waiting for me when I was born in Rapid City, the Gateway to the Black Hills, in the early 1930s. To be precise, May 30, 1930.

Of course, growing up there, I couldn't wait to leave. The remoteness of the place, its quiet, laid-back lifestyle, the rough-edged, matter-of-fact, unpretentious, hardy people were values I had not yet learned to appreciate.

Though our access to art and culture was limited by a sparse population hundreds of miles from any community over seventy thousand people, we did have the movies. Like 80 percent of the population at that time, I went to the movies twice a week. The new pictures opened on Sunday (I couldn't go on Sundays—we were Methodists) and ran through Tuesday. The reruns came in on Wednesday and ran through Saturday.

The first row of the balcony at the Elk's Theatre was the best seat in the house because no one could come between you and the screen. Every Friday night friends and I would sit in our favorite seats with great anticipation. During the World War II years we scanned the audience, curious to see which airman from the local air base had accompanied Miss Biglin, our very attractive social studies teacher, to the movie. Music would play, the curtain would open, and the screen would seductively inhale me into an exciting world of storytelling.

Growing up with no brothers or sisters in the 1940s, I turned to movies as my refuge, and the beautiful people in those improbable stories irrevocably conditioned my life. Those films shaped my attitudes of what it means to be a man, to be an American. My relationships with women, even with God, were shaped by Louis B. Mayer at Metro-Goldwyn-Mayer, the Warner Brothers of Burbank, and Daryl Zanuck at Twentieth Century Fox among others.

Mr. Mayer's Greer Garson was the ideal of womanhood, and all of us seventh graders knew from *Mrs. Miniver* that she saved England during World War II. Betty Grable looked delicious in the musicals she made at Fox, combining limited acting and singing, great dancing, and great legs with a beautiful, innocent-looking face that Technicolor and I loved.

John Payne (Grable's sometime costar), Jimmy Stewart, and Errol Flynn embodied the qualities I most admired in men—charm, sincerity, and bravado. These stars were important waymarks in my life, and I remember them with affection. In spite of their sometimes ridiculous film vehicles and the shallow treatment of important subjects, I am indebted to these stars for instilling within me the realization of the possibilities of having a wonderful life. Thanks to them, I fully expected to.

Recalling some of my favorite films of the 1940s, such as *How Green Was My Valley* with Roddy McDowall and Walter Pidgeon or *Random Harvest* starring Greer Garson and Ronald Coleman, brings back deep emotional feelings—not just memories of the films themselves but vivid, relived moments of my life at that time, which rise up, like *Brigadoon*, through the mists of my memory.

Though I dreamed of being one of those heroes of the silver screen, I had no understanding of the sacrifices, the singular focus, the ferocious drive, or the work and talent required. I have ambition, drive, focus, and some talent, but the movies, as it turned out, were not the avenue to my dreams.

Rather, the potential of television was the call I answered. To me, broadcasting is a calling, like acting or any of the arts. It's something I knew I had to do, I didn't question it, and I vigorously pursued it. Broadcasting is all about storytelling, and for me, reading literature and discovering the power of words was the first step.

While reading Shakespeare's *Othello* in high school, our teacher, Miss Moses, referring to the duplicity of Iago, said, "Do you see how each of us has the power, for good or ill, to affect other people's lives?" That thought became a permanent part of me. Many times someone has said something to me that has made my spirit soar, and at other times words have literally closed me down.

I owe Miss Moses an enormous debt of gratitude for teaching English literature at Rapid City High School. She made reading Shakespeare an exciting experience. Her advice was, "Just start reading, and even though you don't always get it, keep going. Let the words of Shakespeare wash over you. Soon it will all make sense, you'll see." She was right, and she gave me a lifelong love for Shakespeare's plays.

During this time I came across information that could have been a part of one of his dramatic plots.

In 1945, at age fifteen, I made an accidental and important discovery.

During the winter months, we were living in a fifty-year-old faintly Victorian house in Rapid City that during the war had been converted into four apartments, two up and two down.

The downstairs apartments each had a bathroom, but on the second floor the tenants shared a bath located directly at the top of the stairs between the two apartments that had once been four upstairs bedrooms.

Our apartment was considered a notch above the others because we not only had a private bathroom but we were also the one family in the building that could afford a telephone. Since this was during World War II, the other quarters were usually occupied by servicemen and their wives and babies. Our phone got quite a workout by pregnant women calling taxis to take them to the hospital, or calling their families across the country with news that their husbands were being shipped overseas, or sometimes saying, in emotional whispers, that the husband wouldn't be coming back and could she come home?

It was a busy place, filled with active and dramatic lives, and for me, for the most part, 716 Fourth Street was a happy place. My parents paid thirty-five dollars a month rent, and part of each year it was home for my grandmother.

My parents had a modest house in the Black Hills, just outside Rapid City, where they loved to live during the good weather. When winter came and I was in school, they moved back into town. My grandmother would trade places with them, and as my parents were moving back into the apartment my grandmother was moving out. On one occasion she asked me to go down in the basement to help with the packing of her big trunk.

As we were going through her things I noticed an envelope containing a heavy card with formal printing. It was a birth announcement heralding the arrival of Ronald Eugene Hull and containing the usual statistics. Except . . . on the back of the card were the words written in ink, "Adopted son of Mr. and Mrs. Darrell C. Hull."

Adopted? I had never heard the slightest suggestion or hint—nor had any inkling—of such a thing. If this were true, my family had kept a secret extremely well. I stared at the card and then, somewhat puzzled, handed it to my grandmother. She looked at it, and with a rush of words said, "I have no idea what this is about; it doesn't mean anything. I can't imagine . . ." And with that she threw it back in the trunk and closed the lid, declaring that that was enough packing for one day, and taking me by the arm we proceeded upstairs. I am confident this was the only lie she had ever told in her life.

In the ensuing weeks and months, I thought about this possible revelation constantly, but I never had the courage to ask my parents about it. Finally, I confided in Conny Coffield, my best friend. I took some pictures, three or four of my mother, some of my father and some of me, and I laid them all out on the kitchen table side by side.

"Okay, Conny, tell me. Do I look like my mother or my father?"

Conny looked at the pictures, and far too quickly to suit me, said, "Neither one. You're adopted." Mercilessly abrupt.

"Come on," I countered, "Look closely. I kinda look like my dad, don't you think?"

Shaking his head, Conny replied, "Nope. Not at all. You're adopted."

But how could I find out for sure without the fearful pain of asking my parents?

Conny and I decided to go to the records division at the courthouse. We told the county clerk that we were on a school assignment to look up our birth records and then report back to the class about how these records are kept. Our ruse worked.

Conny went first and gave his birth date, November 22, 1930. The clerk opened the ledger and looked up and down the columns. Then, pointing, he said, "Sure enough, boys, right here it is."

And there it was: Conrad E. (his middle name was Eugene also) Coffield, November 22, 1930, Pennington County, South Dakota, with his parents' names listed.

Then, as casually as I could, I said, "Now look me up."

The clerk went to the H's and went up and down and down

this row and up that row and back down this row and up that row. After looking again, he turned to me and said, "Are you sure you were born in Pennington County?" I assured him I was born in Pennington County on May 30, 1930. The clerk said, "Well, there must be some mistake. It's just not here."

After struggling to phrase the question, I asked, "I'm sure I was born in this county. Under what possible circumstances would I not be listed?"

His eyes left the record books and looked at me. With some hesitation he said, "I'm sure this isn't your case, but illegitimate children are not registered in the county of their birth. Those records are kept at the state capital in Pierre. You should clarify with your parents where you were born."

I knew that I had an important clue. Still, it wasn't likely I was going to speak of this with my parents. I felt insecure and confused, and I was afraid of the answer. So for nearly a year I stewed about it. I needed more evidence. I looked for hints. I looked in every family bible. My futile search never uncovered any mention, any sign whatsoever, that I might possibly be adopted. No friends or relatives, if they knew, ever revealed the secret.

Nine months later, when it was again time to switch living quarters with my grandmother, her trunk came back to the apartment. If I could find that adoption announcement card again—that would be tangible evidence giving me the courage, I hoped, to go to my mother and say, "What about this?"

There sat the trunk, unlocked, in the bedroom. It was late afternoon, and as my mother was not home from work, I was alone.

I opened the trunk, took out the shelf, and quickly began searching through my grandmother's things. Desperately searching, pushing things aside and pulling things out, I could not find the card, that vital piece of evidence, anywhere in the trunk.

Glancing out the window, I saw my mother coming home. In a panic, not wanting to be caught in the act, I starting throwing everything back in the trunk as fast as I could. I stuffed things in, put the shelf back on top, and as you would suspect, couldn't close the lid.

My mother, laying her hat and coat on the bed, looked at me. With concern in her voice she asked me what I was doing in my grandmother's trunk. "That's her property," she said. I was caught trespassing. I had no explanation except the truth.

I began by telling her that I had seen the birth announcement card with the word "adopted" on it almost a year earlier, and I was trying to find it again. I didn't have to ask the question.

Looking me squarely in the eye, she said, "Well, you are. Do you care?"

I looked away, into the kitchen. Off the kitchen I saw that the bathroom door was open, and I could see the old-fashioned bathtub standing there on its little claw feet. Without answering I headed straight for that room, closed the door, locked it, and sat on the edge of the tub, feeling light-headed and overwhelmed.

It was five thirty in the afternoon. About six o'clock I heard my father come in the kitchen home from work. He greeted my mother and asked where I was. "He's in the bathroom."

She related what had happened, and that she had told me it was true I had been adopted. My father made no response that I could hear. Nothing else was said, but I could hear them setting the table and getting ready for dinner. Neither parent came to the door nor did they ask me to come out.

While they were eating I heard their conversation recounting the day and the people they had seen. Wisely, they let me be.

Four hours later, at nine thirty, I was still sitting on the edge of the bathtub. For four hours a tangle of thoughts had been exploding through my head.

One of the first realizations that came to mind was the happy observation that I was not related, by blood at least, to an aunt and one of my uncles. I was impressed and frankly surprised that my relatives, to their credit, had not revealed the secret. I'm quite sure my cousins were never told, because they almost certainly would have used that information against me.

It was my relationship with my parents that mattered.

Do they love me? Do I love them? I sat immobile. Do they love me? Really love me?

After calling up my boyhood and early teen memories, I had to admit that I knew they loved me. I had been secure in that all my life. I couldn't use a lack of love as ammunition against them. Further, there was no question about my love for them. I continued to sit because I just wanted to think, to get this through my head.

Embarrassment was a large part of what I felt in trying to accept my new status in the family. Not knowing what to say was the other.

There were so many questions. I wondered about nationality, ethnicity, and cultural heritage. Were my ancestors from Europe, or eons ago did they march across from Asia on the Aleutian Islands chain? Who were those other people who gave me life? Do I have siblings? And, of course, the big one—why didn't they want me?

We can intellectualize everything, but the nagging feeling still remains, that for some reason I was rejected. I realize now that this feeling, although painful, has also been a powerful motivator.

Finally, at nine thirty at night, the rim of the bathtub got to me. My legs were asleep and I could hardly stand up—literally. I hadn't moved a muscle, except those in my head, for nearly four hours. I had been there long enough, so quietly I went out, made myself a sandwich, and then joined my mother and my father in the living room. They were both reading, but immediately looked up.

My mother asked, "Are you alright?"

I replied, "I think I'm fine."

We didn't talk further.

Over the next few months and years I did discuss being adopted with my mother. She told me all she knew, which was interesting but very scanty. My adoptive parents, Nettie and Darrell, had been unable to have children after a number of miscarriages. My mother went to the Rapid City Welfare Office, located in the Alex Johnson Hotel, and asked Mrs. E. E. Benjamin if it would be possible to adopt a baby. Mrs. Benjamin took a liking to Nettie, and just a week later a baby boy was carried into her office and put up for adoption. I was retrieved that very day, on June 5, 1930, from a situation that could have been tough.

Instead, I was welcomed into the home of Nettie and Darrell Hull. She was a housewife carefully managing his meager salary as an auto mechanic at the local Oldsmobile garage. She had a high school education and had even taught in a country school for two years. He had a tenth grade education and a great love and talent for all things mechanical—and they both knew how to work.

3

The Stranger in
the Night

I have great affection and enthusiasm for the theater, plays, actors, and all things that have to do with performance. These interests were nurtured early on. Though my parents didn't attend the community concerts, they always made sure that I had a good seat for all the artists who came to Rapid City during those years, and they had me studying piano since the second grade.

Rapid City in the 1940s had a population of thirty thousand people and was a long way from everywhere. Thanks to recording contracts that demanded concert tours to sell their records, great artists of the first tier made their way to our stage. These included pianist Rudolph Firkusny, opera diva Miliza Korjus, and even violinist Yehudi Menuhin at the peak of his powers—they all performed in the Rapid City High School auditorium. Mario Lanza graced that stage, but I spent most of his concert backstage talking with his extraordinarily beautiful wife, Betty. When I mentioned that she should have a career, she quickly replied that one star in the family was quite enough. This was just before his brief but somewhat dazzling career at MGM.

During one of these concerts I was part of the performance,

because I had been asked to turn the pages for singer Jennie Tourel's accompanist. During that concert Miss Tourel, the great Russian lieder singer, remarked backstage that our auditorium was like "singing into a box of cotton." During intermission she instructed her pianist that she wouldn't be singing a certain group of Russian art songs, because "they would not be appreciated by this audience." Back on stage she announced, "I'm so sorry because vee cannot find zee music." I thought of suddenly announcing, music in hand, "We've found it!" but I repressed that idea and the show went on.

One night, about a year after my "adoption" discovery, I was cast in the Rapid City High School junior class play, *The Stranger in the Night*. It was a mystery of course, and I played a bellhop and wore an authentic uniform borrowed from the Alex Johnson Hotel. Opening night I was sitting backstage in one of the dressing rooms, in makeup and costume, when my friend Myra Garhardt came by and said, "Ronny, your mother wants to see you. She's on the other side of the stage."

That's odd, I thought, because my parents weren't coming that night, and it wasn't like them to go backstage anytime. I left the dressing room and walked behind the set to stage right. There stood a diminutive, slim brunette woman wearing a tailored, and in my eyes, beautiful gray suit that had thin, dark stripes. On her left shoulder was a sparkling lapel pin of some kind. I walked over to her and she said, "I'm waiting here to see Ronny Hull. They told me if I got here at seven thirty I could see him—he's our son."

Nervously, I responded, "That's my name." She said nothing but just looked at me steadily. I repeated, "That's who I am."

She studied me with intent, unblinking dark eyes. Then she said slowly, "I don't see how that is possible. I'm not sure."

All I could manage was, "That's my name. That's who I am."

"Perhaps they made a mistake," she said and quickly turned and left, leaving me standing there.

I was caught somewhere between anger and hurt. How could she say that? And why? What had just happened? Who was she? Was it possible she had been directed to me as the baby she had given up nearly eighteen years before? Then that old, cold feeling of maybe not measuring up crept inside my skin. I was short, skinny, and the makeup probably didn't help any concept of a long-lost son.

The stage manager called out, "Three minutes to curtain!" The junior class play of 1947 was about to begin. Like a zombie I stood in the wings waiting to go on, and I couldn't think of a single line. All kinds of thoughts were churning in my head. Who was this "stranger in the night"? My mother? If not, who was she and why did she come here? She seemed disappointed in what I looked like. Now what do I do?

Then I heard my cue to walk on stage. Before I entered into the play's fictitious world, the thought that flashed through my mind was, "Whoever you are I hope you're in the audience, because tonight . . ."

For the next two hours I was a charming, energetic bellhop having a great time in the part. This was not a polished performance by any measure, but that particular audience of friends and peers found this singularly unsophisticated play a hilarious evening. I hope she was there.

Thirty-five years later, it was 1982; I was driving past 716 Fourth Street, the apartment house where we had lived and where I had sat on the rim of that bathtub. I always looked at the house with nostalgia, and this time I was surprised to discover that I could see blue sky through the rafters of the second-floor roof. The place was being torn down.

Parking the car, I wondered if I could have one more look at our old apartment. I walked up on the porch and opened the front door into the hallway. Our apartment was the one on the left. I tried the door; it was unlocked. It opened into the most surrealistic experience of my life.

I walked into the living room, looked around, and found it exactly as we had left it back in the 1940s, furniture and all. The piano was just to my right. Open on the piano was the sheet music for "San Antonio Rose" ("Deep within my heart lies a melody . . .") The chairs, the davenport, the radio, the end tables, the wallpaper, and the pictures were all there. My own mental time machine had placed me back in our old apartment just as it was. There were no people, but I could hear their voices.

I heard the Evanses and the Danburgs and the Courtneys all chatting while they played bridge, bidding, exclaiming, trumping, and enjoying each other. Playing cards was popular entertainment for people of limited resources.

From there I went into the bedroom and then into the kitchen. The bathroom door was open and the bathtub was still perched on its claw feet. I went in and sat down on the edge of the tub. After closing the door and sitting very still, I didn't have to try to remember anything or conjure up anything. I didn't have to think. I simply sat there, and the old tape in my head started playing.

I heard the backdoor open. I heard my dad come in. I heard him ask where I was. I heard my mother and father talking. As I sat there, every thought I had that day my mother told me I was adopted came back racing through my mind. Wondering whether or not they loved me or I loved them. Was I a member of this family, and if not, what family? All those memories rolled through my head as vividly as when the drama was played out in this space in 1945. When the tape stopped, I looked up, opened the bathroom door, and walked slowly, one last time, back through the apartment.

I knew I had to take something from this place away with me. As I walked out on the porch, it hit me. My dad always kept a variety of tools in the trunk of his car, and I was quickly able to pry the house numbers 716 off the front porch. With those numbers in my hand I returned, exhilarated, to the car and to the present.

This experience rekindled my desire to learn more about who

I am and where I came from. I've never felt the need to know my birth parents, their relatives, or even other siblings, but I do yearn to know their history and mine.

I finally persuaded a judge in Rapid City to release my adoption records on file in the state capital in Pierre, South Dakota. In this process I received a photocopy of my original birth certificate. Here, late in my life, on February 14, 2002, I learned that my name was originally Theodore Vaughn Ramsey, that my mother's name was Jeanne May Ramsey. She was twenty-one years old, she was white, she listed her occupation as "school teacher," and her last mailing address was Yankton, South Dakota. The father's name is listed as Paul Vaughn, age twenty-four, white, no other information. Except this: In the blank under "Legitimate?" is written the word "no." The highlight of this discovery was the line at the bottom for the attending physician's signature. The word "physician" is crossed out, leaving the word "midwife," and it is signed in ink by Dora Du Fran.

Dora Du Fran was a British woman who came to the United States with her parents at age one year in 1872 and settled near Lincoln, Nebraska. In 1886, as a teenager, she went on to Rapid City "to make a living in a country that paid handsome prices for young beauty," according to a biographical account. She eventually became a dance-hall girl in one of the saloons in Deadwood where she married Joseph Du Fran, "a gentleman gambler" who had come to Deadwood on a freight train from Pierre.

Rena Webb, writing in *Deadwood Magazine* in 2004, says, "Dora Du Fran was a brothel madam who brought a chain store concept to prostitution in the Black Hills." Plainspoken cowboys, according to her, called the place "Diddlin' Dora's." Eventually they had "sporting houses" and gambling halls in Deadwood, Belle Fourche, and later in Rapid City.

When I was in high school in the 1940s some of my friends and I used to go to Deadwood and park near the "Cozy Rooms" or the "Pine Rooms," well-known "houses of ill repute," and watch to see if we knew any of the patrons going in and coming out. Every now and then we did, including a couple of classmates. At our fiftieth high school class reunion, while listening to what was left of the boy's octet, Conny and I, referring to a tenor, whispered and nodded, "Remember?"

In Dora's early days in Deadwood before the turn of the century, one of her best friends in town was the notorious Calamity Jane.

Calamity died penniless in 1903, and Dora, whose businesses had flourished, paid for a large, elegant urn to be placed on the grave site on Mount Moriah, a cliff overlooking Deadwood. Her grave is just across from Wild Bill Hickok's resting place. His grave features a handsome bronze bust of this notorious western figure who spent exactly three weeks in Deadwood. Both legendary figures are buried just across the path from the grave of Dora Du Fran. Thousands of tourists each year make their way on foot, or by bus and car, to this repository of western lore, tangible evidence of America's frontier days.

In her later years Dora wrote and published a reminiscence about her friend Calamity Jane and the western mining town of Deadwood. At that time it was one of the last remnants of the authentic Old West.

Dora's husband died in 1909, and she moved to Rapid City and set up her businesses at 224 Second Street on Rapid Creek. Rapid Creek, though it's more like a river, separates Rapid City north and south. True to experience the world over, the town was divided socioeconomically. The "nice" part of town was south of Rapid Creek and the poorer classes lived north. On the creek at Second and Omaha Streets, Dora built two buildings on what became known as Coney Island. Both were two-story buildings, one a gambling hall and bar and the other a house of prostitution. Coney Island was so named because a bend in the creek put water on three sides of Dora's property. The historical lore of Rapid City has it that when the spring rains came, "Coney

Island" became literally an island, thus isolating the patrons of her establishments from the "mainland." When this happened, so the legend goes, the morning sun would find many a prominent husband stranded on the island while the revengeful wives, with rolling pins in hand, were waiting on the opposite shore.

Rena Webb writes in her article that the Coney Island operation is confirmed by the 1910 census. In addition to "head of household," sixteen other people were living at Dora's place. They were identified as "boarders" and included nine women ranging in age from twenty to twenty-nine, a forty-six-year-old female servant, a hired man, and a Chinese cook. Dora's occupation is noted as proprietor of a resort, the girls as resort inmates.

Dora was a remarkable woman, with extraordinary energy, spirit, and style. She had a good business head, too. There are many newspaper accounts about her life, her work, and her exploits which confirm that she was well known and loved throughout the Black Hills. She was, apparently, the proverbial "madam" with a heart of gold.

She took care of the poor, the needy, the disenfranchised. She was always helping people who had less than she had. As a "madam," she looked after her own girls and was a midwife. She took girls off the street who were "in trouble" and delivered their babies for them. She also performed abortions. She went down to the train station and gathered up transients, the lonely, the homeless, and provided them with meals, and every year, Thanksgiving dinner. She was a respected citizen of the town; she not only had many friends but she enjoyed the cooperation of the sheriff and the police department. Her good works for others transcended her livelihood. People loved her because she loved people and took care of them.

It was June 5, 1930, when Dora Du Fran walked with a baby in her arms from her place of business at Second and Omaha Streets to the Alex Johnson Hotel and the Welfare Office at Sixth and St. Joseph Streets. The baby was handed to Mrs. E. E.

Benjamin, and later that day Mrs. Benjamin handed him to Nettie and Darrell Hull—my newfound parents.

When Dora died on August 5, 1934, the *Rapid City Journal* praised her good citizenship in helping suffering humanity: "She stood for the flower of mercy that grew in the hard soil of a hard-lived world."

Was my birth mother "one of the girls" who worked for Dora? Or was she a young woman who came to Dora for her skills as a midwife and the anonymity that would afford? I do not know. I have been searching but have not found out.

Sometime after June 5, 1930, my parents were given my new birth certificate naming them as parents and giving my name as Ronald Eugene Hull. There was not a word about being illegitimate. This I owe to a woman named Edna Gladney from Fort Worth, Texas.

Greer Garson starred in the film *Blossoms in the Dust* which told Edna Gladney's story. She ran an orphanage in Fort Worth, where she grew ashamed that so many innocent children carried the burden of being "illegitimate" all their lives. It was she who coined the phrase "There are no illegitimate children, only illegitimate parents." It was she who persuaded the Texas legislature to create a law allowing each adopted child to have a new birth certificate without the stigma of the word "illegitimate." This was a fight that was eventually waged successfully with the Congress of the United States.

My father would never talk about the fact I was adopted, to me or anyone. If the subject came up, especially after we adopted our first son, Kevin, he would quietly leave the room. Our eyes never met acknowledging this fact. I was his son and that was that. I didn't press him.

Though I cannot speak for other adopted people, I suspect they experience what I do. Always present in the back of my mind is "Why?" Without playing the violin too vigorously, there are questions: why didn't they want me, why did they give me away, what was wrong with me? Throughout my life these questions have kindled that persistent desire within me to "measure up."

One can intellectualize the various scenarios of poverty, unwanted pregnancy, family tragedies, that this was the best direction, that life for me got better not worse. This is almost certainly true, but I still wonder. Who am I? What is my genealogical heritage? Do I have brothers and sisters, and why was I given away?

I like a good story, and someday I hope to have a denouement to this one. I owe it to my children.

In the meantime, they have had the benefit of two sets of grandparents of the first order.

4

The Hulls and
the Kayes

The roots of our lives are not planted in our time. We stand on the hopes and dreams, the sacrifices and the labors, of myriad others who have given us the opportunity to have productive lives.

THE HULLS

It was chance or dumb luck that took me from Dora Du Fran's house of ill repute to the healthy, loving environment of my adoptive parents.

My father, Darrell, was an automobile mechanic who loved cars and was adept with all kinds of machines. He began as a mechanic in the Oldsmobile garage in Rapid City and eventually worked his way up to the position of service manager.

Immediately after World War II he and a colleague started their own business, B&H Auto Service. With new car production suspended during the war years, they did just fine repairing autos and selling used cars.

Later, my parents had Hull's Auto Service. My dad ran the place and my mother was the bookkeeper until he could hire someone full-time. At that point she went to work for a friend selling real estate.

All during these years my ambitious, undereducated, workaholic parents got into real estate on the side. In the late 1930s the town of Hermosa, thirteen miles south of Rapid City, was dying, and anyone could acquire a house simply by moving it away. My parents picked out a house and spent two hundred dollars they didn't have moving it to a lot in Rapid City. They put it on a foundation, and every night and weekend for months the two of them rewired, plumbed, and remodeled the entire place. Sometime later they sold the place for four thousand dollars! Much of that was pure profit. This was the beginning of their buying and selling houses and property in every section of the city.

They kept the business going, moving from house to house, to basements, to apartments, constantly doing the renovation work themselves. Then they rented the place out or sold it for a good price.

By the time I came home for the summer after my sophomore year at the College of the Pacific, my parents were living in a lovely home with a stylish, dark exterior of stained wood and a beautiful interior design. The dining room had a gabled ceiling overlooking a sunken living room that featured a brass planter eight feet long, laden with a variety of plants under an enormous front window. They had worked many years for this level of comfort and luxury. I said to my dad, "A dream home. You've earned it."

"If someone offers me five hundred dollars more than I have in it, it's theirs," was his response.

A year later they had sold the place and had found a large, well-located piece of land they liked, with lots of pine trees on it. The only building was a single-car garage. They pulled the garage door down, nailed it shut, put in some temporary walls and a kitchen and bathroom, and moved in. You could literally step into the shower and come out through the oven, which were back to back. They never mentioned being any less comfortable than before, and soon that place sold for a healthy profit, too. The house they lived in at any given time said nothing about their financial status and little about who they were.

While I was in college my father was still managing the garage, and my mother had earned her real-estate broker's license and hung out her own shingle. With Hull's Real Estate, she was into the business in a serious way. When it came time for my dad to retire, knowing his son had no inclination and could never successfully run a car business, he sold it. He earned his real-estate license and went to work for my mother. Together, they did real-estate deals in Rapid City into their early eighties.

Nettie and Darrell spent thirteen winters in Arizona near Scottsdale. During these years my mother took up swimming and painting. My dad teased her about her painting lessons and once jokingly remarked, "Son, isn't it true that if you put a monkey in a room with a typewriter long enough, he'll write *Hamlet*?" Pretty cruel, but he ate his words. Invited to submit some of her paintings in a local Scottsdale art show, she sold two pieces of her work. One went for sixty-five dollars and the other for eighty-five. My dad quickly changed his tune with, "How fast, woman, can you turn these out?" She painted some pleasing Arizona and Black Hills landscapes, and was particularly adept at creating a nice separation between the mountains and the sky, almost in a three-dimensional fashion.

Retirement brought them into Westhills Village retirement community, a well-appointed apartment in an inviting Black Hills setting.

I joined my parents for dinner there during my visits. One evening, looking across the dining room, I saw the Quarnbergs. They were Rapid City aristocracy and had lived in a very large home on "the boulevard"—West Boulevard. I recall being seven or eight years old and accompanying my dad to their home to deliver their car. When the massive, rounded-top front door opened, I saw a receiving foyer with a winding staircase leading upstairs. I had no idea people actually lived in such houses in real life. And there they were, eating dinner here at Westhills Village.

"Isn't that the Quarnbergs over there?" I asked. "Well, see, the Hulls and the Quarnbergs wound up in the same place. It all evens out."

"No," Nettie said. "They have a three-bedroom expandable." This, as compared with my folk's one-bedroom nonexpandable.

I was in Los Angeles at the Century Plaza Hotel when my mother called and said that my dad had had a stroke and was in the hospital. But she thought he could understand what he heard, though he couldn't speak. She put the phone to his ear, and I had a chance to tell him about the work I was doing with producers in Los Angeles. The last thing I said to him was, "I love you, Dad."

I took a book and went out to the pool for a couple of hours. The sun made its way to the ocean, and when I returned to the darkened room I could see the light on the phone blinking. I knew. I called, and my mother informed me that my dad had died twenty minutes after I had talked with him.

After his death, my mother, in her late eighties, traveled some. She called me from Miami just before embarking on a cruise through the American Virgin Islands. "Ron, this brochure says that if you want to snorkel at Caneel Bay you have to have a 'buddy.' These old women I'm with won't go near the water."

I had been there, and it's some of the best snorkeling I've ever discovered. Remembering my experience, I told her that there's a person on the beach to show you how to use the equipment and that he will assign you a buddy if you don't have one. About ten days later Nettie called and her first words were, "I snorkeled all afternoon with a thirty-year-old man."

Years later, Nettie's 101st birthday was coming up in a month. We had just returned from a vacation in France and hadn't seen her for a while, so we decided to drive up to Rapid City for a visit. We had four fine days with her. When we returned to Lincoln I received a call from Westhills Village.

"Ron, Nettie died this morning."

"But I just saw her yesterday morning. What happened?"

"She was in the beauty shop having her hair done."

I called Lucille, the woman who had fixed her hair for a number of years.

"Lucille, what happened? What were you talking about when my mom died?"

"We were talking about your visit, what a good time she had. I was just putting the last roller in her hair, and your mother looked at me and said, 'You know, this would be a fine time to go.' With that her head fell forward and she was gone."

All I could think of to say was, "Did you finish putting the last roller in her hair?"

"No," Lucille said. "I just stood there with tears coming down."

She was wearing a white blouse, a string of long red beads, a red sweater, and she was having her hair done. I was grateful that Nettie left this life fully alive right up to the last minute. As Neihardt's poem "Let Me Live Out My Years" says,

O Let me be a tune-swept fiddlestring
That feels the Master Melody—and snaps!

THE KAYES

My wife Naomi's parents, Bennie Bee and Albert Kaye, gave their daughter, and later me, a sense of place, of respect for the land and the values of the early people who first settled the Great Plains. They were successful with an insurance and abstract business, and they farmed many acres of land, some of which had been in the family since the late 1880s.

All through the 1960s and 1970s, when our children were growing, up we almost always went "over the river (the Missouri) and through the woods"—well, not exactly "woods," though there were some trees on the way—to Grandmother's house for Thanksgiving.

Grandmother's house, belonging to Naomi's mother, Bennie Bee, was a white-frame, six-bedroom, two-story home with a spacious wraparound porch. It was as big or bigger than any other house in the town of Highmore, South Dakota, population eleven hundred. Bennie Bee's mother built the house in 1911. Mother Kaye, as I called her, was married in the front room and delivered her two children in the back bedroom on the first floor. This was her home until her death at age ninety-eight, though her last two years were spent in a nursing home in Lincoln. During one bedside visit at the nursing home, she said to me, "Ron, call Rube Heckenlaible" (her neighbor in Highmore). "That lamp in the front window has always been on at night and I'm afraid people walking by will miss it. Have Rube turn it on and leave it on." She kept the lights, heat, and telephone all going during those last two years so that when the family gathered for her funeral, her home would be just as she left it and welcoming to all.

Bennie Bee didn't want us, or what family might follow us, to have to be responsible for the disposition of the house after she died, so she willed it to the United Methodist Church Overseas Relief Fund. She had always worried about the starving children of the world. The church sold the house, and the new family painstakingly renovated it room by room. It will serve as a family home for another eighty-some years.

Over the years she often rented out one of the upstairs back bedrooms to a high school girl from the country. Many of the high school students rented rooms in town and went back to the farm for the weekends. They were often young people from large families, and though not impoverished, were raised in exceedingly frugal circumstances. My mother-in-law took these young women in hand and taught them how to clean, do some cooking, and how to take care of a home, skills they could use to earn a little spending money as well. Though "straitlaced" in some ways, she could also surprise you.

One morning about six o'clock I left our upstairs "north bedroom," the one we always used when visiting, to walk down the hall to the bathroom. As I passed the "east bedroom" the door was open and I couldn't avoid seeing that the young female renter had a young man with her in bed. They didn't notice me as I tiptoed by.

Later that morning I said to Bennie Bee, "Did you know that the young lady upstairs had her boyfriend with her all last night?"

Bennie Bee replied, "I know."

"But his pickup is parked out in front of your house. Everyone in town will know that he spent the night here. What will they think?"

"I don't care what they think," she said, "and those kids have so little . . ."

Some of our best times with her were the competitive Scrabble games she enjoyed. One of our rules is that you can't get impatient and tell a player to hurry up. If it takes twenty minutes per play, that means it's going to be a long night.

One night I had just played and it was Bennie Bee's turn, then Naomi's. I had just run out of cigarettes, so knowing I could walk the two blocks to "downtown" and be back for my next turn, I said that I would be right back and got up to leave.

My mother-in-law said, "But it's midnight and nothing will be open."

"There's the tavern. I'm sure they are open."

Quietly she said, "No member of this family has ever been in the tavern." I was not to be the first.

The Kayes of Highmore were second-generation Methodists. The church meant a lot to them, my father-in-law was the church pianist, and Bennie Bee was the Sunday school superintendent for years.

Before the turn of the twentieth century the old Methodist church in Highmore had burned to the ground, and ever since, the bell from that original church had been stored in a shed on the grounds.

In honor of her husband and his love for the church and its music, Bennie Bee hired a contractor to construct a modest eighteen-foot wooden bell tower and install the original church bell in it, so that once again the Methodists would have a bell to call them to worship. It was simple but attractive, and you could see the bell through the perforated steel covering. There was an opening in the covering of the tower allowing someone to reach in and pull the rope to ring the bell.

During one visit the Methodist minister asked me to stop by his office. "Ron," he said, "I know that you have a good relationship with your mother-in-law, and I'm wondering if you would talk to her about electrifying the ringing of the church bell. I don't think it would cost much, but that would allow me to be able to push a button here in the office to make the bell ring and in the winter time not have to wade through three feet of snow to go pull that rope."

That seemed reasonable to me.

I began with, "Mother Kaye, I ran into your minister today and he has an idea that I think will appeal to you."

Looking up from her Scrabble tiles, she said, "If you think I am going to have that bell tower wired so that he can push a button in his office to make it ring, think again."

I went back to my own set of tiles and I knew that was the end of that.

I am in Bennie Bee's debt for the standards she upheld, but most particularly for her daughter, Naomi, my wife.

NAOMI

When we first met, she was an eighty-five-pound, agile package of dynamite, with beautiful, large brown eyes, a serious student with fine musical talent and athletic ability.

Naomi is truly a Dakota girl. Though she never lived on a farm, she has deep respect for the people who settled the South Dakota prairies, and she embodies the character and ethics we attribute to those who are close to the land.

After raising her family, she designed a successful career for herself by becoming an ordained Methodist minister. She didn't work as a preacher but as a minister of visitation, concentrating on clinical pastoral duties. Each day for over twenty years, she visited parishioners in hospitals, hospices, and nursing homes, often counseling the terminally ill. She brought to her work loving, straightforward honesty and compassionate care without sentimentality. Naomi could comfortably sit on the edge of the bed of an old, burly farmhand, put her hand on his, and communicate compassion in a way a male pastor never could. Her honesty is disarming. And her patients were not always aged or infirm.

One January day she came home and told me of a nineteen-year-old woman who had just been diagnosed with acute leukemia. She was given three or four months to live. This young woman with shining hair, bright, beautiful eyes, and perfect skin knew that her time was nearly spent. A few weeks later, while she was coming to terms with her condition, she said, "Mrs. Hull, I am very afraid of dying some night here in the dark all alone. I want to be among the living, with life going on around me, in the sunshine if possible. Can you promise me that?"

"I can't promise you anything, but it could happen the way you want it," Naomi said.

Two months later, Naomi came home from work and said to me, "This morning I stopped by at 7:00 a.m. to say hello and told her I would be back after I had seen a couple of patients going in for surgery. They were just helping her into a wheelchair and getting her ready for the day. She got her wish. Two hours later they found her sitting in her chair in the sunroom, surrounded by people and activities, her head to one side as if she was just asleep."

I said to her, "I would be terrible at your job. I couldn't do it."

She replied, "You would be terrible. You'd pat the person on the back and tell them they're going to be okay. They are not going to be okay."

Naomi brings intelligent, pragmatic, useful, and loving care to her ministry.

5

On Becoming a Storyteller

Experiences create a good storyteller. Some stories come to us with no effort, and others we have to go out and find. Storytelling has been the focus of my life, whether it's around a campfire, in a theater, on television, or projected on the big screen. Initially it was motion pictures that captured me. My introduction to theater came during my freshman year in college. Before that, though I was aware of Broadway stage productions like *Oklahoma!* and *Carousel*, I couldn't imagine a live theater production that actually had a carousel on stage. When your experience is limited to two high school plays per year, how is that possible, I wondered?

Dr. Phillip Kaye, the director of Dakota Wesleyan Theater, my advisor and later my brother-in-law, had started a unique and interesting experiment in religious drama. Carefully choosing his scripts, he brought energy and excitement to these one-act biblical stories.

He worked like a sergeant demonstrating hand-to-hand combat with his actors. He faced us on the stage and literally breathed life into our movements, our motivations, our delivery. He was right there in our faces, infusing pacing and energy and rhythm into our efforts. We lived and breathed those stories, and his emotional energy became a part of our approach to the work. We not only had the enormous benefit of hours of painstaking rehearsal, discussions of character, interpretation, and improvisation, but he also provided us with many wide and diverse live audiences through booking us into myriad Methodist church basements, chapels, and sanctuaries throughout South Dakota, Nebraska, Colorado, and Wyoming.

We brought our small cast to these places in two automobiles, one of which pulled a trailer with the meager scenery, props, lighting equipment, costumes, and makeup. These weekend productions were an outreach program of Dakota Wesleyan University, a means of recruiting students to the college and, for the church, to God.

For us, the student actors, it was a creative mixture of show business and faith. Besides, every actor knows that once you're "out there" on the stage it's just you and God anyway. This was a good fit.

As a freshman, late in maturation and painfully skinny, I could easily play young biblical characters, including the boy Jesus, five or more years my junior, usually wearing a skirtlike tunic and sandals.

Enthusiastic applause followed our performances of *The Chastening*, a well-written one-act drama that involved a mother, a father, and a young son. It was an intellectual, allegorical drama featuring the conversation Mary, Joseph, and Jesus "might have had" after Jesus, at age twelve, had enlightened the elders.

My part, the young boy, began with an awkward line. Looking back, I'll never understand how I got away with saying, "Mother, Father, the ass is wonderful," referring to the donkey that the boy had just ridden out from Jerusalem. It had to be the church setting that kept the audience in line.

One of our jobs offstage was to go into the audience at the conclusion of the play and pass a collection plate. This money kept food in our stomachs and gas in the cars while we were on the road.

During the holiday break we brought these plays to churches in the four-state area. Traveling up from Denver, we arrived in a small Wyoming town later than we had hoped. We hurriedly put up the set and got into costume and makeup just as the audience had filled the church. I had to go to the bathroom, so I looked around but couldn't find it. I should have stepped outside—that's where I later discovered it was. Desperately I said to Dr. Kaye, "I've got to go to the bathroom before we start the play."

Phil said, "Sorry, it's too late, the music is just ending. You'll have to hold it."

I replied, "I can't hold it."

His reply, "Get a rubber band," was not helpful. I had no choice. I held it. I rushed my lines some, but I held it.

Experience in drama is an excellent component of anyone's education. The discipline required of seriously presenting a play is difficult to replicate. Theater makes rigorous demands and calls us to be alert, to work as a team, to be prepared, to be stronger and better than we were the day before. And where else but in performance will your body kick in with those regular surges of adrenalin to keep you going, to keep it moving! After all, there are people out there with high expectations.

Though I did not realize it, the most important event of that first year in college was getting to know Dr. Kaye's sister, Naomi. We met on the steps of Dakota Wesleyan's College Hall. During that first encounter, she stood almost transfixed, a mixture of boredom and puzzlement, as I described in lengthy detail the picture *A Foreign Affair* with Marlene Dietrich and John Lund. She later said that she couldn't believe anyone could be that enamored with the movies.

After that freshman year at Dakota Wesleyan, I spent my first summer back in Rapid City working as a bellhop at the Alex Johnson Hotel. That stately western hotel, with its well-designed

Indian motif throughout, was built by the railroad in 1928 and is still a first-rate hotel.

Being a bellhop was my kind of job, and I was good at it. In a real sense this was my version of the movie *Grand Hotel*. Every day I looked forward to meeting interesting strangers from faraway places, to the pleasure of listening to their chatter while checking them in at four o'clock in the afternoon and then the rush to get their luggage neatly packed in the trunks of their cars when they checked out early the next morning.

Bellhops depend on tips, and to be successful, they have to have inordinate energy. They must be able to charm the customers in the few minutes it takes to grab their bags and carry them into the elevator and out of the hotel to the customers' waiting cars. I was able to pay a good share of my college expenses with the money I made through tips each summer.

Working as a bellhop is an exciting adventure because from sunup to sundown, hotels are teeming with life. Bellhops regularly witness many personal moments in the lives of strangers, and there is tacit agreement that we can be trusted not to talk. Sometimes you walk in on compromising situations when you're bringing drinks or laundry into the room.

At these times, people have a mind-set that bellhops are invisible "see no evil, hear no evil" nonentities. You can almost read the unspoken words "Oh, it's just the bellhop" on their faces, and they go right on with arguments, fights, intimate conversations, desperate phone calls, and pleas for help or other emotion-laden activities, ignoring the presence of a bellhop.

Life—it was all there. "Hey, kid, here's a fiver. Run down and get me some rubbers." "Yes, sir, I'll be right back."

"Young man, don't be in such a hurry." "Sorry, ma'am, I'm the only one on duty now. I have to get back to the floor."

"Hey, kid, how about scrubbing my back?" "Sorry, sir, duty calls."

Human relationships, connections, pain, joy, sorrow, authentic human stories being played twenty-four hours a day. And it afforded me valuable lessons in growing up.

Almost every summer a major Hollywood studio would come to the Black Hills to shoot a Western, and the cast and crew headquartered at the Alex Johnson. I couldn't believe my luck when in June 1950 director George Sherman brought Yvonne De Carlo, Van Heflin, Preston Foster, Jack Oakie, Ann Doran, Rock Hudson, and Susan Cabot to make a film on my South Dakota doorstep.

The picture was Universal's *Tomahawk*, a competent, small-scale cowboy-versus-Indians Western. Thanks to my split shift, I could visit the set every day—a fort built fifteen miles south of Rapid City—and still be around the hotel when they came in from work. Everyone wanted cool libations in their rooms after working in the sun all day, and this gave me daily opportunities for listening to the inside story of how the film was or was not progressing. I was in heaven.

I heard complaints from some about the number of "takes" Miss De Carlo required, but everyone enjoyed working with her. She was "Peggy" to the cast and crew, as Peggy Middleton was her real name. I don't think she would have known you were speaking to her if you addressed her as Miss De Carlo or Yvonne. She was unpretentious, friendly, and courteous, with a beautiful face and figure and dark, exotic eyes.

My aunt Edith was the overnight telephone operator at the hotel at the time. Every night about 10:00 p.m. Rock Hudson would stop by her station and tell her that if he should receive any phone calls from Hollywood at any time, to send them up to Miss Cabot's room. My aunt would comply. Like Yvonne De Carlo, he was one of the kindest, most courteous guests any of us encountered at the hotel.

Susan Cabot was lovely to look at, extraordinarily petite, and had the most curvaceous, perfectly formed female body one is ever likely to see. As the bellhops would say, "Everything about her is standing at attention." When Mr. Hudson, with his Adonis-like, towering presence, walked through the lobby beside the diminutive Miss Cabot, one of the bellhops (we were young), unseen by the couple, would make a motion with his hand like flipping a propeller to get the airplane started. Of course we didn't know for sure if anything was going on between them, but there was constant speculation. They were beautiful physical specimens that cameras—not to mention the rest of us—adore.

Naturally, I took every possible opportunity to serve them with drinks, errands, or whatever they needed, and this led to a number of conversations. I wanted to know about their careers, how they got started, and their perceptions of making it in Hollywood.

Each of them had talent and each had the will to succeed in a very tough business. As they said, acting is one of the most cruelly competitive career fields one could choose. I was losing money every minute I wasn't hustling bags, but I was fascinated listening to these two young people, both in their early twenties, telling me about the rigors of moviemaking; of being cast, of deals falling through, of being excited with a project and then being disappointed with the results; about the elation when they knew they had done a good job and the exhilaration of being a part of a successful film. Listening to them, I learned early on that life is not just about success, it is also about failed efforts and loss.

One afternoon when Susan Cabot didn't have to report to the set, I took some things up to her room. It was a hot, dry, windy, South Dakota June day. She was looking out the window, and there were real tumbleweeds rolling down St. Joe Street amid windy gusts of swirling dust. Turning away, she said, "Do you live here?"

"Yes, this is my hometown."

"How do you stand it?" she asked, not unkindly.

Though I didn't think of it that way, I could see how bleak our town must have seemed to her, and I replied, "I don't plan to stay here forever."

Those days in 1950 were an unforgettable summer. I could watch Susan Cabot and Rock Hudson work with Yvonne De Carlo and Van Heflin, in rehearsal and actually during shooting. Then later, back at the hotel, I could have the opportunity to stand on the edge of their inner circle for a little while. I enjoyed being "just the bellhop."

Rock Hudson enjoyed a fine, accomplished screen career. Though he died far too young, even in death he played a significant, positive role. His prominence brought urgent, needed attention to the dreadful disease of AIDS, and his death contributed to accelerated and intensified efforts to find treatment and a cure for countless others.

Susan Cabot, whose promising career was postponed by marriage, was later tragically killed by a mentally deranged son.

When we're young we look forward to the future with such hope and anticipation. I dreamt that perhaps someday I would be a working actor like these remarkable people.

After that summer, I transferred from Dakota Wesleyan to the College of the Pacific in Stockton, California. This school appealed to me because it was reputed to have a fine drama department, it was originally a Methodist school, and I had met a young woman from Stockton, California, at Canyon Lake that summer. She was a navy brat visiting relatives in Rapid City, and she had the best suntan I had ever seen. Though the romance ended two months after I arrived on campus, the year at the College of the Pacific was a rewarding one.

Unlike Dakota Wesleyan, the College of the Pacific had a few fraternities and sororities that represented a new world to me. I decided to pledge, not because I desperately wanted to belong but because I needed to know that I could get in, that I was good enough.

The pledge process was a nerve-wracking experience of parties and conversations and trying to emulate the behavior of those around me, both members and aspirants. It was during this process I taught myself how to smoke. I was dizzy for days. But I finally learned, excruciatingly, how to inhale.

When the sealed bids were handed out, I knew that inside the envelope was either the name of a fraternity or a blank piece of paper. To shield my possible—and expected—disappointment, I went into a men's room stall, locked the door, opened the envelope, and discovered that I had been accepted.

It was this semester at the College of the Pacific that I had my second encounter with Madame Jennie Tourel. I noticed in the Stockton paper that "world-famous Russian diva Jennie Tourel" was going to be in concert at the Pacific Auditorium. I called the booking agency and said that if Miss Tourel's accompanist requests a page turner to give me a call because I had experience. Not long after, the agency did call to tell me to report backstage by 7:00 p.m. and to wear a tuxedo. That was an expense I hadn't counted on, but with luck I rounded up an ill-fitting one from a fraternity brother. I reported to the auditorium exercising and flexing my hands to ensure I could get those pages turned on time. Three or four of my friends were out front and were quite impressed, though one did mention that the lighting made me look like I had no chin.

Miss Tourel behaved differently at this concert. She had received some poor reviews for a recent Bell Telephone radio broadcast and her self-confidence was somewhat shaken. An entourage of friends from San Francisco accompanied her to Stockton, and after each group of numbers, one or two of them were backstage assuring her that she "never sounded better." The highlight of the evening for me was when, called back for an encore, she walked on stage and announced to the audience that her encore would be from Leonard Bernstein's song series called *I Hate Music* and that she was dedicating this group of songs to her page turner from "Sous Dakota."

That concert was Friday evening, the last day of classes before spring break at the College of the Pacific. Miss Tourel included me with her friends after the concert, and we all went off to a reception and celebrated her resounding success. For me, at age nineteen, this was a night to remember. Later I thanked Miss Tourel, went back to the campus, and returned the borrowed tuxedo.

As enjoyable as that experience had been, it was the next night that offered excitement of a different order.

The following morning, with a small bag in hand and less than fifteen dollars in my pocket, I headed home for spring break. Since I didn't have the money to take a bus from Stockton, California, to Rapid City, South Dakota, I decided to hitchhike. I had some experience hitchhiking short distances in South Dakota, but this was a new and major undertaking.

After finally getting deposited on the edge of Stockton, and with the eastbound highway beckoning me onward, my spirits were high. At first I did pretty well, thumbing my way east through the mountains in only three different rides. Then I found myself, by nightfall, standing on the outskirts of Winnemucca, Nevada. It was dark and there was very little traffic. After standing on the highway for over two hours and not connecting with any ride, I was beginning to be concerned.

To my consternation there was another hitchhiker standing nearby, but he decided to give up. As he walked away he said he would probably find a freight train to hop.

"Hop the freight?" I wondered. When he was out of sight, I too gave up and walked the short distance to the small station where a train was standing.

I didn't even know which direction the train was headed. I knew I had to go through Salt Lake City so I went in to the agent and asked if that train was going to Salt Lake City.

"Yes, but that's not a passenger train, young man. That's a freight."

"Oh, is that all?" I responded, trying to sound disappointed.

I went outside the station, and when there was no one around I began walking quickly back toward the end of the train. There was boxcar after boxcar, carrying I know not what. About half-way back were two gondola cars loaded with logs piled high and held in place by two-inch metal straps. Gondola cars are open and have walls about four feet high. I climbed up to look in and saw approximately ten feet of space between the end of the logs and the end of the car. That seemed adequate, so I dropped down into the car and settled back against the logs, somewhat wary of what I was doing but feeling a pleasant tinge of excitement as well. I had never "hopped" a freight before, but the crisp night air, the clear sky, and nearly full moon heightened my anticipation for the trip to Salt Lake City.

The train started moving slowly along the tracks, and then shortly the pace quickened. I could see the light poles of the town receding faster and faster into the night, and I was on my way at a pretty good clip. I also realized I was a captive—I would be going wherever the train went and could not get off until it stopped. It was picking up speed and logs were beginning to shift and rub against each other, noisily creaking and groaning. We were dashing north through the night and I was beginning to understand the meaning of "hopping a freight." Hopping on was easy, but something told me that hopping off might be much more difficult.

About an hour into the ride, it was now very dark, the temperature was dropping, and I was getting cold. I had on a light fraternity jacket suitable for April in California, and I had a small zippered duffel bag with underclothes, socks, a pair of jeans, a clean shirt, my toothbrush, and a couple of books. My hands were getting cold and numb, so I used two pairs of socks as gloves. Moving around briskly at the end of the car, I looked over the side and back at the other cars.

With a sudden pang of surprise, I saw the legs of men hanging out the open side door of the boxcar behind me. I was not alone. Apparently there were a number of us hopping the freight, and every now and then a spent cigarette, glowing red, was hurtled from the train. My hope was that no one was aware of me.

That inner discontent was soon magnified.

The logs were not only beginning to shift a bit from side to side, they were slowly inching forward and taking over my space. Fear was replaced by panic.

The logs, fastened down by metal straps, had not been secured well enough, and suddenly, with a loud snap, one of the straps broke, freeing the logs at my end. With a grinding screech, one log swung out away from the car, held by just the rear strap. Gasping, I stared at that log protruding eight to ten feet from the train.

Before I could think of what might happen next, we came to a bridge, the log hit the girders, and with a thunderous crack broke in two and hurtled up overhead, coming down and hitting the top of the boxcar behind me, then bouncing off to the ground.

Following suit, another log came loose and swung out to the side, though not as far. The logs seemed almost alive, and the noise they made shifting in that metal gondola car was deafening and paralyzing. I cowered down, looking up to the logs. With mixed wonder and horror I saw a man working his way along the top of the car ahead, coming to secure the metal straps. Thinking I might be arrested, though my alternatives were probably worse, I decided I couldn't let him see me.

With a double thickness of socks on my hands, grabbing the ladder with one and clutching my bag with the other, I scrambled over the side of the train. Hanging on to the metal side ladder, I put my head down and held on with one bunched-up, sock-filled hand. I was literally waving in the wind off the side of the train, enduring this terror while the man repaired the log situation.

I was not detected. When I could finally throw my numb, aching body back in the car next to the logs, I was, by this time, prepared for anything. Or so I thought. Suddenly, it was not just a dark night but total engulfing darkness. The stars disappeared. A mountain had swallowed us in a tunnel. I couldn't see anything. Then the smoke came back to envelop me. It was thick, sooty, particle-laden coal smoke. I unzipped my bag and put it over my head as a filter and tried to breath as little and as carefully as possible. Finally, we shot out of the tunnel, and I sank, exhausted, to the floor of the car.

Bring on the logs, bring on the carbon monoxide, wreck the train: with barely six feet of space left for me in the car, I knew I was not going to get through this journey anyway. On we rumbled through the night.

At last, as the welcome morning was breaking, the train came to a lurching stop. Salt Lake City? I wondered as I peered out. Afraid not. We stopped in the middle of the Great Salt Lake Desert of Utah. No matter. I was getting out of here. I clambered over the side and ran away from the train as fast as I could. Luckily there was a highway nearby. I held out my thumb for the first truck to come along. It stopped, the door opened, and the driver looked down at me incredulously and said, "Where in hell have you been?" I glanced in the side mirror of the truck and staring back was the image of a chimney sweep, my face covered with a thick layer of ebony soot. He laughed, I got in, and like Lewis and Clark, "we proceeded on." I was happily confident that by the next day I would be home in Rapid City. There was never a second experience in hopping a freight for me.

After my sophomore year in Stockton my best friend, Conny, and I decided to forgo our college educations and enlist in the air force before we could be drafted to serve in the army in Korea. Since we were going to take this dramatic step, we played on the emotions of our parents and were allowed to reward ourselves with a dream trip to San Francisco, Los Angeles, and Catalina Island before we left.

It was a fabulous time for us, and we spent all the money we had made that summer. We knew that would happen, but we didn't think we'd need it since we were enlisting. What we didn't know was that after the trip we would change our minds. The reality of joining the air force hit us pretty hard and we decided we'd be better off in college for the next two years. Our parents, more than somewhat disgusted, agreed to give us even more money than they had planned to in meeting tuition and other costs. This decision prompted me to return to Dakota Wesleyan, because I truly missed my girlfriend, Naomi Kaye, who was still attending college there.

I felt at home back in Mitchell, South Dakota, and enjoyed two great years concentrating on theater, music, and speech. This gave me the opportunity to play George in Thornton Wilder's *Our Town*, the young soldier in Christopher Fry's *A Phoenix Too Frequent*, and the young man in Anton Chekhov's *The Boor*. Looking back, I realize that some highly sophisticated teaching took place at that small college on the windswept South Dakota plains in the early 1950s, and it prepared me well.

In 1952 we graduated from Dakota Wesleyan University. The very next day my wife-to-be, Naomi, and our friends Zona Zeitner, Leona Rice, David Yamada, and Ben Burns (who was one of my best friends) got into the little '41 Chevy borrowed from my dad and drove off to New York City to find fame and fortune, or at the very least, jobs.

Zona was engaged to Ben, and they were going to Union Theological Seminary for her to study organ and piano and for him to become a Methodist minister. Leona was a voice major, and David, who hailed from Hawaii, simply wanted to see New York City.

Naomi, Zona, Lee, Ben, and I had rooms at a place called the Fairholm College Club just across the street from Columbia Teacher's College on 121st Street between Broadway and Amsterdam. The girls were on the sixth floor and Ben and I roomed together on the third. Though Ben was engaged to Zona and I was engaged to Naomi, in those days you didn't live together until after marriage. We lived in cooperative apartments where Ben and I shared a room together, and the bathroom and kitchen were shared with seven other tenants. The girls had the same arrangement upstairs.

I walked the streets for over a week, looking up at all those towers of Manhattan and dodging the traffic and the people. While I marveled at the architecture, the commerce, the literal drumbeat of the city, I kept thinking that surely somewhere in this metropolis there was a job for me.

Finally, after paying a search firm, I landed a job downtown, just across the street from Pennsylvania station, as a clerk with Gibbs and Hill Construction Company. I was responsible for locating blueprints of major international hydroelectric dams from enormous files and delivering them to the desks of the project engineers. Naomi, Lee, and Zona were hired as waitresses at the Stoddard Restaurant on Morningside Drive, which was a popular eating place for Columbia University faculty. Their day was made when Virgil Fox, the renowned organist for Riverside Church, dropped by for lunch.

New York City in the summer of 1952 was welcoming to all newcomers, a place where we were truly free of obligations, parents, and our midwestern conditioning. We rarely thought of crime, never feared being robbed, and thought nothing of walking in Central Park hand in hand late at night. Every dime we made we spent on theater and concerts, and every now and then an expensive nightspot.

We saw *Pal Joey* with Harold Lang and Vivienne Segal, *The Fourposter* with Betty Field, *The King and I* with Yul Brynner, Jack Carson in *Of Thee I Sing*, and Martha Scott in *The Male Animal*. We heard Carmen Cavellaro and his orchestra with singer Dick Haymes at the Astor Roof, and we pretended we could afford it when we went to dinner in the Starlight Room of the Waldorf-Astoria.

We knew instinctively that we needed this experience in New York as a vital part of our education, a feast that would always be with us. Fifty years later, Manhattan is still the place we are eager to return to. It replenishes our spirit, it lets us appreciate the arts and relive memories of our youth.

When fall came, Naomi returned to South Dakota to teach elementary music education. I stayed on in the city because I expected to be drafted at anytime and I needed to continue working before I was called up.

During this time I met an attractive young woman who worked at *Time* magazine. That impressed me, and since I was now alone in the city, one gets lonely, and plays and dinners have to be shared, and I was twenty-two years old. I rationalized that seeing her from time to time could be a lot of fun and wouldn't jeopardize my engagement to Naomi. After all, I thought, New York City is a very big place, so who would know?

Henry Fonda was starring in a new play, *Point of No Return*, and I asked Ann to see it with me. The show was playing at the Alvin Theatre, one of New York's biggest houses. Since my budget didn't allow for orchestra seats, we were relegated to one of the last rows in the center section of the balcony. Though we were far from the stage, we found the play an exciting, relevant story about making it in the business world.

October brought the inevitable and I received my personal "greetings" from Uncle Sam. I drove back to South Dakota in the borrowed Chevy to report to the draft board, see Naomi, and say goodbye to friends. During one of these farewell gatherings in Mitchell, arranged by Naomi's aunt, one of her friends, a woman I didn't know, walked over to me and said, "Who was the young woman I saw with you at *Point of No Return* in New York City?" I stared at her. How was it possible that she knew me, that night, in that theater, way up in that balcony? She had, I later learned, seen me in plays at Dakota Wesleyan.

On the spot I resolved: Do anything you wish, but remember, someone is always watching.

6

Front and Center

Drafted, I was shipped off to Fort Sill, Oklahoma.

Being subjected to rigid discipline—facing tough situations that test us both physically and mentally—is important for developing young men, particularly young men who've had it relatively easy all their lives. That is, young men who have had stable homes, parents, schools, and college. For a large share of middle-class kids, those early years of their lives are prescribed and largely decided for them, which was pretty much my case.

The army was just what I needed. There were healthy amounts of discipline, and importantly, the army serves as a great equalizer. Every new recruit is brought down to the same level, to the same physical and psychological existence and state of mind. We all experienced every daily routine together. We dressed alike, worked together, marched together, and learned the value of a being part of a group.

As I was raised an only child, privacy was a given in my life. I had my own room, and having never spent time around siblings, I was accustomed to having my own space. This was quickly shattered during basic training when I went into the latrine and saw two rows of ten toilets each facing each other. There were no booths, no walls, just twenty stools side by side in one room. Since we were limited even to the amount of time spent in the latrine, you had to sit there with people across from you and on both sides. At first, this was extremely embarrassing and unpleasant, but it helped accomplish the purpose—no one is special in the army. Also, it taught me not to waste time in the bathroom.

Basic training included a number of lecture courses. I did my best to pay attention because, as the cadre (the noncommissioned officers training us) kept repeating, "You guys are going to need to know this stuff when you get to Korea." Korea in those first few months after I was drafted in October 1952 was still an active war.

One morning our battery commander came into the class and said that we had to look especially sharp, sit up straight, and stay awake and alert because our class would be honored by a visit from Brigadier General Brittenham, the commanding general of the post. We had to look good, thus making our cadre and officers look good, too. After this announcement they gave us a smoke break. Nearly every young man smoked in those days—it was the manly thing to do and cigarettes at the post exchange were only fifteen cents per pack. I went outside for the break.

The classroom buildings at Fort Sill were old converted mule barns formerly used by the artillery. The barns still had large, heavy sliding doors that hung on rollers, and it took at least two people to push them open or shut. Since my closest friends weren't in my classroom but were in a similar barn down the line, I walked over and joined them for the break. When I returned a few minutes later, I saw that my classmates had already gone in and the big sliding door was closed.

What to do? Should I skip the class and hope they wouldn't miss me? That could have repercussions, and I knew that I needed what they were teaching in that room. Further, with the general arriving, I knew I had to be in that classroom. I couldn't slide the door open by myself, so I knocked on the door while composing my apology for being late. With effort the door was slowly pushed open.

I heard my commanding officer yell *Atten-hut*! There before me stood the officers and the whole class at rigid attention. And worse, the officers had formed a line and they were all saluting—me!

Staring straight ahead, I quietly, as humbly as possible, quickly scurried past them and slunk into my seat. The recruits unsuccessfully repressed their laughter while the officers and cadre fumed.

By the time I finished basic training, the Korean armistice agreement had been signed. Rather than being sent to Korea, I was assigned to Special Services at Fort Sill. My job was working in the "cage" at Honeycutt gymnasium, handing out basketballs, paddleballs, paddles, gloves, and all the athletic equipment available for soldiers to check out and use. This job was boring beyond measure but one that afforded lots of time to read.

One lazy afternoon my reading of a book of Edna St. Vincent Millay's letters was interrupted when along came a sergeant from the Public Information Office.

"According to your MOS [military occupational specialty], you have experience in theater?"

Since I was a speech and drama major, I said yes.

"What do you know about television?"

I knew nothing about television; my family never even owned a TV set. The first and only television I had seen was Roller Derby—women on roller skates—in a bar on Amsterdam Avenue in New York City the previous summer. But not knowing the point of this interview, I said "some."

He continued, "The major has just been assigned the responsibility of producing a weekly television show featuring the men and activities of Fort Sill. We would like you to try out as the producer or director or whatever the person in charge is called."

I put my book down and said, "This would be a good fit for me. What do I have to do?"

I knew that minute that I wanted this job because it would take me out of the cage and its tedium. I learned a long time ago that if you can read, you can do anything. The sergeant replied, "Write a script for a variety show and bring it over to the office Wednesday."

That night I went in the post library and found a book about writing for television. It had illustrations that showed me how television scripts are divided down the center of the page, the right-hand side containing the "audio" or words to be said or what the audience would hear, and the left-hand side containing the "video" or what the audience would see. This was quite clear and made sense. But I had no idea how to describe the video or what the camera saw or what the camera could or could not do.

I called KSWO-TV, the station in Lawton, Oklahoma, and I talked to a young man who was a TV director. I explained that I had to write this script and I didn't know where to begin.

"Well," he said, "it's easy."

Over the phone he told me that on the left-hand side you tell what the cameras are going to do. Cameras, I discovered, can only do certain actions or maneuvers.

The director in the control room through a headset tells the cameraman in the studio what he wants the camera to do. If you tell the camera to "dolly in" or "dolly out," the whole camera—pedestal, wheels, and all—moves in and out, closer to the subject or farther back. If you have a zoom lens, you say "zoom in" or "zoom out" and the mechanical action of the lens gives you a closer or a wider view. The camera remains stationary. To move the whole camera to the left, that's a "truck left," and a move to the right is a "truck right." You get nice effects, I learned, with a long arc to the left or the right. Later, as a director, I became "truck happy."

But then, if you want to go from, say, a close-up of a person's face on the left to the face of the person on the right, you just swivel the camera on the pedestal to the left or the right. That's called a "pan left" or a "pan right." The camera can also move up and down vertically for a "tilt up" or a "tilt down." And that's it.

The left-hand side of the script will tell what the camera sees and what the camera should do. It can tilt up, tilt down, pan left, pan right, zoom in, zoom out, dolly in, dolly out, truck left, truck right. I thanked the young man on the phone and wrote all of this down. I was ready to write the script.

It took me an afternoon in the cage to imagine a show with a girl singer, a band, a military interview of some kind, and a spot for some talented soldier to perform. All of this I made up out of whole cloth, but I got the job.

We decided to call the show *Front and Center*, and for the first program I lined up the Eighty-Seventh Army Band for two numbers, the director gave me a lead on a girl singer, Betty Black, the young wife of a major serving in Korea, and for the interview section I invited a young WAC (Women's Army Corps) captain who had just returned from the war zone. We rehearsed the band and the singer on the stage of theater number 1 on Thursday afternoon, and on Thursday night at 6:00 p.m. we all headed for the studio for our first broadcast at 8:00 p.m.

To a person, none of us had ever seen the inside of a television broadcast studio. But no one knew that.

With as much authority as I could muster, I took a look around the studio and said, "Let's put the band there at that end of the studio. The interview set should go between the band and the 'Cockles and Mussels' street scene set for Betty Black's number."

Fortunately the young director I talked with on the phone walked in and said, "Yeah, that's fine."

There was a big washtub in the middle of the floor, so I picked it up—and then jumped at least three feet into the air. There had been a nature program broadcast an hour earlier, and I had just given freedom to a huge snake that immediately began to slither all over the place, emptying the studio in seconds. This episode did wonders for our energy level. Once we had him safely under the tub again, we went on with our work.

I was not only the producer but also the master of ceremonies for *Front and Center*. We got the cue, and the Eighty-Seventh Army Band "struck it up." During that first number I was called to the telephone just outside the studio door. It was Major McKechnie from the Public Information Office—my boss.

"Private Hull, are the lights on out there? The music sounds fine, but all I can see are silhouettes of the band members." I opened the door and the studio lights were bright and glaring. Then I remembered a comment someone made about their TV set.

"Major, I've heard there's a button on your set called a "brightness" button and you should turn it either to the right or to the left."

"I'll try that." He came back to the phone with "You're right. The band looks fine. Carry on, Private Hull."

Then I introduced the singer. The set was a backdrop of an Irish street. Our space in the studio was limited, so I told Betty to push her wheelbarrow with the cockles and mussels a few feet while singing, then stop and turn and push it back so that the street scene would always be in the background during her number.

Though nervous, as we all were, she assured me that she understood the limits of the scenery. The problem was, she hadn't rehearsed the number in the studio, only at the base, and the spaces were different. I introduced her and she sang the first chorus: "As she wheeled her wheelbarrow, through streets broad and narrow, crying cockles and mussels, alive, alive-O!"

Watching on the studio monitor, I was pleased that her number looked and sounded just fine. She turned on cue and continued singing, but somehow she got lost in the song and forgot that she had to stay in front of the street scene set. Here she came, our young major's wife, pushing that wheelbarrow, not only through streets broad and narrow but right on past me sitting with the WAC captain, on past the Eighty-Seventh Army Band, and ultimately past the control room, the other cameras, the crew, and even the tub with the snake underneath. It was a singing tour of the studio, so to speak.

That wasn't the only problem on the premier night of *Front and Center*. The interview with the WAC captain was scheduled to follow the "Cockles and Mussels" number. Though we had rehearsed the music earlier, Sal Ferrante, the music director, did not give me the order of the numbers until we got to the studio. A few seconds before air time I filled in the blanks with the song titles, paying no attention to which music went where.

The WAC officer gave us a vivid account of what was going on in Korea and life in the Women's Army Corps. I thanked her, looked down at my notes, and announced that the Eighty-Seventh Army Band would now play "The Lady Is a Tramp."

The next day Major McKechnie called me in and said that for our first effort, the program was pretty good. "There's one thing, Hull," he said. "You've got to watch your juxtapositions." That sent me straight to the dictionary before I realized what he meant.

Thus ended the first program in the ninety-six-week run of my tenure with *Front and Center*. This was my initial experience working on a television program and being on camera. Fade to black! As rough as it had been, our soldier show, everyone agreed, was better than the public service film *Industry on Parade* that followed, and all of us had a wonderful time.

Betty Black and I became friends. She was a fine singer, trained and experienced, and since her husband was serving overseas she was always available for gigs at the service clubs and on our show. Often I doubled as her accompanist. She was, to me, an attractive "older" woman in her late twenties.

That fall a message was posted near the barracks ordering all personnel of the headquarters battery to fall out (be in formation) at 6:30 a.m., wearing the winter dress uniform. This was a ritual we went through twice a year, changing from summer dress to winter and vice versa. I went into my bunk area to make sure my uniform was presentable. The required Eisenhower jackets and trousers were not hanging with my other clothes. They weren't packed in my foot locker either. Aghast, I could not remember where my winter uniforms might be. This was a real problem because the inspection was set for the next day. Then I remembered.

In the spring I had complained to Betty Black that the barracks were bereft of any place to store my winter uniforms. She said that she had plenty of room, so I took them over to her house and hung them up in one of her closets, and promptly forgot about them.

This realization was doubly disconcerting because a few weeks back, Betty Black had joined her husband, who had been transferred directly from Korea to Austria, and the household goods had preceded her—household goods that included my dress uniforms and shirts. I've often wondered what the major thought when he discovered two sets of dress uniforms complete with corporal stripes in that shipment.

By now, my office was behind the big, new CinemaScope movie screen in theater number 1. Twentieth Century Fox's *The Robe* was one of the first films displayed in this new marvel of projection, and it was an exciting event for all of us in Special Services. I saw Doris Day in *Calamity Jane* and many other films from behind that screen. Though you were seeing everything backward, still, it was like having your own private show.

One morning I received a call that pop singer Johnny Ray was coming to the post and would my office please work with him on a show for the troops. He was a big name and his songs like "Cry" and "The Little White Cloud that Cried" were at the top of the charts. His style was truly distinctive. The passion in his voice was unique and appealing, and his sense of rhythm was remarkable.

With him we designed a Christmas show for all the troops, and it was filled with nostalgic and joyful music. Everyone was spellbound with his interpretation of "I'll Be Home for Christmas," half sung, half spoken, and totally emotional. His "Walking My Baby Back Home" is, in my opinion, the best of all recordings of that song. With the right management and promotion, Johnny Ray could have and should have been a long-lasting troubadour of significance and popularity in America. At least that's what I thought as I stood in the wings watching him perform at theater number 1 just before Christmas 1953.

Naomi and I were married the previous June, and she was living with me in Oklahoma. I knew I had married a good sport when Naomi welcomed the entire Eighty-Seventh Army Band, the girl singer, and the person interviewed from *Front and Center* into our small apartment every Thursday night after the show. They usually left sometime after midnight. The other building tenants didn't complain, largely because they were young and in the service, too—and more often than not, they came in and joined the party.

A few months later we were in South Dakota, home on leave.

While visiting my parents we took in a production of Noel Coward's *Blithe Spirit* at the Black Hills Playhouse. During intermission I ran into an old acquaintance, and he made a comment, one of those pivotal remarks that had a lasting impact on my life. Oh, the power of words and the power we have over each other with just the slightest comment! He said that he heard that Syracuse University in New York was now offering a master's degree in television.

By this time I had over a year's worth of *Front and Center* under my belt, and I was in love with television. It combined every aspect of the theater—music, speech, and drama—all my interests and passions. My two-year stint at Fort Sill would soon come to an end and I would have to face the real world and get a real job. I was quite certain I wanted to make a career in television, and to formalize the experience I was receiving, it seemed that Syracuse University might be the place to do it.

We were released from the army two months early in order to enroll in school. We packed up my dad's trusty little '41 Chevy and drove to Syracuse, New York, and the study of television—with high hopes for an exciting future.

7

With Thanks to the GI Bill

Our apartment in Syracuse was two bedrooms upstairs in a late-nineteenth-century house. One of the rooms was our kitchen and dining area, and the other was our living room and bedroom. We slept on a couch that folded out at night. The bathroom was a converted closet with a shower stall and toilet added. We had no furniture, so suitcases doubled for end tables. (For years our luggage had rings on them where we had set glasses.) At least our apartment consisted of two contiguous rooms. The other apartment on our floor, inhabited by another young married couple, also consisted of two rooms, but the two rooms were separated by the hall. In the morning when leaving our apartment for school, it wasn't unusual to intercept one or the other of our neighbors in various stages of undress going from the bedroom across the hall to the kitchen or visa versa.

We couldn't afford a telephone, but fortunately, Mrs. Hooker, our landlady, had one. The water pipes in the building were all exposed; you could see bare pipes running up the side of the wall in our kitchen. When the telephone downstairs was for us, Mrs. Hooker would take a pair of pliers and bang on the water pipes.

That provided a startlingly loud signal to come to the phone, which meant going downstairs and running outside around the house, often through three feet of snow, to Mrs. Hooker's door to take the call. Even today, whenever I hear water pipes banging I think the call is for me.

Naomi paid our bills that year working as a secretary in the speech department at the university. My check for $135.00 per month, from the GI bill, paid my tuition. Naomi's supervisor, Ethel Deisinger, was a warm and loyal friend to both of us and an important mentor and colleague for Naomi. During the late spring semester the big happening in that department was the unexpected disappearance of Dr. Allerdyce, a tenured, respected teacher in the speech department. One day, as far as we knew, she simply didn't come to work. Gone. Though the department was abuzz, no one seemed to know what had happened. She didn't come back.

On the other side of the campus I was busy in the TV studio with "Sequence Seven," our class studying for the master's degree in television. This class included some bright and interesting people who were to make their mark in television—Michael Ambrosino for one. He and I produced a series on social agencies called *Casebook*. One episode had Naomi and me introducing the program in a vignette of a young couple talking about adoption. Since I was adopted, I always held the idea that someday it would be good to do the same for someone else. He's our first son, Kevin Ron. We credit him for triggering the three siblings who came to us the hard way.

Mike Ambrosino would later initiate and produce the acclaimed *Nova* science series on public television as well as other important national work.

Owning a TV set was mandatory to successfully completing our assignments. Our first set cost sixty-five dollars and was, of course, black and white. Color TV was just an experiment at that point. One of the exercises we were put through was to watch assigned dramas on television and write down and identify each and every shot used. For example, a long shot is LS, a medium shot is MS, and a close-up is CU. This was an efficient way to get us to look at the visual sequence of shots being composed by the director cutting from camera to camera in telling the story.

Not all the students could afford their own TV set, so many nights Naomi would go to bed on the couch scrunched up next to the wall while I and four or five classmates sat along the edge of the other side of the couch watching the *Studio One* or *Playhouse 90* dramas and furiously making notes of the myriad shots the director was calling. It was all live television in those days, and this brought heightened energy and vitality to the productions. Keeping track of each shot, we learned how to quickly edit in our heads.

Over Thanksgiving break Naomi and I and our friend Bob Spearman and one of our classmates, Lela Deshmuk, from Bombay, India, set out to spend the long weekend in Manhattan. We had two goals: to see a Broadway show and to get into Steve Allen's *Tonight* television program. We secured box seats at the Winter Garden Theatre for *Peter Pan* starring the magical Mary Martin. Appearing as Wendy was Kathleen Nolan, who was later to become a friend.

At the end of the first act Mary Martin casts her spell, and like the Pied Piper, leads the Darling children flying through the nursery window, out among the stars on their way to Never Never Land. The set opens up and the sky is filled with Peter and the children, with London down below as they soar high over the Winter Garden stage. It was exciting, it was breathtaking—most of the audience was on its feet cheering them on. This was the New York theater I had always yearned to experience. We returned to Syracuse in high spirits and ready to complete the work necessary for a master's degree in television.

With a U-Haul trailer fastened to the '41 Chevy, we left Syracuse in September 1955 and made our way back to South Dakota, first to Naomi's home in Highmore and then on to mine in Rapid City.

This was one of those pivotal points in life when an era, a phase—"the old order"—ended and nothing would ever be the same. It was now time to enter the working world, and I needed a job.

8

Our Town

Like many of my peers, I was unsure of myself and filled with insecurities when I went off to college and later marched off for the mandated two years in the army. Making a career decision is a major process filled with anxiety, and for me, each new step in my life since I was a teenager has been accompanied, and motivated, by the gnawing feeling that I had to prove my worth. Would I ever be good enough? Did I measure up? These questions are always present, even today.

I had discovered at Syracuse University that it was the newly arrived "educational television" that seemed to hold a promise of worthwhile work that could make a difference in people's lives. By chance, serendipity, and luck, I found a new world peopled by educators, producers, teachers, actors, writers, scholars, and artists—people who have something to say.

In college I would hear cynics remark that everything depends on luck and "who you know," implying that you have to know the "right" people to get ahead. Everything does depend on who you know, but we make our own luck. Connections are essential. Relationships are the most important aspect of our lives. We create these ourselves and through them build the life we want.

My dream was to live in California and make it in television broadcasting in Los Angeles. However, in my search for a job the paths seemed to lead in other directions, and I didn't get there. This was partly due to the fact that when I finally did find a job, in Lincoln, Nebraska, I was so exhausted from looking that I simply decided to give this place a try for a while. California could wait, and it remained a lifelong, elusive goal.

I put together a résumé of my experience which, even double-spaced, didn't quite fill a page. There was college, the army and *Front and Center*, a master's degree in television, and a few summer jobs—busboy, bellhop, Western Union delivery boy—and that was it.

With this in hand, the first week of September 1955, I boarded a Continental Trailways bus in Rapid City and headed, I wasn't sure where, on the job quest. Denver was the first stop. Unannounced, I called on all three television stations, talked with whomever would see me, handed off my résumé, and got back on the bus. It was headed south, so I got off in Amarillo, Texas, and followed the same routine. From there I traveled on to Lawton, Oklahoma, to see old friends from my army days, and then east to Oklahoma City. I liked the station there—it was a new and shiny building and I enjoyed a thoughtful, encouraging interview with the program director. His courtesy to this kid who literally came in off the street is still appreciated. After that it was back on the bus to Little Rock and from there on to Memphis, Tennessee.

There's a special place in my heart for Memphis. By this time I was tired of being "on the road," bouncing around in those noisy, uncomfortable buses, walking from TV station to TV station, being rejected here and receiving some encouragement there. After checking into a third-rate hotel, I went out into the streets to find a place to eat. As I was passing a bar I saw a big television set through the window. Eating and watching television would be a luxury for me, so I went inside and took a place at the bar and ordered a sandwich.

Unfolding on the screen before me was a carefully crafted, inspiring production of a musical version of Thornton Wilder's *Our Town*. This was producer Fred Coe's *Producer's Showcase* broadcast of September 19, 1955. Featured were Eva Marie Saint as Emily and Paul Newman as George. Eva Marie Saint's performance in the drugstore scene, at her wedding, and reliving her twelfth birthday was achingly beautiful, heart-stopping perfection. I had enjoyed success playing George at Dakota Wesleyan University and was immediately captured by this version. "Love and Marriage," a lovely song written for the show, was sung by Frank Sinatra, who played the stage manager, and I was in heaven even as I was beginning to yearn for this journey to end, not forgetting that I needed a job.

As I looked at the screen and enjoyed the power of that story and those artists, I knew with certainty that this was the work I wanted to do, and these were the kind of artists I hoped to work with. This experience was a positive mental transfusion. I was back on track and almost eager to get back on the bus and into my professional future. Many years later I told that story to Eva Marie Saint, and she and her husband, television producer-director-writer Jeffrey Hayden, sent me a videotape copy of *Our Town* starring Eva Marie. It's as moving to me today as it was that Memphis September evening in 1955.

Our Town is, of course, a universal statement about life in America at the turn of the twentieth century, and for those of us living here in the Midwest, its magic still resonates. When I first read the part, I knew that I was George Gibbs in essential ways. Ten years later, I had another opportunity to bring him to life when actress Sandy Dennis—early in her career in her hometown of Lincoln, Nebraska—and I played Emily and George in scenes from *Our Town* in a benefit performance for her college sorority. I know George pretty well. By this time Sandy had Broadway's

Tony Award to add to her "Best Actress Award for 1956" from the Lincoln Community Playhouse, and our friendship began that award night when I won for "Best Actor." She had come a long way, and the night we played Emily and George, her talent inspired me to give the best theater performance of my life.

I left Memphis and proceeded on to Auburn, Alabama, for a job interview and from there rode the bus to Atlanta, Georgia. A telephone call alerted me to a producer-director position in Lincoln, Nebraska, and by now, newly exhausted by the bus ride, the new cities, and the job interviews, I decided to splurge. Spending money I didn't have, I flew from Atlanta to Chicago and there caught a Western Airlines plane to Lincoln.

At the Lincoln airport I told the cab driver to take me to a hotel, and he suggested "the Cornhusker."

"What a strange name for a hotel," I remarked.

The driver slowed down, and pulling over to the curb, fairly snarled, "You do know that you are in Cornhusker football country, don't you?"

"Oh, yes, of course," I laughingly lied, realizing the gravity of the situation and feeling lucky he didn't ask me to get out. I've learned a lot since then.

My first interview was conducted by the founder of what became the Nebraska ETV network, Jack McBride. That evening he invited a colleague, Bob Schlater, to join us for dinner at the Italian Village Restaurant. I was bemused by the fact that they had brought their own liquor and had to keep the bottles on the floor. Everyone in the place was constantly bending down and pouring drinks from under the table, as it was against the law for bottles to be in public view on top. Drinking out of bottles in brown paper bags left under the table detracted from the sophistication of the place. It was 1955, and Nebraska was not only a "dry" state but it was also known as "the white spot of the nation" for its constitution that prohibited the state from going into debt. Nebraskans, I was to learn, are sensible people who make it a point to live within their means. This was my first visit to Nebraska, and from the start I knew it was a singular place.

Fatigue from nearly three weeks on the road, those buses, the dust, rough highways, and no little boredom had claimed my energy as I arrived for the concluding interview with George Round, director of University Public Relations. We had barely begun visiting when he abruptly asked me in a gruff tone of finality, "Do you want the job or not?" This directness is a Nebraska trait. With diminishing vitality, I heard myself answer, "Yes, I do." It was a welcome realization that my wayward bus trip had almost come to an end. I would be a Cornhusker, too.

This time, a Greyhound bus took me out of town to Rapid City where my wife and the '41 Chevy were waiting.

Naomi and I carefully packed every inch of space in the backseat, the trunk of the car, and the awkward U-Haul trailer. We were ready to say goodbye to my parents and head for Lincoln when my father approached the car and said, "What are you doing?"

I reminded him that we have to be in Lincoln to start the new job in just a few days.

"Yes, I do know that," he said, "but what are doing with the '41?"

I knew this was his car, but we had been using it for over three years. Did he really expect it back? The car didn't mean anything to him. He certainly didn't need it and it had little value.

He interrupted my thoughts when he said, "I loaned you that car."

"Well, yes," I replied, "but Dad, that was three years ago. We've used it in Oklahoma, New York—and you don't need it. You'll probably sell it to some high school kid for 150 bucks, and . . ."

"That's right, I probably will," he said, "but that is my car and I expect you to buy your own car now that you have a job."

He wasn't angry and he didn't raise his voice, but he stood his ground and kept his word.

Muttering, we unpacked the Chevy and looked for options. One appeared. Naomi's father had learned that there was one last unsold new 1955 Chevrolet in the showroom of his friend's dealership in Faulkton, South Dakota. Though quite a distance away, this car dealer fortunately was a private pilot, and he picked up Naomi and me and flew us to Faulkton where we committed ourselves to the most gargantuan financial obligation of our brief married life. We drove back to Rapid City to repack our belongings, and from there we drove to Lincoln and entered the city in style in our "toast and cream" '55 Chevy.

That car is still dear to my heart and I consider it one of the best automobiles ever built. We paid two hundred dollars down on this two-thousand-dollar masterpiece, and in four years it was completely ours.

My dad was an honest man and he knew how to work. Though he was not able to stay in school beyond the tenth grade, he brought a broad intelligence and common sense to his life. Beginning as a mechanic in the local repair shop in Miller, South Dakota, he dreamed of one day having the resources to purchase his own car. Sweat and perseverance allowed him to achieve that dream many times over, and though I was initially frustrated by his action concerning the 1941 Chevrolet, I never resented him for it. Rather, I respect him for his tenaciousness in following through on his own word. I also knew what his life had been growing up in a large family with literally nothing, and how hard he had worked so that I could have something.

The first Sunday we were in Lincoln, we chose to attend the large downtown Saint Paul United Methodist Church because we suspected it would have a good choir and a fine organ. We were right. We even filled out the attendance record that morning. The senior minister at Saint Paul Methodist Church was Dr. Frank B. Court, a distinguished preacher well known throughout the national Methodist Church. In addition, he was a busy, respected speaker on the national circuit and was paid a healthy annual retainer by the General Motors Corporation Speaker's Bureau for many years. A natural, gregarious politician, he had friends in high places throughout the country. Of course we didn't know all of this that first Sunday, but we were impressed by his style and intellectual command and authority in the pulpit.

That evening about seven thirty we answered a knock on our apartment door and were astonished to see the Reverend Frank B. Court himself standing there. We would not have been more shocked if he had been the governor of Nebraska.

"Well, are you just going to come to church or what?" was his first comment. He was like that—blunt, just shy of being rude. We managed to mumble something about having sung in church choirs in the past, and he said, "Fine, I'll meet you Wednesday night [always choir night] at the corner door at seven thirty." And he was gone.

From her childhood, Naomi had always wanted children, specifically four girls. I wasn't opposed to children, but having been raised an only child I hadn't given children of my own much thought. That attitude changed after our first one, and he came to us the easy way.

We had been married four and a half years and we wanted a baby. Nothing was happening. We used to sit on the edge of the bed and wonder what we were doing wrong. Thanksgiving Day 1957, we took the wishbone from the turkey, dried it, and hung it on a lamp in our bedroom for good luck. Our friend Hodson Hansen, MD, stopped by one Sunday morning two weeks later. When he came into our apartment, his first words were "What do you kids want for Christmas?"

"Last night," he said, "I delivered a baby boy and the mother does not want to keep him. I would like you to have him if you want him. Don't tell me now. Think about it and give me a call later today."

Numb, we put our coats on and decided to take a walk around

the nearby park just off J Street. Halfway around the block we looked at each other and together we said, "Do we want him?" We rushed back to the apartment to call Dr. Hansen.

The following Thursday the mother signed the papers releasing him for adoption. Since we were doing this through a doctor and not a social agency, we were participating in what was called at that time the "gray market." That didn't matter to us. The following Monday, when our new son, Kevin, was eight days old, we brought him home. We were told that the adoption could be completed in six months but that the mother could change her mind in the meantime. It was a chance we had to take.

By the third month we had bonded. Kevin was our child and we knew we couldn't stand to lose him. We actually thought of contacting friends of ours, the Moores, who were living in Jakarta, Indonesia, managing the Goodyear plant there, in case we should have to leave the country. Fortunately we didn't have to jeopardize our citizenship to keep him. The six months elapsed and Judge Ronin signed the papers, making him ours.

A year later, December 1958, while Christmas shopping for Naomi's present I discovered an attractive necklace that featured a small silver wishbone with an embedded diamond chip. A wishbone, like the "lucky" Thanksgiving wishbone, was to become our family symbol, and I bought it.

Our new year began with Naomi feeling extremely tired and nauseated, but since she had recently been in for an examination, she knew she wasn't pregnant. Her mother and I were worried that she was seriously ill. We finally insisted that she see my general practitioner, and it only took him a few minutes to announce, "She's pregnant." She was over three months pregnant! We hadn't been doing anything wrong after all.

Brian ("the Lion") was born October 17, 1959. With our two boys, the wishbone became even more symbolic. October 17 was Saturday, a Big Red football Saturday, with Nebraska playing Missouri. To earn extra money I worked on Saturdays at the local CBS commercial station as a director. That morning I directed an hour-long children's show, *Juvenile Theatre*, and then went home for lunch.

That afternoon Naomi's water broke and we rushed off to Lincoln General Hospital. She went into labor and in three hours delivered Brian David. Naomi's timing was perfect. It was four o'clock in the afternoon, giving me time to get back to the TV station, rehearse the live commercials, and at 6:00 p.m. direct the news. At six thirty I rushed back to the hospital to be with Naomi and Brian, at eight thirty I reported back at the station to rehearse more live commercials, and then at 10:00 p.m. I directed the most important news block of the day.

In Nebraska everyone watches the ten o'clock news, at least through the weather forecast, and then goes off to bed by 10:20 p.m. The Nielsen audience measurement reports confirmed these viewing habits for years. If memory serves me, Brian's delivery cost us one hundred dollars. But I had in a single day made ten dollars for directing the kid's show and another ten dollars for each of the news blocks. Saturdays were a thirty-dollar day for us, and with our budget, this was essential income.

Two years later we were flying to New York City, and a friend, Marian Schimmel, owner of the Cornhusker Hotel, offered to take us to Omaha since she was leaving for New York City on the same plane.

After takeoff she leaned across the aisle saying, "I loved your story about the wishbone. My grandmother in the 1880s came to South Dakota in a covered wagon. She brought this with her, and I want you to have it." Reaching in her purse she handed Naomi a gold wishbone lapel pin. Naomi became pregnant during that trip in the Pennsylvania Hotel just across the street from Madison Square Garden.

Brandon joined the family the following August. We now had three boys, and Naomi did not have even one of the four daughters she wanted. Three boys, to me, was a big family, but we decided to take a chance even though it might mean four boys. It didn't. Kathryn arrived and made three boys worth it.

We lived on a beautiful street, Rathbone Road, which was lined with seventy-five-year-old elm trees that framed some old but charming homes. Our neighborhood was often referred to as "Fertility Flats" due to the predominance of children. This we blamed on the railroad. Not far away behind our street, each morning about 4:00 a.m. the Burlington Northern train made its noisy way past our bedrooms. Almost everyone woke up. We now had four children, our neighbors the Lawlors had seven, the Smiths had four, and the new neighbors, the Griffins, also had four.

One afternoon Sheila Griffin was setting out party favors and chips and dip for a cocktail party in an hour or so. Mrs. Berger from across the street dropped by to welcome her to the neighborhood. Seeing the party preparations, she said she'd come back, but Sheila insisted that she come in for a few minutes. Mrs. Berger, accompanied by a little boy about three years old, entered and the visit began.

The little boy went immediately to one of the bowls of dip and began scooping it up and eating it. Sheila was disconcerted, but Mrs. Berger said nothing, and the boy was able to continue having all the chip dip he wanted—while Sheila squirmed.

With the visit over, Mrs. Berger said goodbye and started out the door. Sheila cried, "Wait, you've forgotten your little boy."

Mrs. Berger turned around and said, "My little boy? I thought that was your little boy!" It was Brandon, our little boy, from the second house down.

Life was beautiful for us on Rathbone Road. We had a healthy, active family. With the ETV staff we were making significant progress developing educational television in Nebraska, and we were cultivating a coterie of stimulating friends, most of whom, like us, were from out of town.

Though we enjoyed Lincoln, we found it to be a rather closed society to newcomers. It seemed to us that most people here had gone to the University of Nebraska, had pledged a fraternity or a sorority, with the women coveting membership in the Junior League and the men taking part in myriad discussion clubs that dated back to the nineteenth century. These affiliations still played an enormously important role in their lives, but it was all unfamiliar territory for us.

Our first year in Nebraska we were dumbfounded by the overwhelming devotion people had for the Cornhuskers and Big Red football. We had never before witnessed anything like this kind of sports mania, but we were beginning to bond with Lincoln and the people, and we decided that if this was going to bother us, then we should leave Nebraska, because this was not going to change.

Lincoln was, I was learning, a father's son town. The third generation of the "old guard" was in place when we arrived. Most people were hospitable to us, though we always said we lived here twelve years before they stopped referring to us as that new couple from out of town.

In the 1950s the Lincoln business community was controlled by the "O Street Gang." These were the leading citizens who owned the businesses and industry of the community, and most of them were situated on or had offices hovering near the main thoroughfare, "O" Street. Like so many midwestern towns and cities, Lincoln was a grid: east–west streets were given letters, and north–south streets were numbered. "O" Street bisects the city, and property values have traditionally been higher on the south side as opposed to the north side of the street. When we arrived, the community leaders were the second and third generation from the "old" families dating back to the 1880s. This reminded me of Booth Tarkington's *The Magnificent Ambersons* and how certain families had always been in control of the business and social life of the community.

The first generation was the immigrants—hardy, determined,

admirable people who knew the hardships, work, and joy of building the city and state. While many in the second and third generations built on the successes of their parents and contributed significantly to the life of the city, some carried themselves with a sense of "entitlement," which runs contrary to my nature. Perhaps this comes out of my insecurity of not knowing who my ancestors are or where they came from, or from my bottom-rung beginnings, but it also reflects my deep belief that each of us must earn our own reputations and respect from our peers, and not justify our status by who our parents or grandparents were.

In 1939 Nebraska author Mari Sandoz wrote her book *Capital City*. Her premise was that the capital city was the home for the state university, state government, state penitentiary, state mental hospital, and myriad other related agencies, and that the inhabitants made their living off the backs of the honest, hardworking people (the "real" people) in ranching and farming communities spread across greater Nebraska.

She maintained that the book was a composite of all the capital cities in the Great Plains, including Austin, Oklahoma City, Topeka, and Lincoln. That may be, but if you read the book, you know it's about Lincoln. In this novel some of the old families are still identifiable, as are the physical descriptions of the various sections of town.

My view is that this was her hate letter to Lincoln, and when it was published the people living here thought so, too. In those early years, she never felt accepted or appreciated by the townspeople and their social circles. It was the late 1920s and the early 1930s, and Mari Sandoz lived her life her own way. If that meant she would be criticized for socializing with some "avant-garde" intellectual, independent writers and poets in the Teepee Room at the Cornhusker Hotel—all the while smoking "in public"—then so be it.

It didn't help that in *Capital City* she wrote about the annual Aksarben (Nebraska spelled backward) weekend and the coronation of the king and queen of the mythical kingdom of Quivira, though she changed the names. This is the annual highlight of the Nebraska social season, and in her account one of the prominent "dukes" of the kingdom is discovered dead with his feet sticking out under a stall in the men's room in the basement of what is clearly the Cornhusker Hotel.

By 1960 times had changed. Sandoz was a prominent writer on everyone's guest list whenever she was in Lincoln. One of the "families" had a party for her to honor the publication of the *Son of the Gamblin' Man*. Alone briefly, Mari and I were standing under an elegant Venetian chandelier in front of a large cut-glass punch bowl. As I was filling her cup she turned to me and remarked, "Twenty years ago I wouldn't have been invited across this threshold," and with a slight grin and nod to me, she added, lowering her voice, "and frankly, you wouldn't have gotten in either."

9

We Had a Dream

KUON-TV, the educational television station of the University of Nebraska, came into being through an unusual relationship with John Fetzer, owner of the local commercial station, KOLN-TV, Channel 12. In 1953 KFOR-TV, Channel 10, was the competitor for the advertising revenues of the area, and this station was losing money. In an "enlightened self-interest" proposal, Mr. Fetzer bought KFOR-TV in February 1954, took Channel 10 for himself at KOLN-TV, and offered the University of Nebraska the opportunity to apply to the Federal Communications Commission (FCC) to have Channel 12 changed from a commercial to an educational designation—thus creating for himself a one-station monopoly in a lucrative market.

Once that was accomplished through the forward thinking of Chancellor Clifford Hardin and his new director of television, Jack McBride, KUON-TV became a reality. But there were challenges.

We had no studio, no cameras or equipment of any kind, a meager five-person staff (which included our shared secretary), and literally no production or programming budget.

We did have the educational resources of a major university, many ideas for programs, dozens of eager students volunteering to serve as members of our crew, and plenty of faculty members who wanted to be on television. Under daunting circumstances, we set out to create a worthwhile television service with a young, inexperienced staff—all of whom had big dreams, vaulting ambitions, and inexhaustible energy.

Again the generous Mr. Fetzer stepped in and invited us to share the KOLN-TV studios and to use their old transmitting tower next to the building, which gave us a coverage area of a little over a thirty-five-mile radius. KOLN-TV broadcast their programs from a new tower west of Lincoln on Channel 10, covering vastly more territory. This partnership was one of the most unusual and ultimately successful commercial and educational cooperatives in the history of American broadcasting.

At Channel 10 we had only two program sources: we could produce a "live" studio program or we could broadcast a film. This was five years before videotape entered the scene and before there was a national PBS educational network for us to carry. We did have 35-millimeter slides for use between programs, which we put on the screen while we played recorded "dinner music" from 6:00 to 6:30 p.m. We called this "Evening Prelude." To comply with FCC rules we changed the visual every ten minutes; usually the record-album cover of the classical music we were playing. We felt that it was a real public service to offer a quiet half hour of classical music on television during dinner.

Since we were sharing a studio, we could produce one of our live shows on Channel 12 and then immediately get out of the way so that KOLN-TV could go live with their program on Channel 10. The engineers were the heroes of the day, not to mention their prowess as track stars.

At the close of one of our programs, an engineer had one and a half minutes to run out of the control room, stampede down the hall into the studio, and unplug all the audio lines and all the camera video lines from transmission over Channel 12 and quickly plug them into the transmission system of Channel 10, and then, at breakneck speed, race back up the hall to resume their work in the control room. This feat was accomplished during the station breaks of both stations, and we had hired students whose responsibilities included opening and closing the proper doors so the engineers could run this mini-marathon through unobstructed hallways. This was live television—not only in front of the cameras but behind them as well.

Every now and then, after one of these frenzied skirmishes, I would look up from the director's chair at the Channel 12 monitor to discover that we were broadcasting *The Price Is Right*, and Channel 10 was carrying *Backyard Farmer*. Somehow the switch had not been made, and when this happened both stations would be faded to black until the proper wires could be unplugged and plugged in again. This modus operandi lasted from November 1, 1954, our first day of broadcasting, until the fall of 1957 when we inaugurated our own studio in the basement of the Temple Building in what was once a cafeteria on the university campus.

Our new studio on campus was a big improvement over Channel 10's because ours didn't have a pole smack in the middle of the staging area like the one at KOLN-TV. Every day we had to disguise that pole in some imaginative manner. Sometimes it was a chimney, or a column, or a tree, but it was *always* in the way.

I miss those days of live television. There was that electric sense of excitement, of importance, when you sent that signal, at that very moment, directly into people's homes. That sense of urgency is diminished in the refinement of perfecting everything through multiple tapings until the talent and production crew get it right. Often during this process the original vitality is lost along with that sense of power, of instantly connecting with the audience.

Gone are the wonderful "bloopers" of yesteryear when mistakes were made and couldn't be retrieved. One of our favorite expressions was, "Well, it's just 'poof in the night.'"

For example, one evening I was doing a live introduction on air of *The Play of the Week* (David Susskind's wonderful series of great dramas featuring Broadway's finest actors). These were made possible by the new Ampex videotape technology we gratefully received from the Ford Foundation in 1959. The play was *Victoria Regina*, featuring actress Helen Hayes, first lady of the theater. After extolling the merit of the drama and the actress, I said, "Now enjoy this remarkable drama, *Rictoria Vagina* . . . of course I mean *Victoria Regina* with Helen Hayes."

Or when one of our hosts mentioned Thanksgiving as one of the great sexual holidays (he meant secular) in America. Or on another occasion when he introduced a film from Hawaii, describing it as the "Land of flat sandy women and beautiful beaches."

Weather is always of prime importance in Nebraska, and at that time the weather reports were always given as the lead story on the nightly news. One night the fellow giving us the latest temperatures and weather forecast while standing in front of a map of the upper Great Plains looked directly into the camera and said, "You Nebraskans are in for some very severe weather," then turning and referring to the map, continued, "because there is a large, cold mare's ass coming down from Canada." Those of us in the control room were transfixed with surprise. Of course he insisted he had said air mass.

From the beginning our only mission was to provide an alternative to commercial television and to produce programs of educational and cultural merit. Some of those early programs are worth remembering. For example, we had programs with such titles as *Red Cross Wife Savers* (it was the 1950s), filled with household tips and hints on running a successful home. Then there was *Bugs and Things* from the Entomology Department. I hated producing this one, because inevitably half the cast found a new home in our studio. In the late 1950s we even had a series called *Sports for the Mrs.* ("Hello, ladies, today the coach is going to teach you how to enjoy a football game.") Try broadcasting that today.

The summer of 1956 I was assigned to produce a six-week series designed to teach beginning swimming through the auspices of our local YWCA. For this we had to do some substantial creative thinking because we had no remote television facilities to go on location. We couldn't afford to shoot on film, and there wasn't a swimming pool within miles of the studio. We did have, however, some black drapes for the background and to cover the floor, necessary when creating "limbo lighting." This lighting directs the attention strictly on the people in a black or limbo background, thus eliminating the need for expensive scenery, a technique very popular in the early days of live television.

I brought in an ironing board and painted it black. By placing it in front of the black background and black floor it was virtually invisible. Our student swimmer was a nine-year-old girl in her bathing suit. I had her lie prone on the ironing board, facing the same direction as the ironing board's front end, allowing her arms to be free. The instructor, also in a bathing suit, was standing behind her explaining the various strokes as the young girl demonstrated them.

Over this scene, with a second camera, we superimposed the water in a fish tank, in which one of our volunteer students made waves with a stick just out camera range. By carefully shooting the scene, superimposing the water over just the lower half of the "swimmer's" body, it appeared to the viewer that she was following the coach's instructions and splashing away in a pool. Viewers accepted these programs, and the YWCA was very pleased with the registrations achieved as a result of that summer effort.

Another of those early programs was *Backyard Farmer*. Viewers call in with lawn and garden questions for a panel of agriculture experts from the university. Wayne Whitney, the program's "star," was a university extension agent, as we called them in the old days. Wayne was a man who would drive halfway across Nebraska to help some family figure out what disease was ruining the trees on their place, and he was invaluable to the show. His robust countenance and delivery and his ribald sense of humor attracted people in much the same way the personality of Julia Child brought viewers to our screens some years later with *The French Chef*.

Wayne, almost every season, couldn't resist saying that a lady had just called in and wanted to know what to do about the "fungus on her flox." And if that wasn't bad enough, another of his favorites was "This lady has aphids on her asters." In the early 1960s *Backyard Farmer* was for a time the highest Nielsen-rated program in all of educational television in the country, and it flourishes to this day, a staple of the Nebraska network television schedule. This extraordinarily high audience rating was achieved by one of our network transmitters in the early days when the people in North Platte, Nebraska, could get only one other station.

Working in educational television is continually fascinating. It's the best place to get a liberal arts education every day. Anyone who has anything to say can cross your studio threshold and share their talent and their years of research and experience. We are constantly sitting at the feet of scholars.

10

Shapers of the Dream

Extraordinary people came to us in the early years and immeasurably helped us design and shape the statewide broadcasting service we became. The alumni of Nebraska public television are a wide assortment of people from all over the United States, from every economic and social level of society. We came together in the mid-1950s on these beautiful and prolific plains united in our belief in the potential for educational television. Our origins and early leaders came out of higher education, and we were dedicating ourselves to something worthwhile, something that would have lasting value and give meaning to our lives and the lives of those who watched.

Here are some of the indelible people who saw the promise of educational television and were important to our growth and success.

VIRGINIA FAULKNER

Virginia Faulkner was the editor in chief of the University of Nebraska Press at a crucial time in its history. We were fortunate to have her working with us on scripts and program ideas. Virginia, born into a wealthy insurance family in Lincoln, was an eccentric, gifted, often brilliant writer and editor. In the 1930s she had written *Friends and Romans*, which predicted auspicious success for a young writer. She worked writing scripts on national radio programs in New York such as *Duffy's Tavern* and *The Fred Allen Show*. In California, MGM put her in their script department where she contributed to the scripts for two Greta Garbo films, among others. In 1947 Virginia returned to the East, and with her composer friend Dana Suesse wrote a Broadway comedy with music, *It Takes Two*, which featured Vivian Vance, a young actress who later became Ethel Mertz alongside Lucille Ball in television's *I Love Lucy*.

While working in New York City she created a popular continuing character for the magazine *Town and Country* called "Princess Tulip." This audacious character was often used in advertising and graced the windows of stores on Fifth Avenue. As Virginia described her, "Princess Tulip got up with the birds and went to bed with anything." Later she found time to ghostwrite *A House Is Not a Home*, the autobiography of Polly Adler, Manhattan's most famous "madame."

Looking back to her New York days, Virginia, afflicted with alcoholism, told me that she never saw *Gone with the Wind* all the way through because she couldn't go four hours without a drink.

Virginia was fortunate that her career path intersected with distinguished professor Bernice Slote's, and they forged a truly productive friendship. Recognizing Virginia's uncommon abilities, Bernice was there for her when she most needed her. Every few months when Virginia would slip back into her old habits with alcohol, Bernice, keeping a close eye, would make arrangements for someone to teach her classes, go to the university press, pick up Virginia, and the two of them would drive out through the countryside of Nebraska, stopping only for a McDonald's hamburger now and then. These "side trips through Nebraska" lasted two or three days, allowing Virginia time to sober up. Bernice would drop her off at her apartment, and in a day or so Virginia was back at work at the press with renewed vigor and clarity of mind, eager to be back at work. It was Virginia who suggested that Bernice focus her career on the work of Willa Cather, and Bernice is acknowledged as one of the foremost Cather scholars.

The alcohol didn't seem to diminish her writing and editing talent, her wit, or her gift as a raconteur. One Christmas, shopping for her present, I found a handsome, heavy brass paperweight in the form of the letter *F* for Faulkner. She opened the package, held it up, and said, "Where are the other three letters?"

She was a woman of no pretense. She dressed in simple tailored suits, kept her gray hair rather short, and wore no makeup. But due to her singular personality, one would never call her "plain." Her eyes flashing with ideas, her command of the language, and her articulate, rapid-fire manner of speaking enhanced her appearance and kept us fascinated. One afternoon during a program planning meeting with our program director, Bob Schlater, Virginia asked if we could arrange a meeting the following Tuesday at 2:00 p.m. Bob, who had just returned from his first visit to London, reaching for his calendar said in the British manner, "Just a minute, I'll have to check my *shedual.*" Virginia came back with, "Oh, *scit!*"

Her acerbic, razorlike wit was the exterior of this woman, the part you got to know first. In time you realized that she was indefatigable in the amount of hours, energy, creativity, and thought she brought to her skills as a writer and an editor, not to mention the high standards she maintained and the auspicious reputation she earned for the University of Nebraska Press.

Virginia Faulkner set the University of Nebraska Press on its way to enviable heights. She convinced Mari Sandoz to let her publish a book of Mari's short pieces, essays, vignettes, and stories. The work is *Hostiles and Friendlies*, and Sandoz told me that Virginia Faulkner was the best editor she had ever worked with. "She took this vastly disparate collection of material and made sense out of it. I didn't think it could be done," she remarked.

Virginia died unexpectedly while watching *Monday Night Football*, a true Nebraska Cornhusker.

JOHN KRIPPS

As we were launching educational television in Nebraska in the mid-1950s, improvisation was our bottom line. With an annual budget barely over sixty thousand dollars and five staff members, we were always scrambling to borrow set pieces or make them ourselves or recruit volunteer help—anything to get the show on the air and to save money we didn't have. Volunteers and students were the backbone of our production crews, and we were always looking for new recruits to work in the studio. We were paying students one dollar an hour to run our cameras and audio and carry out all the other duties of the studio production crew. Then, quite unexpectedly, we tapped an unusual source.

In 1962 Maurice Sigler, warden of the state penitentiary, asked if we could use some additional manpower at KUON-TV at no cost. He offered to make available one of the inmates from the penitentiary if we could provide transportation and lunch for him. We would give this person hands-on training in the hope that it could help him find employment after his incarceration. Warden Sigler's experiment is regarded as the first informal "work release" program for inmates at the Nebraska State Penitentiary.

Our first "trainee" was a young man named John Kripps. He was in his midthirties and had been in and out of jail since his teens. Mostly he had been a thief, stealing cars primarily, and apparently not a good one. I drove to the penitentiary and picked him up at eight o'clock every morning and delivered him back to that walled fortress at 5:00 p.m. each day, or if he worked on a show during the evening we would drive back at 10:00 p.m.

There were some employees and parents who had serious questions about bringing an inmate into a college setting. We had certain rules that we agreed to. John could not work closely with women. Most of our student crew members at that time were men, so that worked out pretty well. We could always use women in the control room while he worked in the studio and vice versa.

Someone had to be with John every minute of the day, including assigning someone to accompany him to the men's room. He was never to be out of our sight.

Everyone followed the instructions to the letter, and fortunately John understood and cooperated fully. He had never been guilty of any violence of any kind, and after we got to know him, he became one of us.

When we first met I noticed that he had the grayest, coldest eyes I had ever seen. His face, handsome in a way, had a fixed look—rigid with a firm, unsmiling, thin-lipped countenance—almost as if he were wearing a mask.

John was a success story for all of us. After his release from prison, he eagerly worked hard with us, learning television engineering quickly and making many friends at the university.

Later John shared an apartment with John Eutzy, an inmate he had known in "the place," who was out on parole. Two parolees living together was against the rules. John knew it, and I insisted he either move out immediately or I would report him to Warden Sigler. He moved out. Years later I heard that John Eutzy was on death row in Florida.

One afternoon I had a call from a woman who said that she and her husband were going to leave the country for a number of months. They had a lovely home filled with expensive acquisitions from their travels, and they were looking for someone they could trust to "house sit" their property. A young man had applied to them and given my name as a reference. His name was John Kripps. They were impressed when they spoke with him and wanted to know if they could safely entrust their home and possessions in his care for nearly a year.

This is one of those times when you want to help someone, but at the same time you feel the obligation to be honest and forthcoming to innocent people who will put weight in your opinion.

The question was, of course, do they have a right to know about John's prison record? I couldn't hesitate, either, or ask if I could call them back. I had to respond immediately.

"John can do anything," I told them. "He can fix or repair any machine or part of the household. I know that he would respect your property, take care of it, and would be an ideal person for this situation." I did not mention his history. She thanked me, and John got the job. I liked John and I knew that this would be a big test for him—and for me.

I couldn't sleep that night worrying about the possible outcome of this decision. He would have every intention of taking good care of the property and valuables, but would he be tempted, could he be trusted? Despite my doubts, the deal was concluded and I was responsible.

The next day I called Warden Sigler and asked if I had done the right thing. He replied, "Absolutely. We can't hold a person's past over his head forever. Give him a chance, give him a break." I felt better.

Time was to prove that John gained self-esteem, took excellent care of the house (even insisting that every guest remove their shoes at the door), and lived in the best surroundings of his life. About nine months later the couple returned, well pleased and satisfied to find a well-maintained home and their treasures intact.

After a couple of years John decided to get married. His bride, Sue, was pretty, intelligent, and an exemplary student studying drama in the theater just above the television studio. He asked me to be his best man, and my wedding gift to him was to pay the rental on all the men's tuxedos.

Standing alongside John in front of the congregation and looking at the assembled guests, I quickly noted that a self-selection process had put the university crowd on the left-hand side of the church sanctuary and the penitentiary alumni on the right—a new twist on the concept of "town and gown." The differences were most apparent in the women. "Prim and well coiffed" was on the left and "let's party" was on the right.

For the wedding reception we were given an address on North Forty-eighth Street. I had to wait for the ushers and groomsmen to change clothes so that I could collect the tuxedos and return them the next day. Naomi and I were the last to leave the church.

We found the address on a large nondescript building. Our instructions were to drive around to the rear of the building and enter through the back door. We drove around to the back, but there wasn't any back door. There was a telephone booth attached to the building, but no door. We started walking around the building looking for some other entrance when we encountered another couple. We said we were looking for the wedding reception. They said, "This is the right place. Go around in back."

"We've done that," we said, "and there's no door."

They replied, "Didn't they tell you? Go through the phone booth."

The phone booth? We walked back to the phone booth, pushed back the door, stepped in, and knocked on the back wall. Sure enough, the back of the booth opened and we were inside. We had our first experience in what had once been a speakeasy, a secret from the cops, a place used for gambling, drugs, or illegal liquor. Just the kind of rendezvous point John Kripps and the penitentiary crowd would know about.

The reception was noisily underway, and repeating the scene in the church, the university crowd was clustered on one side of the room with the ex-convicts and their partners on the other. The two groups were mingled only on the dance floor, but still at some distance. This convergence of two cultures was our own *Guys and Dolls* with the Damon Runyon underworld New Yorkers mixing it up with the Salvation Army.

About halfway through the evening, John angrily came over to me, saying, "Someone stole my mother-in-law's purse."

"What should we do? Call the police?"

He sternly replied, "You never call the cops when you been in that place yourself."

The purse was stolen, apparently, during the ceremony at the church. He was sure he knew who did it, so he walked over to the fellow, grabbed him by the front of his jacket, and slammed his head up against the wall, saying, "Okay, you son-of-a-bitch, where is it?" John wasn't acting tough, he *was* tough. After three or four slams against the wall the dazed guest handed over the money he had taken and allowed that he had stolen the purse.

"Come with me," John said. "I know where the purse is."

Later, after driving a couple of miles and borrowing a ladder from a nearby filling station, we climbed to the roof of the Safeway grocery store and found the purse. The culprit had taken it, removed the money, and tossed the purse onto the roof of the store on his way to the reception.

It was a lovely, starlit midnight, and I remember looking out at the lights of the city and thinking, "How the hell did I wind up on the roof of the Safeway store looking for a stolen purse?"

John Kripps was a valuable employee for us for a number of years. After nearly twenty years in prison he managed to support himself, have a family, and for the most part enjoy a productive life. His salvation was a caring "family of friends" at Nebraska educational television who persisted with him and insisted that he have a good life.

ESTHER MONTGOMERY

One of those friends was Esther Montgomery. Not unlike Mari Sandoz in her devotion to teaching and books, she was a smart, dedicated master English teacher at Lincoln High School, where she had taught both Dick Cavett and Sandy Dennis during their high school careers. At age fifty-seven she left Lincoln High and for the next ten years taught literature to thousands of students from our educational television studios.

Esther possessed an innate sense for the visual. Through her research and travels she had collected artifacts, models, pictures, and books that she used to bring American and English literature lectures to life in the classroom. She would haul out an Elizabethan stage, castles, riverboats, and busts and models of literary characters. Hers was a truly impressive collection. Begun in the 1920s, it had come to fill a whole separate room at Lincoln High. Because of these visuals, her transition from the classroom to the television studio was a seamless process.

When teaching poetry and short stories during her television classes, she often roped people like me into doing readings or dramatizing certain sections of American literature. These daily literature broadcasts were seen in dozens and dozens of high schools across Nebraska. At one point the students were reading James Thurber's *The Secret Life of Walter Mitty*. As you know, Walter Mitty was living in his own daydreams more than the real world most of the time. The scene has Walter (me) standing in front of the wall of a department store his wife has just entered, but in his mind it becomes the wall behind him as he bravely faces a firing squad.

Heroic Walter, with square-jawed defiance, asks for a cigarette as he squints his eyes and stares his assassins down. Then, when a blindfold is offered, he gruffly exclaims, "To hell with the blindfold." Very tough stuff. Taking a deep drag on the cigarette, Walter bravely exhales the smoke. The sound of firing is heard. Fade to black.

Playing Walter, I stood defiantly facing the firing squad and pantomimed nonchalantly taking a drag off the cigarette, but when the arm came into view offering the blindfold, my mind went blank. Shaking my head, I gallantly said, straight into the camera, "Never mind the hankie" (which it was). The sound of firing was heard.

I still miss live television.

Esther worked with us at Nebraska public broadcasting until she died at age eighty-nine in 1989. Our staff considered her our confidant, our mother confessor, our friend. After she retired from her on-camera teaching role, we kept her on staff as a resident librarian, researcher, and grammarian. In her corner of the building she also served as banker, cashing checks before payday for strapped employees, and our country store operator, always stocked with a good supply of cigarettes, candy, and plenty of hot coffee and herbal tea. She was always there for us with unconditional love and that reliable shoulder to cry on or celebrate with. She took care of people in a sincere, unsentimental way.

A loyal advocate of education via television, Esther was always on the lookout for good program ideas and knew just which buttons to push with certain producers to get an idea into production. After she learned that the transcripts of the famous 1879 trial of Chief Standing Bear were available, she was determined we would tell his story.

The poignant story of the Ponca chief's defiant stand against the U.S. government established for the first time that "an Indian is a person within the meaning of the law." Esther's insistence and tenacity was the catalyst for the research and fund-raising that resulted in *The Trial of Standing Bear*, a major drama presented nationwide in prime time on PBS.

In December 1971 we moved into the new telecommunications building. For the first time we had a spacious staff break room complete with vending machines with coffee and tea, candy, soft drinks, sandwiches, and everything. The company that owned the vending machines told us that we could no longer have our own individual "wildcat" coffee pots throughout the building. They explained that the coffee vending machine is of primary importance as it subsidizes the other machines. Therefore, people had to buy their coffee in the break room for the company to make a profit.

I dutifully sent an individual note to each of the 250 people working for us explaining that "wildcat coffee pots" had to be a thing of the past. Esther received my note, and in response she sent a memo to all 250 people on the staff, which read, "Well, I've been called a bitch and a whore, but I've never been called a wildcat before." Coffee and hot herbal tea continued to be served in her library until her last working day.

In the 1970s when the Dick Cavett Show was the most artic-ulate, urbane, witty, intelligent talk show on the air, Dick inter-viewed writer Truman Capote. The next morning Dick called Es-ther, saying that Mr. Capote told how he knew Willa Cather when he was a young man of eighteen and met her a number of times at the New York Public Library. Only, Capote called her Willa *Cay*-ther, not Cather. "What about this, Esther?" Dick asked.

Esther said, "Dick, I taught with Willa Cather's sister Elsie, and she said Cather; Mildred Bennett and all the Cather aficionados in Red Cloud [Cather's hometown] say Cather, but if you'd *ray*-ther say *Cay*ther, go right ahead."

For over thirty years Esther was an essential part of the heart and spirit of Nebraska educational television. Her one debilitating fault was that she smoked—all the time. When she was eighty-six she had severe emphysema and one night was quickly hustled off to the hospital. She was not in good shape.

I called her doctor and told him to keep us informed, as we were literally her family. We were prepared to deal with the insur-ance and financial details that would need attention. I asked him to be completely honest with me about her condition. The doctor said, "Well, Ron, we almost lost her last night, but with the help of oxygen she pulled through. Fortunately, she doesn't smoke."

"Who told you she doesn't smoke?" I asked.

"She did," the doctor replied.

I had to tell him that she certainly does smoke and has been smoking for the past sixty years.

When I went into her room she was sitting halfway up in the hospital bed with tubes in her arms, her nose, and her mouth. She could barely talk with all of that paraphernalia.

"Esther," I said somewhat sternly, "how could you tell the doc-tor that you don't smoke?"

With a great deal of effort she whispered, "I don't."

I looked at her suspiciously and said, "When did you stop?"

"Yesterday," she replied with a good deal of satisfaction.

True to her word, she had quit yesterday. She never smoked again.

Three years later she was back in the hospital, eighty-nine years old, weak and tired. When I came into the room she motioned the nurse to help her out of bed so she could sit in the chair and visit with me eye to eye. With the oxygen and respirator to assist her breathing, and all the other tubes, it was too difficult for her to speak, but she could write notes.

"How is Kathryn?" one of the notes read. She had a close relationship with our daughter, since Kathryn had lived with Esther and assisted her during the summertime during her college years. She wrote questions and I brought her up to date on the activities of the station and the people she loved.

One of her doctors stopped by. Taking her hand, he looked her in the eye and said, "Esther, I want you to get a good night's sleep, to get a good rest, because I think tomorrow we'll try to get you off the respirator and see how that goes for you. What do you think?"

There was a vivid flash in her eyes as she looked at him, a fierceness of recognition, and just as fiercely, she nodded her head in agreement. I kissed her and said goodnight. The next morning we had a call that Esther had died peacefully at nine thirty that morning.

Esther loved the works of John Neihardt. Her favorite was *The River and I*. Her will stipulated cremation and a request that her ashes "become one with the Missouri River." The Nebraska Highway Department assisted us by closing, for half an hour, one lane of traffic on the bridge over the Missouri River at Nebraska City. Eighteen staff members took turns pouring her ashes into the river while the others threw garden flowers with them. The trees and foliage along the river were glistening in their fall splendor, and the river majestically carried a long, narrow, serpentine rope of bronze and yellow flowers in honor of a great teacher and friend.

11

My Two Friends
John Neihardt
and Mari Sandoz

From those earliest years in the 1950s, this new medium of educational television attracted the interest of major creative and intellectual people, and we were eager to make these connections.

JOHN G. NEIHARDT

John G. Neihardt, Nebraska's poet laureate and author of *Black Elk Speaks* and *The Cycle of the West*, brought literacy, history, poetry, and exciting storytelling to some of our earliest efforts. He also brought viewers by the droves to our fledgling KUON-TV educational television station, and we brought him book sales and helped reestablish his fame and literary prominence.

The handsome bust of Neihardt in the rotunda of the Nebraska Capitol, signifying him as a member of the Nebraska Hall of Fame, was created by his wife, Mona. She had studied sculpturing under Rodin in Paris. While she was there she read some of Neihardt's poems and began corresponding with him—he in Bancroft, Nebraska (that prosy little village, as he described it)—and she on the Left Bank. They fell in love and she agreed to meet him, for the first time in person, in Omaha and get married. To save money he walked down the railroad tracks from Bancroft to Omaha, nearly seventy-five miles, and met his bride, who may have been surprised to find that she was nearly a head taller than he.

In 1961 he came to Lincoln from his home near Springfield, Missouri, to appear in three taped television programs about his life, his writing, and his poetry. People still boast that Neihardt was one of their teachers at the University of Missouri and most often mention his remarkable television lectures, *The Twilight of the Sioux.*

Neihardt, extraordinarily photogenic, was a television natural, and unlike Sandoz, took to it easily. With a great mane of white hair framing a handsome countenance, even the camera sensed the meaning in his piercing, azure blue eyes. As distinguished university professor Bernice Slote described him, "He was a mystic—craggy, quick-eyed, and alive as spring."

We had Dr. Neihardt for only one day, and I had to complete three half-hour videotapes in that time. This was a heavy schedule considering all the production details that can go wrong and the reality that he was eighty years old. My plan was to produce two programs in the morning and one in the afternoon, thus leaving some time to pick up anything we may have missed for editing later.

By 10:00 a.m. we had successfully completed the first program, with the English Department's Professor Robert Knoll interviewing him in *Neihardt: His Life and Times.* Robert Knoll was to become one of the most respected and distinguished professors in the history of the university, and late in his career he published *Prairie University*, the definitive history of Nebraska's land-grant university. Elated and feeling confident we could get the second interview completed before lunch, I went into the studio, thanked everyone, and said we'd take a ten-minute break before proceeding on with *The Lyric Poems.*

Raising his hand, Neihardt said, "Wait a minute, young fellow, the boys [the crew], Dr. Knoll, and I have decided we want to go down to Lebsock's for a beer."

Hesitantly I replied, "But, Dr. Neihardt, I don't think you want to have a beer before you tape a television program . . ."

"I had two before I taped this last one."

We went to Lebsock's. This was Lincoln's version of a "pub," a unique, dark gathering place that served beer and great beef sandwiches. Neihardt used to say, "Give me a Coors beer at 10:00 a.m. and 2:00 p.m. each day and an Ex-Lax at noon, and I'll live forever."

The third program we taped that day was "The Death of Crazy Horse." Neihardt recited this twenty-six-minute narrative from *Black Elk Speaks* from memory, with no flaws, in one take. Not bad for a man his age—or of any age. A few months later we were working on another program with him, and I remarked that his memory was extraordinary for an eighty-one-year-old man. He replied, "That's just two numbers. Turn them around and I'm eighteen."

Neihardt became something of a regular on KUON-TV. We gained permission to broadcast his University of Missouri television course, "The Twilight of the Sioux," and every year we produced a new Neihardt interview in which he would tell some of his famous stories and recite from his works.

One story during the 1960s had particular relevance for young people. He related a conversation he had with one of his students at the University of Missouri. He was concerned that the young man, one of his best students, was doing failing work and only intermittently coming to class. When Neihardt questioned him, the young man said, "Why should I try to excel? Everywhere I look I see the insanity of this war in Vietnam, the unhappiness of people, racial riots, hunger, poverty, horrible things going on around me, so what's the use?"

Neihardt responded, "You're quite right, there are terrible things happening all around us. This world in many ways is a depressing place. We could take twenty-four hours and spend the time talking about how bad things are in our lives. But, you know, if we do that we must also take twenty-four hours and talk about the good things that are happening. Young man, when you walked over here this morning to my office, did you notice what a fine, sunny day it is? Did you see the myriad flowers, the trees? This is a beautiful world we live in. Let me ask, do you like to eat?"

The student replied, "Of course."

"I'll bet you like chicken, and steak, and ice cream, and mashed potatoes."

The fellow nodded.

"Do you eat the swill we throw out to the pigs?"

"Of course not," the boy replied.

"Why not?" Neihardt asked. "There's plenty of it. No, you choose not to. We all have to make choices in this world, and you can choose to do the best you can."

Neihardt was at home with students. He mesmerized them with the power of his poetry, literature, and storytelling. Embracing life was central in his teaching, and often I heard him say, "The most beautiful music of all is the music of what happens." There was no age barrier between him and his audience.

Unlike Mari Sandoz, who admitted she did a very practical kind of writing, Neihardt was a writer of another kind.

As Helen Stauffer writes in *Sandoz, Neihardt, and Crazy Horse*, "He would get up in the morning, take pen in hand, and the words would literally flow out of his brain, down through his arm, and on to the page. He did very little editing (outside of the editing he did in his mind) and none of the laborious, painstaking work that was Mari's style."

This, I think, is partly explained by the fact that Neihardt was a mystic—he was always seeking spiritual truths and experiences. *Black Elk Speaks* eloquently testifies to this. Spiritually allegorical, symbolic material was always important to him in his work. That's the way he thought, and his long narrative epics in *The Cycle of the West* and his lyric and dramatic poems are good examples of this. He often said that he didn't know where the material came from, he was the instrument that wrote it down.

As Stauffer relates,

> Neihardt, secluding himself, usually in a separate room or a little building away from his house, for a certain number of hours each morning, followed a rigid, but limited, schedule of writing hours.
>
> He would begin each day by rereading his previously written lines in deep concentration. He immersed himself in the atmosphere until he reached a near-trance state, waiting for the next lines to form in his mind. When the line had formed, he polished it in his mind, perfecting it before he moved on to the next line. He seldom revised once the lines were on paper.

Neihardt and Sandoz shared a deep respect for the Native American cultures and people in the Great Plains. Neihardt created his *Black Elk Speaks* through interviews with Lakota chief Black Elk, and Neihardt stated that through this seminal book he had become the instrument to preserve the wisdom and culture of the Lakota.

Mari Sandoz, in a 1952 letter to Mr. D. H. Stroud, explained why she never developed any work around Black Elk. In Helen Stauffer's *Letters of Mari Sandoz*, Mari says, "Black Elk was rather the find of John Neihardt, and so out of courtesy I was against cutting into his territory. Neihardt and Black Elk, both vague, visionary mystics, seemed so peculiarly compatible."

Mari Sandoz respected John Neihardt. Though they spent little time together, they knew each other and occasionally wrote to each other. In a letter from Sandoz to Neihardt dated December 20, 1960, published in Helen Stauffer's *Letters of Mari Sandoz*, she writes, "You must know that I wouldn't doubt your statement about anything including your sitting up alone with Tibbles and his dead wife, Bright Eyes." (Tibbles was a lecturer on Native

American problems and wrote an account on Standing Bear in *The Ponca Chiefs*. Bright Eyes was the translator in court, and both toured the country with Standing Bear.) She ended the letter with "May the year 1961 be a magnificent year for you and in the good Sioux way, for everyone."

During one of my visits to Mari Sandoz's apartment in the West Village, she commented that she did much of her writing right there, in a wingback chair in front of the fireplace. To get herself into the mood for writing about the great Trans-Missouri region, the Plains, and the Plains Indians while sitting in New York City, she would often take down one of Neihardt's books and let the rhythmic flow of his writing help her capture the mood for her own writing. This reading helped her to mentally return to the High Plains country while working far away in Greenwich Village.

The last time I interviewed Neihardt for public television we had the usual crowd of students sitting on the studio floor just out of camera range. Sitting beside him or on his lap was Neihardt's dog, Jocko, a devoted French poodle. Neihardt, caressing Jocko, once said, "Let me live in her heart for one week and I will tell you what love is." Before beginning the interview we were testing the microphones. At age ninety-two Neihardt was hard of hearing, so at the direction of the audio engineer I turned to him and asked, "Dr. Neihardt, can you comfortably hear me?"

He replied, "What?"

Raising my voice a little, I asked, "Dr. Neihardt, can you understand me at this level?"

Those blue eyes I mentioned sparkled as he said, "I can understand you at any level."

Mona preceded Neihardt in death by many years. She was cremated, and Dr. Neihardt instructed that when he died, their ashes should be mixed together and poured into the Missouri River—"Not in any specific place where the grandchildren might remark that this is where Grandpa and Grandma ended up, but on the river somewhere."

A month before his death Neihardt said it was time to return to Skyrim Farm, his home outside Columbia, Missouri, and he died there with Jocko at his side.

After the memorial service we all gathered at the home of Julius and Myrtle Young, Neihardt's home away from Missouri, for cake and coffee. While talking with Neihardt's daughter Alice, I said, "When do you plan to mix the ashes of your parents and pour them into the Missouri River?" I noticed when I said this that Hilda, Neihardt's eldest daughter and executor of the estate, glanced in our direction.

Alice, moving closer and lowering her voice, said, "I'm not sure that's going to happen. Hilda doesn't like the idea."

This was a family affair and I knew that this would be my only opportunity to make a comment, so I replied, raising my voice just a bit, "But that's what he wanted. The river meant everything to him." I made sure Hilda heard me.

Three weeks later, Hilda telephoned. "Ron, today I went out to the airport and rented an airplane with an Indian name, an Apache. We flew up north over the Missouri and we found a wide, beautiful bend in the river. I opened the little window and emptied the combined ashes of my parents out into the sky. I was taken by surprise when the wind picked up the ashes and carried them straight up, up into the air. The sun shining on those fragments turned them into a sparkling shower of diamonds as they fell down into the waiting Missouri. I thought to myself, today, Hilda, you did something right."

MARI SANDOZ

It was her curiosity about this fledgling idea of "educational television" that connected me to writer, historian, and chronicler of the West Mari Sandoz. Mari was author of the Atlantic Prize–winning biography of her father, *Old Jules*, and followed by *Cheyenne Autumn*, *Crazy Horse: Strange Man of the Oglalas*, and many other nonfiction books and novels. My friendship with

Mari Sandoz was one of those serendipitous relationships that significantly helped "point the way" for me personally and for the programming focus my television efforts would take.

Yesterday in Nebraska was the first television series I produced at KUON-TV after joining the four-person staff of University of Nebraska educational television station in 1955. It was the awakening of my interest in exploring American history.

While doing some research at the State Historical Society I saw Mari Sandoz in the lobby admiring some of the Indian artifacts. She was congenitally curious, particularly about worlds outside her own. During this initial encounter and subsequent conversations, the newness of television prompted her to agree to create with me the seven-program series *Creative Writing with Mari Sandoz*.

I was her producer and director on this live series, and we spent weeks together in daily meetings at the Historical Society shaping the content of the programs and discussing the various points to be included or given further emphasis or dropped. The primary contribution I made in these sessions was suggesting that she make the series more personal by illustrating her major premises with examples and anecdotes from her life and experiences in creating her books. I was the objective sounding board she depended on and learned to trust. During these program discussions she related to me her philosophy about writing and revealed so much of herself. These meetings ultimately forged a deepening friendship that lasted until her death seven years later.

I recall with warm nostalgia one midafternoon in 1959, while we dangled our legs off the loading dock of the Nebraska State Historical Society and each of us enjoyed one of my Pall Mall cigarettes, Mari said, "Why do you always call me Miss Sandoz?"

I asked what she would prefer.

"My friends in New York call me Sandy," she replied.

I knew I could never manage that level of informality. Sensing this, she said, "Alright, call me Mari."

She meant it when she said that she would rather face a rattle-snake than our two DuMont television cameras, but true to her own work ethic, she "faced them down" and brought intense determination, dedication, and a compelling on-camera presence to seven half-hour programs.

Her literary mantra was, "Anyone with the power of literacy can learn how to write well enough to publish." She would quickly add that there is wide disparity between writing for a country weekly and *Harper's*, but to her, all writing was important.

Old Jules, the book that launched her writing career in 1935, was not her first book. Her first book was what women often write as first books. She said, "About 75 percent of men's first books are autobiographical—and that tells you something. About 50 percent of women's first books are psychological studies." This, of course, is what Mari's was.

Late in her life she said, "I didn't realize it then, but even now at my advanced age I wouldn't think of trying a psychological study—that's too difficult. But as a new novelist, I didn't know that, so I started on that."

She sent her first book out at the beginning of the Great Depression in 1930. The publishing house, Dodd, Mead and Company, kept it for eight or nine months and then sent it back and said that if by September 1931 times were better, they would publish it.

Well, by September 1931 times were much worse, and Mari said, "But by then I had no intention of sending it back. As soon as I got the book back, these eight months of being away from it gave me a detachment that I needed very much. When I opened the package and looked at the thing, looked at it and read it . . . and then I thought, 'Oh my,' and took it into the backyard and burned it. It never saw the light of day."

"This was the bride's first biscuits that never poisoned the husband," she said.

So *Old Jules* was her second book. Though her father told her he considered writers and artists the "maggots" of society (who lived off the sweat of others), on his deathbed he asked Mari to write his story.

Mari was always encouraging people to tell their own story. It's important, she said, to stay with material that means something to you personally, something with which you have emotional identity. Further, she advised peopled to pick out a geographical area to write about. Then, any research you do for one book is always useful for the next, and the one after that. This system worked well for her.

"Writing is not writing so much as it is rewriting, refining, polishing, throwing away, and starting again," she would say. Everyone has a story to tell, and Mari would say that it takes inordinately laborious work and excruciating honesty. This is often difficult, for if you are writing about family or friends, people you know, the tendency is to soften everything a bit. Mari Sandoz didn't soften anything.

She mentioned that often her publishers would say, "Mari, you can't say that. Those people out in Nebraska are still alive and they will sue you and sue us, and we don't want that."

Her reply was, "The people back there know the whole story and I always leave just a little bit out. They know that if they sue me or my publisher, I'll go ahead and tell everything. No one has ever sued me yet." As an aside, she would add that you seldom have trouble with those you include in a book. It's usually with the ones you leave out.

That ability to invest years of work and the courage to bring unadorned honesty in telling your story are essential. Further, she would say that there are as many ways to write successfully as there are people who try. "Though publishers," she remarked, "have funny notions about novels, readers don't. All the writer has to do is keep the reader turning the pages."

She considered herself apart from the very gifted kind of writer. That kind of writer, she said, didn't always know where their material came from, but they had this gifted slant on things that made them great. People who did her kind of writing did a lot of thinking about it, perfected their own methods, and refined their own approach. This is what she hoped she was—a combination of being a significant researcher and creative writer. She had to do a practical kind of writing, but she had an uncommon ability to use simple words in powerful ways.

One of her memorable sentences—"There was no training school for the pioneer, he went out and he either was one or he wasn't"—is an example of the forthright, pragmatic way she looked at life and wrote about it. It's an outlook shared by many High Plains country people, and certainly by the members of the Old Jules clan.

Her sister Flora was honored at the 1992 commencement exercises of Chadron State College with the "Distinguished Service Award." This meant donning a cap and gown and providing some remarks to that year's graduating class. Flora strode to the podium with serious intent, no notes in hand, looked out over the expectant faces, and delivered her address. This is it in toto:

Hitch your wagon to your star.
Get in harness and pull your own load.
There's lots of work to be done. Thank you.

As she returned to her seat, the class of '92 and their parents and friends all rose to their feet with tumultuous applause. How very Sandoz, how very western Nebraska.

One evening after I had given a speech, "Mari Sandoz—A Personal Reminiscence," for the annual Sandoz Society meeting, Mari's younger brother, "Young Jules," remarked to me as we passed each other leaving the event, "Well, you sounded better than you look." Walking on, I wondered what he meant by that.

So turning back, I said, "Mr. Sandoz, what do you mean I sounded better than I look?"

"Well, looking at you I couldn't tell if you knew anything about my sister or not, but after listening to your story I've decided that you knew her well."

Her burning interest was in the history and life and culture of the Native Americans of the High Plains country of northwest Nebraska where she was raised. Of her twenty-two books about the American West, *Crazy Horse: Strange Man of the Oglalas* was, in her opinion, her best. She fell in love with Crazy Horse, the revered Sioux chief and General Custer's nemesis. She admired his intelligence, his tactical skills, his leadership abilities, his reverence for the people and the land, his manliness, and his spiritual powers.

Though she lived in New York City in the West Village at 422 Hudson Street, disdainfully referring to her apartment as her "outpost among the aborigines," there was no question about it—she loved living in Manhattan near her publishers and the center of culture in America.

Mari worked for over three years on *Crazy Horse*, and when she sat back in her wingback chair in Greenwich Village and read the final manuscript through, she felt only despair. She knew she was doing the book entirely wrong. This realization set her on a course of reflection. In writing the book, she not only had to get back into a past that she knew nothing about from personal experience, but she also had to get into the psychology of another race. And all of this had to stay within the facts, because this was a work of nonfiction. So, she had written it the best she could in white man's words and in white man's form, but it just wasn't saying what she wanted it to say. It lacked an authentic voice.

It was remembered sounds that propelled Mari Sandoz to change the writing of *Crazy Horse*. Sounds remembered from childhood can quickly transport us into the past. The peel of certain church bells, the haunting lament of train whistles, echoes of voices, stairs that squeak, someone's laughter—all are there in our memory waiting to take us back. Mari recalled from her childhood the sound of the little dog lopes of the Sioux horses coming down the hill behind Old Jules's place on the Niobrara River. On the hard ground in the summertime you could hear the rhythmic "thrump, thrump, thrump" cadence of the horses' hooves, and she decided to build that cadence into her writing. She rewrote the entire book building in that little rhythmic cadence, and this stylistic change, she said, did what she wanted it to do. Many Native American scholars have said she got it right. But she would say you will have to judge that for yourself. For her, the stylization worked, and she remarked, "This one came the closest to what I was trying to achieve."

Mari said the high point of writing is that first wonderful conception—that flash through the mind—of the book you're going to do. Then, somehow or other, it never reaches that peak again. In the end you do the best you can, and you make compromises, but—and this is important Sandoz psychology—by this time you have this other idea, and this other idea—this is going to be the one. One time she mentioned this in a speech in Denver, and at the end of her talk a large, buxom farm woman came up to her and said, "I want to shake your hand, Miss Sandoz. I know just what you mean. We had eighteen children before we gave up getting the perfect one." Mari loved telling that story.

Finishing a novel, according to Sandoz, is an emotional time for the writer. Mari had extremely strong feelings about this. As she said, you put in years and years with these people, they are your creations and they take on a reality that is beyond the reality of your friends, your relatives, or your family. Because of that strong emotional tie, you hate to give them up. She said that you will find no less a reaction after your tenth or fifteenth book than after your first, except that with your first you are not so able to cope with it. Sometimes it's almost impossible to give up those interesting people you've created. It's like killing them. It's not humorous; it's very serious, because unless you have something else started, some new book, you may find yourself paralyzed.

Don't think for a moment, she said, that you don't get a little God complex. The excitement of finding a publisher and the grief of being torn from a world you've created may be major stumbling blocks to your getting going on another work. That is why it is so important to be working on more than one book at a time. Get involved as emotionally as you can in your next book before you leave the book you are finishing.

She cited the example of Ross Lockridge Jr., a young writer she knew. He had given her the first few chapters of a novel he was working on and asked for her evaluation. She told him that the work was excellent, that the rest of the book would write itself, and suggested he get started on another idea.

His book, *Raintree County*, was published, and within weeks, according to Sandoz, he had made $250,000, which included $150,000 from MGM, and the novel had been accepted for the Book of the Month Club and for condensation in *Reader's Digest*. This was an enormous amount of money in 1948.

He was lionized from the beginning, sought after for book signings, radio interviews, and personal appearances. As she said, "I didn't see him very often, but he wrote to me every once in a while, and I suggested that he might get started on something else." But he kept saying, "No, it's such a fine time now." He had been writing for a long time. He wanted to enjoy his success, sit back and enjoy the attention. We know what happened—he couldn't get started on another book. He would put a piece of paper in the typewriter and start typing, then look at it, and, we surmise, say to himself, "That's no *Raintree County*." He went out into the garage, started the car, and they found him dead of asphyxiation at age thirty-four.

Mari also cited Margaret Mitchell as a woman with enormous creative push. She had written *Gone with the Wind*, and she never wrote another book. "Get committed to another book," Mari told her students. "Sometimes your first is just so-so, and so is your second. Never mind, keep trying. Maybe your third book will hit, and by that time you've grown as a writer, matured as a person, and if that third book sells, the publisher will usually re-issue books number one and two and they will start selling, too." Perseverance was Sandoz's middle name. She was a pragmatist and she loved it when her books did well commercially. Though she made money, her books were expensive to finance, because she spent at least three years in research and writing on each one.

About this time, in the late 1950s, I was working on a program called *Land of Their Own*. The audio consisted of actors reading from the authentic 1870s diaries of the Uriah and Mattie Oblinger family of Fillmore County, Nebraska. The video consist-ed of hundreds of still photographs from the famous Solomon D. Butcher collection of pioneer photographs taken in Custer Coun-ty, Nebraska, around the same time the diaries were written. In a way this was like producing a Western with the original cast.

Most of the pioneers, including Uriah and Mattie, lived in houses "made out of the self-same sod that they plowed in the fields," as John Neihardt said. In posing for Mr. Butcher, these pioneer families, wanting to impress the folks back home, brought everything of value out of the house and into the photograph. All members of the family were there, surrounded by the sewing machine, furniture, washtubs, farming equipment, and even the family cow, and the sod house is in the background. Many of the pictures show the father and his two or three sons all wearing shirts of the same pattern, cut from the same bolt of cloth, and often identical to the cloth on the table. The pride on those faces and the dignity of their postures are forever indelibly eloquent.

And so are their words: "Ma, someday we will make this des-ert blossom as the rose" or "Ella never seen a tree 'til we went to the Little Blue."

By experimenting with the printing process of those glass neg-atives, Historical Society photographer Kenny Kopta and I were able to lighten the darkness of the open doors of the sod houses. It was like opening a long-locked safe and discovering hidden treasures, because revealed inside were a table, dishes with vivid patterns, cups and ladles, the utensils of life, unseen until now. Ours were pioneer efforts compared to today's far more sophisticated and revealing digitization technology.

When Mari Sandoz screened *Land of Their Own*, she turned to me and said, "This kind of thoughtful work rises to the level of publishing."

She believed that the beginning of every book was the creation of a "thematic statement," that you should be able to state the core premise of your story, including the characters, the locale, and the conflict, in two or three sentences, and that everything you write should amplify or edify that theme.

It was, she said, like the facets of a diamond. We look at a diamond and see the overall beauty, but when we look closely we see that each facet is reflecting the other, each commenting in a different way and making the stone sparkle.

Mari was a stickler for detail and a sense of reality. She had an acute eye for noticing everything around her, and she was always taking notes on bits and scraps of paper. In her apartment she had a shopping bag hanging open from a doorknob in the kitchen and another hanging on the door into the living room. One bag was labeled "People" and the other was "Places and Things." The scraps containing her notes were bits of reality she saved. When she needed a detail on how someone looked, acted, or sounded, she reached in the bag. Here's a man with an ill-fitting jacket or mismatched socks, a woman with an unusual hat or gait, or uncommon makeup. People on the street, in the restaurants, or on the subway were all under her scrutiny, as was her physical environment. She used these details to heighten her creations.

Mari Sandoz was a courageous woman, and she devoted her life to writing about the courageous people of the High Plains—the Native Americans, the trappers, the buffalo hunters, the ranchers, the homesteaders, the cattlemen. These are the people who populate her books, and this is the land she celebrates.

On the mantelpiece of the faux fireplace in Mari Sandoz's apartment stood a statuette of a gaunt, lanky ranch hand. This realistic portrayal of the "cowhand" was one of the many awards marking her publishing achievements. As I admired it, Mari Sandoz, sitting in that wingback chair in which she had begun in longhand many first drafts of her work, said to me, "That's the kind of man I like." Looking at her, I knew she meant it.

Here was a woman with an eighth grade education who simply would be a writer. She willed it for herself. Many of the characters in her books are what she calls "will-to-power individuals," and much of herself is infused in these characterizations.

Any writer or teacher or dramatist will tell you that the essence of storytelling is conflict. That, of course, goes back to Aristotelian theory: without sustained conflict you simply have a narrative. Sandoz maintained that the kind of conflict that interests a writer will vary from person to person.

Mari grew up in a harsh environment, an underprivileged home. Her father, whom she made famous in *Old Jules*, was a violent man. At the turn of the twentieth century, there was much discord in their home and a great deal of dissension in the surrounding communities of northwest Nebraska. It was a time when people used hired killers to get what they wanted—Mari Sandoz had an uncle who was killed by one. People on homesteads faced many daunting hardships, not least finding enough to eat. She often said that her interest was in the kind of conflict that people from privileged backgrounds would not have. *Old Jules* is testimony to that. It is no surprise that Mari Sandoz, after experiencing at a young age all the privations and daily work demanded by homesteading, would later, as a writer, become interested in social justice issues, in the destruction of discrimination between economic, racial, and national levels. It was on these subjects she felt she could do her best writing.

People from privileged backgrounds, she said, were protected from these kinds of privations and weren't aware of this kind of conflict. The privileged, in her view, were more interested in conflict between siblings, or in the conflict between fathers and sons, mothers and daughters, or between generations, or between economic and social supremacy.

Often you hear that success depends on talent. Mari Sandoz would say that people with talent are a dime a dozen. Many talented people never do anything because they don't have the stamina or the interest to absolutely apply themselves in learning the craft and, most importantly, doing the work that is required. But somewhere along the line, talent or not, the person must have the power to see human conflict—because out of this comes the important writing.

The last time I saw Mari Sandoz, she was sitting up in bed at Saint Luke's Hospital in New York City, dying of bone cancer, and stoically correcting the page proofs of her Custer book, *The Battle of the Little Big Horn*, which was published posthumously. Her once-beautiful bronze-colored hair was now white, held together in one long braid. She asked me to stay, at least through dinner. "Everything tastes like cardboard," she said, "and I have to eat for the energy I need to finish this work."

She remarked that day that it wasn't the dying she regretted, it was just that "I have so much work left to do." I knew she had planned out two or three more books, which would never be written. Her books, she said, were her children, and there are twenty-two of them in libraries all over the world.

Mari died March 10, 1966. Her sister Caroline accompanied her body on the train from New York back to the Sandhills of Nebraska. For her gravesite, Mari wanted a spot just off Highway 29 on the top of a hill overlooking the Old Jules place.

When the snow and cold prevented them from getting the casket all the way to the top of the hill, Caroline, in her typical Sandoz "that's the way it is" attitude, said, "Put her down here." It was only halfway up the hill, but "that's the best we can do." And it's fine. Even from there the gravesite has a sweeping view of the rolling hills of Old Jules country.

The following May I went to the hospital to visit Mari's long-time friend Mamie Meredith, an English professor who, like Mari, was dying of cancer. Mamie had believed in Mari's work back in the early 1930s. Those were tough times, and Mari, despondent over dozens of publisher's rejections, coerced Mamie to help her burn more than eighty short stories in a washtub in the backyard of her home. While Mari poured the kerosene, Mamie raked the pages back and forth, enabling them to burn. These two friends' tears were plentiful, but as Mamie said, they dried quickly in the blistering summer sun.

Mamie Meredith spent a lot of time reading and clipping articles out of magazines and newspapers for her friends. She knew that I couldn't afford the *New Yorker* or *Variety* or the *New York Times*, so once a month she would bring to my office a manila envelope filled with stories about the theater, television, and books—subjects I like best.

Barely five feet tall, Mamie always wore a colorful hat: one of those busy creations sprouting lots of pink and blue cloth flowers sticking way out in front. Not only was she short, she had a penchant for standing extremely close to the person she was talking with. In my case, she would stand toe to toe with me, looking directly up into my face with those stems and flowers tickling my nose. I tried backing away, but the flowers always followed.

That morning at Lincoln General Hospital I told Mamie I was leaving the university to join the U.S. Foreign Service to serve as the television advisor to the government of South Vietnam. Our State Department had decided to bring television to Vietnam to help "win the hearts and minds of the people."

Mamie, frail and lying very still, motioned for me to bend down closer to her, and in a whisper remarked that Mari had always been captured by a sense of adventure, which is reflected in all her books, and that she liked people who took control of their lives and had the lives they wanted.

"Don't you wish she knew what you're doing?" she asked. I

thanked Mamie for all of the clippings, and we wished each other Godspeed on our new journeys.

A few days later I was seated on a stool at an outdoor restaurant in Saigon, Vietnam, sweating, eating rice and fish, fighting back homesickness, and struggling to remember why I decided to go to Vietnam.

In July a letter arrived from my wife, Naomi, telling me of Mamie Meredith's death. One night, two months later, I came back to the Astor Hotel on Tu Do Street, picked up my mail, and went up to my room. With a 6:00 p.m. curfew in Saigon there was plenty of time to write letters, and happily, they produced lots of incoming mail.

This particular evening I noticed a large manila envelope with a return sticker from "Mamie Meredith." I emptied it of clippings from the *New Yorker* and other publications, and sure enough, there were a couple of Broadway reviews, an article about Noel Coward, and a story about the movies from the *Times*. Glancing upward, past the gecko on the ceiling, I saw this stout, gray-haired little angel with flowers in her hat, sitting up there in the clouds, clipping away.

A note from her brother told me he had found these among her things and knew that she would want me to have them.

12

Bringing Television to Vietnam

Foreign travel has always been an irresistible magnet to me. I yearn for faraway places. When my best friend and I were fourteen years old, we used to look at the world atlas and choose where we *had* to go. There were three places we chose that intrigued us beyond all others. One was Greece, with Athens, the Parthenon, and all the monuments and ruins of that glorious civilization. Peru was high on our list, because outside Cuzco were the spirits of the fascinating Inca people and their mysterious Machu Picchu. This city, high in the Andes, was firmly secured in our imaginations. Cambodia was on our list because when we found an article dealing with the history of French Indochina, we were awestruck by the description of the ancient Khmer temples hidden away in the jungles of "Kampuchea." We were determined to walk the paths of these people of Europe, South America, and Asia.

Many years later, I still felt the pull of foreign lands. I wanted to work overseas. I wanted my family to have that experience. In 1960, when John F. Kennedy visited the University of Nebraska campus while campaigning, I was a member of the audience when he expanded on his idea for a Peace Corps. Every word he said resonated with me, and I desperately wanted to be in the Peace Corps! The problem was that by that time I was married with two children and all the attendant responsibilities.

Then, six years later, I had an opportunity for my own Peace Corps. Only the setting wasn't peaceful; it was 1966 and it was war-torn South Vietnam.

In the early 1960s Bob Squire was the program manager of the public TV station in Austin, Texas. I was program manager for KUON-TV in Lincoln, Nebraska. We became friends while attending the many national educational television meetings scheduled in those days.

During these years when our careers were parallel we improved each other's broadcast schedules by exchanging our best locally produced programs, primarily music ones, because they traveled best between our two stations. Perennial lack of funding made trading programs an early staple of public broadcasting. Among others, Nebraska broadcast an opera from the University of Texas, and with Austin we shared the extraordinary piano talent of our own Audun Ravnan and a series called *From Bach to Gershwin.*

Bob, handsome in the mold of Alan Ladd, verbal and intelligent, left Texas to manage the United States Information Agency (USIA) television production center in Washington DC, and later developed an agency advising Democratic candidates. He became one of Washington's most successful political advisors and was a prominent factor in the successful campaign of Bill Clinton and Al Gore.

Bob knew his way around USIA and knew of my desire to have a foreign working assignment, so he alerted me to an opening for a cultural affairs officer with the United States Information Service (the overseas name of USIA) in Tokyo, and was an advocate for me. This opportunity was all it took. I was ready to join the Foreign Service.

This meant a battery of written tests and two days of interviews in Chicago with Foreign Service officers from a variety of foreign posts. That process successfully out of the way, we put our house up for sale and made arrangements for me, my wife, and our four children to get the necessary shots in preparation for a grand family adventure.

A few weeks before we were to leave, I was summoned by the Foreign Service Office to Washington DC. They would not disclose the nature of the emergency and insisted on a face-to-face meeting. I had a premonition those shots for my family wouldn't be necessary.

President Lyndon Johnson, I was told, had stopped off in Pago Pago on his way home from Vietnam to observe an educational television experiment. Due to a shortage of teachers, students on a number of the islands were going to school via television, and the president was impressed.

Although we fell painfully wide of the mark, at this early stage President Johnson, Secretary of Defense Robert McNamara, and others were saying, "We have to win the hearts and minds of the people of Vietnam." The president was convinced that television was one way to do this. Television could teach people how to make their water potable, how to avoid diseases, where to get adequate vaccinations; it could teach them about their country, about good citizenship and being loyal to the government, and is an excellent tool for government propaganda.

In the early 1960s the government of Vietnam repeatedly asked the United States for assistance in developing a national television network. Those earlier overtures were denied until 1964 when Ambassador Henry Cabot Lodge directed the U.S. Mission Council to prepare a report analyzing the problem and to make recommendations.

In November 1964 the report was submitted recommending U.S. government assistance in developing a four-station network in Vietnam, with the U.S government providing both broadcasting and receiving equipment, and assisting the government of Vietnam in training Vietnamese staff to operate the stations.

The report was approved in principle, and was recommended to the consideration of the U.S. Agency for International Development) (USAID) and USIA for action. By the early fall of 1965, it had been agreed in Washington to begin planning and training for Vietnamese television around January 1, 1966, with the commencement of broadcasting scheduled for late 1966.

Unexpectedly, by December 1965 the Department of Defense (DOD) decided it was of critical importance that American armed forces television be established in Vietnam as an information, education, and entertainment facility for U.S. military personnel.

Since DOD had almost immediate television transmission capability available through two "Project Jenny" aircraft—*Blue Eagle II* and *Blue Eagle III*—it was planned that armed forces television could commence broadcasting from these "flying broadcast platforms" in Vietnam by January 1966. This was almost a year ahead of time.

The U.S. Mission Council, with concurrence from Washington, decided that it was highly undesirable to bring television into Vietnam for the U.S. military forces unless it could be provided at the same time for the government and the people of South Vietnam.

Thus, on February 7, 1966, through public outdoor TV sets, which were receiving pictures from a circling aircraft ten thousand feet above Saigon, the Vietnamese audience watched its first television program. That first program, broadcast at 7:30 p.m., featured a videotaped discussion with Ambassador Lodge, General William Westmoreland, and Prime Minister Nguyen Cao Ky, which had been taped in the VIP suite at Tan Son Nhut airport on January 21, 1966. The television cameras were connected by cable to the videotape recording machine on *Blue Eagle III*, parked just outside the terminal.

This was all happening in late 1965 as the U.S. government

was building up troop strength in Vietnam from a few thousand "advisors" to hundreds of thousands of fighting men. Like most Americans, I was just becoming aware of our commitment to South Vietnam. Using television to help accomplish our goals seemed like a good idea to me, though all the time I was listening as they described this assignment, I was struggling to place Vietnam on the world map. I knew approximately where it was and I knew problems there were building up, and that the guerilla war going on in this remote place was about to be escalated.

Though I had just been recruited by the Foreign Service to serve in Japan, it was decided that my qualifications were exactly what they needed in the effort to bring television to South Vietnam. The officials at USIA in Washington were eager for me to accept the position of television program advisor to the government of South Vietnam. The plan was to build a four-station television network, which would reach the entire country, and to construct a production center in Saigon. We were to produce cultural programs, news, and programs dealing with health, history, and nationhood. A post in Tokyo was no longer in the cards for me.

As they waited for my response, I had to acknowledge my profound disappointment, and then came the rush of questions concerning my family, their safety and mine, working in a war zone, and how to deal with these new revelations.

Vietnam, they explained, is not a totally safe place and the government pays an additional 25 percent of your salary as a financial differential for serving in a war zone. That struck me as an interesting caveat. As for the family, they could stay in a "safe haven post," the choices being Manila, Bangkok, or Hong Kong. Manila was just a couple of hours from Saigon, Bangkok about the same, and Hong Kong was somewhat farther. I could "probably" plan to visit my family "perhaps" once every five weeks.

This information rested heavily with me. They understood that I would have to think about this and talk with my wife. It was Friday afternoon, and they needed an answer by the following Tuesday.

I knew I would not subject my wife and four children, all under the age of eight years old, to living in a strange environment in a foreign land and culture without me on hand. That seemed out of the question. But I had to wrestle with this opportunity. It had exciting appeal.

I entered the plane for the trip back to Lincoln in a trance. My thoughts were a whirling jumble. I don't have to do this. I hadn't yet taken that final action and stepped across the line and been sworn in as a foreign service officer. But . . .

I was flying in a Stratocruiser between Washington and Chicago. This wonderful old propeller-driven airplane had a "lower deck," via a circular stairway, that served as a lounge. I planted myself there, ordered a glass of wine, and proceeded to numb my sensibilities as I tried to figure out what I wanted to do and/or what I should do.

I knew two things: though I had been in the army, there was no shooting going on then. The Korean armistice had been signed and I had never left the continental United States. Further, my experiences in the army were all positive, because it was Fort Sill, Oklahoma, that introduced me to a possible career in television. I enjoyed every minute of service there—that is, everything except basic training.

Further, as I thought about these things, I was determined not to turn this opportunity down because I was "afraid" to go to Vietnam—though I was. There was also the feeling that perhaps it was now my turn to answer the call to serve my country in a different, more substantial way.

I did not forget the fact that just the idea of bringing television to a country in a faraway land was a palpably exciting prospect. But—there was Naomi and our four kids, and first I must talk with her.

I explained the situation to her, and with only the slightest pause, she said, "Is this something you feel you have to do?"

She didn't say, "What about us? What about me? Do I have to raise these four kids all by myself?"

She said none of that. She waited for my answer.

I told her that yes, I had to do this. Just then, in my thoughts, I recalled the voice of the lady seated next to me on the plane saying, "I'm glad you're not my husband."

Naomi said, "Alright then, we should immediately begin making our plans to accommodate this change in our lives."

She never made me feel guilty, and she never used this against me later. If she had said one word indicating that she didn't want me to go, I would not have gone. She knew that. She knew her husband. I have been forever grateful to her for giving me freedom with no strings. She knew that was important, too.

We did just that. We made the arrangements. The house hadn't sold, so that wasn't a problem. I went to Washington DC for a month of "Southeast Asian Studies." Professor Bernard Fall, a Frenchman and one of the U.S. State Department's leading and most respected Southeast Asian scholars and historians, was the memorable teacher. His books *War in a Very Small Place*, *The Two Vietnams*, and *The Street without Joy* were required reading and, I later discovered, had been read by most of the Foreign Service officers with whom I worked in Vietnam.

I was much taken with this articulate, learned, charismatic man and teacher. My never taking my eyes off him during lectures and hanging on to his every word sometimes prompted him to stop speaking, look at me, and say, "Something?" Shaking my head, I wanted him to continue. His breadth of knowledge and experience in Vietnam confirmed for me that this Frenchman knew Vietnam and its people and what he was talking about.

With this preparation accomplished, I stepped across the line, raised my right hand, and became an FSRO-4, Foreign Service reserve officer rank number 4, and was soon flying out across the Pacific on my way to Vietnam.

When I stepped off the plane at Tan Son Nhut airport in Saigon, I had no notion of the titanic impact this city and this country would have on my life.

The humid air was blistering hot and heavy, perfumed with a ripe odor that was new to me. Though I had an official passport, one of the red ones that is supposed to give you some priority in the immigration line, it didn't work because there were so many other red passport holders and not a few black passports (diplomatic and the highest rank), which made the lines extremely long.

I asked someone to hold my place while I went to the men's room.

"By the way," I asked, "what sign do I look for?"

"Ong" (man), I was told.

I found the door and walked in. The stench was overwhelming. This place had never been cleaned. On top of that, there were no toilets. Just the "bear claws," as I was later to learn they were called, where you planted your feet and the porcelain tray below you sloped back to a hole. Though common to world travelers, this was a first for me. What if you fall over backward?

I remember thinking, "I can't do this." You'd be surprised what you can do if you really have to.

After I made it through customs, someone met me and we joined the swarms of pedicabs, bicycles, taxis, and pedestrians, all making their way, in a cacophonous river of humanity, to Tu Do Street, the center of Saigon. There, the eight-story Astor Hotel would be my first home in Vietnam.

"Is it air-conditioned?" I asked the driver plaintively.

"Yes, it is. Welcome to Saigon."

It was the end of May 1966. I had flown across the international dateline on my birthday, thus "losing" most of May 30. This, I decided, was ample reason to knock a year off my age.

Believing that television can be effectively used as an educational tool in nation building, the United States invested over 10 million dollars in the Vietnamese Television Project during its first four years. Its aim was to achieve specific political goals: to provide a common spirit among the people of South Vietnam—to help establish a viable, stable non-Communist nation. For our part, we started with the activation of THVN-TV (Truyen Hinh Vietnam), Channel 9, in Saigon. Almost immediately, the coming of television to Vietnam attracted media attention.

As writer Neil Hickey said in *TV Guide*: "In an important sense, the birth of television in Vietnam is one of the most hopeful and optimistic occurrences in a country where hope and optimism are chronically in short supply. TV has the potential of bringing to the nation a thread of unity it has not had in its brief history."

The Vietnamese had long been served by radio, and they had a history of producing quality films at the MoPix Center, but television was a brand new enterprise.

The work started the minute I got there. Living and working in Saigon, my life alternated between exhilaration with the work and loneliness and homesickness for my wife and family. Pushing those feelings aside, I devoted all of my mental and physical energy in teaching Vietnamese personnel how to produce and direct television programs for broadcast to the citizens of South Vietnam.

We built four TV stations in Vietnam. The first was in Saigon and was the production center for the country. The other three included a transmitting station near the demilitarized zone in Hue, one on the coast of the China Sea south of Hue in Quin Nhon, and one south of Saigon in the Mekong Delta at Can Tho. These four stations, with their construction begun in 1966 and completed in 1970, provided television signals to the entire country.

As the programming advisor, it was my responsibility to teach the people, most of whom had worked in the motion-picture center, how to produce, direct, plan, and program a television service. My "counterpart," Mr. Le Hoang Hoa, an extremely talented, well-educated filmmaker, was the official programming and production manager of the station. In teaching production classes and conducting workshops in the studio, I discussed everything first with Hoa. We worked closely and successfully together, and he was always the person of authority. The staff were hardworking, intelligent people who immediately endeavored to put into practice everything I could tell them about television production. They applied their experience in film to their work, and we had a small but efficient production team working diligently with the new and awkward oversized equipment provided by the U.S. government.

I advised our government to buy the new, small Sony cameras from Japan because the Vietnamese are much smaller people than we are. But I was told that the USA buys from the USA, so it took two men to run one RCA television camera: one to stand on the pedestal and manipulate the camera and one to push the pedestal across the floor.

Later, when the new production studio was under construction, the U.S. government also ignored my advice to install the kind of toilet fixtures the Vietnamese were used to. But the Department of Defense brought the latest stools from home. The Vietnamese were used to "squatting," even when just sitting around the edge of the studio, and when you went into the new restrooms, if someone was in one of the stalls, you never saw any legs or any feet on the floor. They simply hopped up and did it their way.

The eighty-seven employees of THVN-TV and I had a wonderful time making those early black-and-white programs for the Vietnamese people. Often the video was somewhat shaky as the camera with two men, one riding, one pushing, made its way over an uneven studio floor. All this began in a thirty-by-thirty-foot studio in the old motion-picture production center.

After two or three months, our programs were beginning to look pretty good—years behind American standards but almost acceptable. We had interview programs with South Vietnamese officials, many music programs, a quiz show, and the daily news. Happily, the people at the U.S. embassy, knowing that we were starting at ground zero, thought I had what it took to be an effective advisor. I also scheduled some of the Vietnamese film productions that had been produced in earlier years so that all could see that we were dealing with actors, singers, artists, writers and technicians of estimable talent. Now they just had to learn the ABCs of television.

English is the international language, and this is especially true in the field of television. The very language used in directing television programs, such as "zoom in" or "pan right," "dolly in" or "dolly out," are indigenous to America, where the equipment was invented. These words, which are not translatable, are memorized phonetically and have been adopted throughout the world.

The first day, I was introduced to the staff at THVN through the work of a Vietnamese-English interpreter. Everyone listened politely as I suggested ways we could organize our work at the station. After these preliminaries I asked for comments.

A dozen hands went up immediately. I called on a young woman in the first row. Looking down at the floor, she shyly began speaking in low, soft tones. Though I couldn't understand her, she seemed to be speaking deferentially to me. Occasionally she would look at me while she was speaking and then away to the group and then to the floor and then back at me. The majority of students were nodding in agreement with what she said. Le Hoang Hoa, who was serving as my interpreter, turned to me and said, "They want you to teach them English."

This came as a surprise. I wasn't sure I could teach English. I didn't think I knew how.

The expectant looks on their faces prompted me to say, "Tell them I will look into this possibility. There's some checking I have to do." Everyone seemed satisfied with this response, and I left suspecting that if I could meet this need, I could establish a positive relationship with them quickly. But I had no idea how to accomplish this.

An America friend advised me to go to the USAID Mission and tell them that I needed support in teaching English to Vietnamese. I was soon on my way down Thong Nhut Avenue to the headquarters. From there I was told to go to the offices above a theater in the downtown area and ask for the people in charge of English language instruction. It was gratifying to learn that the U.S. government was way ahead of me.

I found the place and took the stairs up to the second floor where a young woman directed me to an office toward the back of the building. As I walked through a vast storage area, I was excited to be surrounded by stacks of teacher's guides, textbooks, and all kinds of materials useful in a classroom. On the office door was a sign indicating that this was the person in charge of English language instruction for the American efforts in South Vietnam. I knocked on the door with optimism that I was about to become a teacher of English.

As I entered it was obvious the woman I had come to see didn't recognize me, but I was stunned to recognize her.

"Dr. Allerdyce," I said with amazement in my voice, "we have wondered for years where you went when you left Syracuse University." I felt like saying, "Dr. Allerdyce, I presume."

She didn't remember me, but she did remember my wife, Naomi, who had worked with her in the speech department at Syracuse University while I was completing my master's degree in television. I related to her that one evening, after work, Naomi came home and said that the whole department was abuzz. One of their best speech teachers, Dr. Allerdyce, had left without notifying anyone where she was going. She simply said she was leaving, and was gone.

"You just disappeared," I said.

"Well, in a sense, I did," she replied.

She recounted to me that she had never married, was the sole support for her mother and father, had taught at Syracuse a long time, and was, frankly, bored.

"I found this position. The pay was good; I could continue the support for my parents and have some adventure in my own life." She had been in Saigon for nearly ten years. She had many friends, both Vietnamese and American, she loved her apartment, and Saigon had afforded her stimulation, a variety of experiences, and the opportunity to see the world. This was a happy woman who chose a different path.

She made arrangements for me to receive all the texts and teaching materials I needed. Julia Child once said on *The French Chef*, "If you can read, you can cook." And I say, "If you can read, you can do anything." In Saigon, with the ability to read, I became an English teacher for my Vietnamese colleagues.

Thereafter, every morning at eight o'clock in our studio, eighty-seven students and I spent the first two hours of the day reading, reciting, and practicing English. Anna Leonowens of *The King and I* fame was right—"By your pupils you are taught." Watching their progress was a daily pleasure. I would give them English instruction and for the rest of the day they would do anything I asked. Their eagerness to learn, their desire to be serious students, made teaching a rewarding time, a great way to start the day.

I learned that being an advisor is difficult work. Nearly as difficult, Hoa would remind me, as "being advised."

There are language and communication problems and frustrations, particularly when you're teaching not only English but television programming and production and an interpreter, Hoa or someone else, was not always available. My advisees were intelligent, experienced, sensitive people with feelings of pride and self-worth. I learned quickly that I would succeed only if they become engaged and enthusiastic about our work. I was immensely gratified when they would take what I had to say and adapt that information to their frame of reference, or what we used to call "the Vietnamese way," and run with it—and nearly always with improved embellishments and results.

There is no question that I was learning more than I was teaching. I learned early not to equate intelligence with language proficiency. It was very easy to favor the English-speaking Vietnamese in matters of personal attention and work assignments because it makes your job easier. You will encounter much resentment if you fall into this trap, and you will miss some wonderful friendships. Remember your own language deficiency.

My zeal for getting things done "right now" was tempered by my colleague's different concept of time. Like most Americans, I was raised to believe that people are placed on this earth for a short time, during which time we must accomplish something definite. This concept was not always congruent with the Vietnamese way. The Vietnamese place emphasis on their ancestral lineage and tend to see themselves as a small part of an ancient continuum stretching from the past on into the unforeseeable future. This philosophy is reflected in their patient demeanor, their acceptance of things "the way they are," and their reluctance to become engaged in personal confrontation. Though we may say, "Don't do today what you can put off until tomorrow," I wasn't prepared for the expression from my Vietnamese counterparts, "If not now, next life." They simply resisted meeting deadlines, and in time they encouraged me to slow down, relax, and develop patience. I learned to enjoy just sitting quietly alone and mentally, unhurriedly, thoughtfully taking ahold of my life.

Another aspect of Vietnam that I miss to this day is that in Saigon, in that situation, material goods were no longer important. The government provided my housing and paid the bills. I had no need for a car. If someone were to steal my radio, wristwatch, typewriter, camera, and my stash of paperback books, I would have no possessions. I truly felt free from materialistic tyranny. Another aspect of this freedom was the absence of society's expectations. When you're working in a foreign land, you are an outsider. Though you can develop strong friendships, you are not likely to become an indigenous part of someone else's country.

I liked the feeling of having no business or social obligations and did not miss the social competitiveness of our American culture. Of course that competitiveness exists in Vietnamese society as well, but I didn't have to be a part of it. I was fully occupied physically and mentally for ten to twelve hours of every stimulating day and fully enjoying working with the Vietnamese.

There were a few times, however, when things were moving agonizingly slowly at work, or when some message from home was depressing, that I experienced deep, genuine feelings of despondency. If I thought about how I missed my wife and our four children, and looked at their pictures in my room, I felt a desire to chuck everything and go home. At these times I yearned to be alone, but living in a hotel did not always afford that luxury.

Living in a hotel, one can expect the "American plan" or the "European plan," but at the Astor Hotel in Saigon the government had me on the "rotating roommate plan." Rooms were at a premium in 1966 Saigon, and my room had twin beds. One was for me and the other was usually occupied by a diplomatic envoy, foreign national advisor, or someone from a branch of the armed services. There were always people on official business who needed a place to come in out of the rain or the war or both.

One evening, after a particularly stressful, tiring, depressing day, I was walking back to the hotel, dodging the motor scooters, cyclos, and bicycles, not really noticing what was going on around me. It had been a tedious, unrewarding day, and in a blue, funky, self-indulgent mood, I was hurrying to the quiet privacy of my hotel room.

I unlocked the door and to my great disappointment, there, sitting on the bed, was a new roommate waiting for me. He had been informed that I had been in Saigon a few months and was therefore "an old hand." I wanted to be friendly, remembering how lost I felt my first day in-country, so I gave him a brief overview of where the U.S. offices were located, the restaurants, and most importantly, directions to the PX (post exchange). While he was making himself at home in the room, my desire to be only in my own head was still strong, so in spite of threatening weather, I ventured out into Tu Do Street and began walking toward the Saigon River.

Facing the river are massive French-built buildings constructed in the early part of the twentieth century, the largest of which was the Bank of Vietnam. These old buildings, with their deep inset doorways, were like fortresses. The walls appeared to be at least three feet thick. It started to sprinkle, and experience told me that driving, heavy warm water was soon to follow. For refuge I ran to one of the nearby doorways to wait out the deluge. There I sat, out of the rain but still carrying my selfish thoughts, when suddenly I realized I wasn't going to be alone here either.

Out of the darkness emerged a young Vietnamese lad. He was soaking wet and wearing no shirt, no shoes, with shiny wet, glistening black hair, and running straight at me. He sat next to me, sharing the doorway, smiling and looking at me expectantly with the largest, darkest, happiest eyes I have ever looked into. He was one of Saigon's street kids who get up in the morning and sell the *Saigon Post* to English-speaking readers. Once the papers are gone they roam the streets, equipped with rags, brushes, and polish, looking for shoes to shine. An entrepreneur to be sure—living on the edge from day to day, every day.

Those flashing eyes spoke to me. Here was someone who had nothing—and he wasn't feeling sorry for himself, he was busy being himself. That face reflected a human spirit that revitalized mine. I was grateful for this encounter. It was one of those unexpected moments that remind us of the joys of being alive. When the rain subsided, I gave him some coins and hurried back to my hotel room. There was a new man in town, and I could help him properly assess where life had brought him and assist him in how to cope.

Another temporary roommate, a Brit with twenty-five years of experience in Malaysia, was assigned to Saigon as a traffic engineer. His expertise was desperately needed. Le Hoang Hoa once asked me when we were driving through the chaos of downtown Saigon, "Ron, why should I stop at a red light if no one is coming?" Hoa also liked the French custom of driving at night with only the parking lights on, drastically cutting one's visibility. Those tiny lights in oncoming traffic looked like fireflies dangerously darting here and there.

One night, after the loudspeakers from the mosque just down the street had stopped wailing, my roommate stepped out onto the balcony of our fifth-floor room overlooking Tu Do Street. At that moment, shots burst out immediately below us, and one round came zinging up to our balcony, hit the metal railing with a loud "ping," whizzed past his head, chipped a piece of plaster off the ceiling, and then dropped to the floor right at his feet. He rushed back into the room, collapsing on the bed with "What has the Queen done to me?" Or me, I thought.

In some ways, Britain manages its Foreign Service smarter than we do. This new roommate, typical of many British Foreign Service officers, had lived in this part of the world for twenty-five years. He had learned two or three of the region's languages; he knew the history of Southeast Asia and was acclimated to the climate, culture, and geography. He had married a Malaysian woman. And, to my surprise, he unrolled his prayer rug at 5:00 p.m., turned toward Mecca, and said his prayers like every good Muslim, all while I sat at my typewriter tapping away.

Arguably, leaving a diplomat in a single post for such a long period of time erodes any objectivity he or she might bring to their official duties and quite effectively erases any strong feelings of citizenship to the home country. But they do know the territory and the people who live there, and this information is very useful to a government's foreign policy deliberations.

At that time, we Americans on the other hand sent people to a point in the world, left them there for three years, brought them home for a year, and then sent them out to some other place for three more years. They became citizens of the world but were not as valuable to the State Department as they might have been if they had been steeped in the language and history and culture of the place to which they had been sent. Few American Foreign Service officers were fluent, most could barely speak any Vietnamese at all, and most were bereft of any significant understanding of the history or culture of Vietnam. Further, most Americans that

I knew socialized exclusively with other Americans after work. They were living in enclaves, long referred to by the nationals as "golden ghettos." There were notable exceptions.

American dollars bought a lot of piasters, the Vietnamese currency, and there were plenty of beautiful, available young Vietnamese women.

After leaving the Astor Hotel I shared an apartment with a fellow Foreign Service officer. Our rank afforded each of us our own private bedroom and private bathroom—though this policy was soon changed.

The State Department became alarmed at the amount of "cohabitation" with local women taking place among some embassy officials and foreign service officers. It was logical and inevitable, due to the nature of the war and not always being sure who the enemy was, that some officials (of both high and low rank) were sleeping with sisters or relatives of the enemy—the Vietcong.

I remember more than one dinner party when a person of rank took a phone call from the State Department in Washington, and everyone, including the female Vietnamese guests, overheard every word of the conversation. English was often understood by the Vietnamese at a higher level than we suspected.

In a simple but brilliantly effective directive from the embassy, the situation was corrected. They dropped the policy giving every officer his own private room and bath and made people double up, sharing bathrooms. Once that privacy was curtailed, state secrets became much safer. And many disgruntled and unhappy people were getting a lot more sleep.

13

Actors, Politicians, and Airplanes

Our days at THVN-TV were enlivened by Vietnam's talented performers. Among them were Tam Tuy Hung, possibly one of the world's most beautiful women and a popular Vietnamese actress; Kieu Chinh, who later distinguished herself in American films and television; and Le Quinn, the most popular actor in South Vietnam. Composer Pham Duy brought his musicians and his beautiful ballad *The Rain on the Leaves*. All these talents enhanced our work when we brought television to Vietnam.

Politically important people came, too, along with their aides and assistants. President Nguyen Van Thieu regularly broadcast his messages to the people via television, and accompanying him was his prime minister, Nguyen Cao Ky. Ky was the glamour boy, wearing sharp military dress set off by purple or white scarves. He was a handsome man, about thirty-five years old, with a thin black mustache—it was easy to see him as the Vietnamese Clark Gable, which is close to how he saw himself. Judging from his television appearances and performance as prime minister, one would say that he wasn't such a bad actor either.

Ky carried a black briefcase. One afternoon, while I was

chatting with him as the lights were being set up for an interview, he opened it. I was curious to know what a prime minister carries in his briefcase—state papers, secret documents? I had a perfect view. There were two items, a pearl-handled revolver and a pack of Salem cigarettes. He was prepared to shoot and to smoke. He survived the war and moved to California.

Early on, as we were getting the TV operation under way and beginning to produce our own local programs, it was evident we needed a larger trained cadre of people who could operate television cameras and produce, direct, and write programs, as well as all the attendant personnel needed to support these efforts. There were sets to be built and lighting plans to be designed. A professional decorum had to be established in the studio. We needed people who knew how to accomplish all this and work together as a team.

At the time, I was the only teacher. I had an interpreter mornings only, and the rest of the time it was all "silent language"—touches, hand signals, and pantomime, plus lots of grimaces and sighs. Television is a voracious creature, and we had to feed it programs every day. We had a film library of Vietnamese motion-picture documentaries and other productions from years past, which were a valuable resource for programming. Though English-language programs were prohibited, the Vietnamese government allowed French-language cultural programs to be broadcast. Regardless of their attitudes toward France, the educated people of Vietnam loved the French culture.

Our local efforts were rudimentary at first, and training the production crew went slowly. Although many had film experience, learning television techniques was a new discipline. In film the scenes are shot and then edited together later, consuming weeks and months of time. In television you tape a half-hour program in half an hour, editing as you go along by switching from camera to camera while you are recording.

Even when production people know how to do something, it

takes a good deal of practice to do it well. Perfecting such things as dollying the camera smoothly and professionally, following the action, and synchronizing the action with the cameras and audio only comes with experience. Somehow we managed to put together a two- or three-hour package of programming to meet our daily deadline while a Lockheed Constellation aircraft waited at Tan Son Nhut airport.

These two old four-engine propeller-driven Constellation airplanes, with the insignia *Blue Eagle II* and *Blue Eagle III* emblazoned on their noses, made it possible to bring television to Vietnam in a timely way. Earlier both planes had been part of an experimental educational television project in the Midwest called MPATI (Midwest Project for Airborne Television Instruction). During the experiment they flew in an arc over Illinois and Indiana, and with transmitting equipment on board, broadcast instructional programs to schools on the ground. Though not in orbit, the Constellation was in a sense the precursor to satellite transmission. President Johnson wanted a television service provided to South Vietnam, and he wanted it now. It takes a number of months to build a transmitting tower that is several hundred feet high, and that was too long to wait—thus the airplanes.

Before construction work began on the tower in Saigon, THVN-TV used the *Blue Eagle* "flying platforms" from February through October 1966 to serve the huge population in that area. The plane would take our day's work into the air. It flew in a circle at an altitude of ten thousand feet over Saigon's ocean of lights and broadcast our videotaped programs and films to the people below. When the tower in Saigon was completed, the planes were diverted to the southern delta region of Vietnam to provide the programs to the people there. In this manner we were able to bring television to Vietnam while the transmitting tower in each locale was being constructed. As one of the crew put it, "We're Vietnamese Television aloft!"

For our work each plane would fly on alternating days, thus

keeping one plane on the ground for maintenance, which included patching the holes sniper bullets had made during take-off and landing. Once during a Vietcong mortar attack, *Blue Eagle II* was disabled when the tail assembly was severely damaged. During repair the broadcast schedule was cut back from seven to five nights a week, with *Blue Eagle III* doing the job alone. Tan Son Nhut airport, where the planes landed, was a favorite hunting ground of the Vietcong.

Crammed into the aircraft was the kind of equipment a television station needs to transmit pictures and sound to receiving sets, in this case thousands of feet below. Included was a two-thousand—kilowatt transmitter with a telescoping antenna that, after reaching an altitude of ten thousand feet, was lowered out the rear of the plane. Additionally our flying TV station was equipped with a one-hundred-kilowatt diesel generator to supply the power to operate all the equipment: two Ampex videotape recorder–playback machines, two sets of "telecine" film projection units, two audio control panels, and a rudimentary switcher that allowed us to go from the video recorders to film or slides during the breaks between programs. We even had a tiny "studio" about the size of a closet and a small camera aimed into this lighted area for an announcer, should we wish to speak to our audience or do the breaks "live."

Station THVN, Channel 9 (Truyen Hinh Vietnam), was providing a broadcast signal that reached nearly fifty miles in each direction for a potential audience of more than 3 million people. That is assuming they sought out a public television set placed in public squares, bus terminals, community halls, markets, and parks, or purchased one of their own. Not surprisingly, soon after we began, TV sets came flooding in from Hong Kong, many paid for by relatives who had left Vietnam, and the angular television antennae sprung up on rooftops in every section of Saigon.

Our broadcasts began at approximately 7:00 p.m., depending on the weather, enemy activity around Tan Son Nhut airport, and the efficiency of the young navy pilots and crew on the plane.

Each day our small, thirty-by-thirty foot studio was virtually a frenzied assembly line for television as we turned out two to three hours' worth of programming. We had to be ready for the delivery van that took the tapes to *Blue Eagle* at 5:30 p.m. so the plane could be in the air broadcasting the test pattern by 7:00 p.m., with the first program hitting the air at seven thirty. The half-hour test pattern allowed time on the ground for the sets to be turned on, the loudspeakers set up, and the audience to find their places to sit.

Though I flew on the plane only once or twice a month, I grew to enjoy it and I was intrigued by this "flying platform's" capability. I felt surprisingly secure, once we were in the air, because that *Blue Eagle* symbol emblazoned on the nose of the plane proudly represented my country and was a visual reminder that, hopefully, we were making a positive contribution to the people of Vietnam.

Most of the seats in the passenger area were taken out to accommodate the equipment, but there were two or three rows of seats in the rear near the transmitter. As I started up the steps the first time I flew, one of the crew handed me what was obviously a bulletproof vest. I put it on, tied it in the appropriate three places in front in three neat bows, found a seat, and sat down. Shortly, the navy fellow who had handed it to me came over and said, "You don't wear that thing, you sit on it. The bullets come from the ground up." Realizing the truth of it, I quickly complied.

The worst part was getting into the air. Tan Son Nhut was constantly being surrounded by the Vietcong, who shot at the planes daily. To counteract this the pilots would get the plane positioned for takeoff, then spend a few minutes revving up the engines, faster and faster, louder and louder, until with plenty of power built up they would lurch a short distance down the runway and as quickly as possible point the nose into the air. The goal was to get the plane as high into the air as fast as possible, thus shortening the length of time and the angle at which someone could shoot at us. The effect in the plane was that we were soon literally lying on our backs with our feet pointed to the ceiling as the plane laboriously fought its way into the sky. Once we leveled out, the antenna was lowered and we were soon transmitting the sign-on slide with the voiceover greeting and the Vietnamese national anthem to the TV-hungry populace below. The first program of the evening was soon to follow.

It was spectacular to look down on Saigon as it stretched out along the Saigon River, then to look off to the west toward Cambodia, south to the Delta, and north to the highlands. I thought about the people for whom food and money were in scare supply, living in makeshift huts, hovels, and alleyways, daily trying to raise their children and make it safely into the next day. And I thought about the magic of television and how it could reach out to them, entertain them, inspire them, and give them some pleasant time away from the deprivations of their lives.

What ideas could we give them that would sometimes, somehow, make their lives better? Would the imaginations of those children down there be sparked in ways that would help them reach their dreams and potential? Were we doing anything that would be meaningful to them? And would it be lasting? Of course I didn't know the answers to these questions, but I felt thankful that I had a job that was both wrenching and rewarding, and one so full of possibilities to serve people as a catalyst for hope.

My work on these flights was to see that the broadcast requirements were met by the crew: making sure we signed on and signed off at the beginning and end of the broadcast day and filling out the broadcast logs for each program. The crew and I watched and commented on the programs, while they constantly surveyed the various equipment. After two or three hours it was time to return to my seat, check my bulletproof bottom protector, and brace myself for the return trip and a reversal of the experience taking off.

This time the pilots would take the plane as near to the Tan Son Nhut runways as they could, then turn the nose practically straight down and head for the tarmac, putting that giant plane into a steep dive. Then, at the last possible moment—what always seemed to me to be far too late—we would suddenly level off for an abrupt landing. This time, of course, rather than lying on our backs with our feet on the ceiling, we were hanging by our waists from the seatbelt, nearly upside down. I felt I was in a carnival "Loop-O-Plane," with blood rushing to my head and the speeding plane straining like mad to do as it was told.

After one harrowing landing, I commented to one of the crew, and his reply still rings in my ears as one of the war's defining expressions: "No sweat."

14

Like Dragons Take to Maidens

The *Blue Eagle* planes were retired when transmission towers were completed in Saigon; at Can Tho in the delta; at Hue in the north near the demilitarized zone; and at Monkey Mountain near Qui Nhon in the highlands. The Saigon, Quin Nhon, and Hue towers were constructed on schedule, but Can Tho was a catastrophic exception.

On October 23, 1967, work began to install the seventy-five-foot antenna on top of the 325-foot tower near the city of Can Tho. Construction engineers decided to install the antenna by helicopter because the one-hundred-foot gin pole, a device for lifting heavy objects that is normally used in such work, had fallen off the tower and had stuck deeply in the soft delta ground. It was left there with no way of pulling it out.

A large helicopter was brought in to lift the antenna up to the top of the tower. The trick was to get the antenna positioned correctly on top of the tower so that a waiting engineer could secure and then bolt the equipment in place.

While maneuvering the antenna into position, it caught at the top of the tower, partly positioned but not completely so. The helicopter crew could neither get it placed correctly nor pull it back up for another attempt. It was stuck, but at an angle, and could not be secured until it was upright, which, after many tries, they were not able to accomplish. The hovering aircraft had left the ground with forty-five minutes worth of fuel. After thirty minutes of trying unsuccessfully to position the antenna, the fuel supply was becoming dangerously low. With only fifteen minutes of flying time left, it was imperative to get the helicopter back on the ground. The crew cut the cable connected to the antenna and returned safely.

The antenna, however, fell to the ground, damaging the tower every foot of the way. Like a pretzel, the antenna lay demolished at the foot of an irreparably damaged tower, which had to be dismantled and completely reconstructed, a process that delayed transmission for months. The shipment of the new tower from Sacramento, California, also included a new gin pole. Rumor was that the person in charge of the operation that morning took the next plane out of Saigon and never returned.

The budget of the project provided public TV sets in hundreds of locations. Wooden stands were constructed to hold the twenty-seven-inch black-and-white TV sets off the ground. The sets were enclosed in wooden housing with roofs (to repel the monsoon rains) and doors that locked (to prevent thievery). Loudspeakers were placed on either side of the set to amplify the sound. Vietnamese guards were hired to protect the public television sets by day, and to be on hand at night to unlock the housing, adjust the antennae, and tune the sets in.

These television sets were positioned in every conceivable public place in the cities and safe hamlets. Some were in village and city squares, at the Central Market, in auditoriums, classrooms, cafeterias, intersections, and open buildings—any space that would accommodate one hundred to two hundred people and within the broadcast signal of *Blue Eagle* hovering above. The loudspeakers amplified the sound so that large groups could hear what was going on, and the people came and watched—transfixed—squatting on the ground, as intrigued by television as we had been, standing outside furniture-store windows back in the early 1950s.

We were providing that television signal to reach the people who lived in the culverts, hovels, cardboard boxes, and shanties that were home to much of the population. Our goal was to create images and sounds that could inform them and be useful in their lives. And our efforts were beginning to be noticed.

Neil Hickey, writing for TV Guide, said, "It lasts for only an hour each night, but the South Vietnamese have taken to it like dragons take to maidens. Television has come to Vietnam and this disputed sliver of land on the South China Sea will never be quite the same."

Through television they could watch how to make water potable and how to avoid the plague. They could enjoy traditional Vietnamese operas, dramas, and music. They could learn where to get their shots and how to keep their children healthy.

Fortunately, USAID came through with the money to fund a six-month training period for twelve Vietnamese men and women who would be working in the production department of THVN-TV. This training was to take place in Taipei. The Taiwanese knew what they were doing because they had a flourishing television service in their country, and they were Asian—a good fit for the Vietnamese.

1. Ron Hull's birth certificate, signed by Dora Du Fran.

2. Esther Montgomery, TV teacher of literature and NET "house mother" from 1957 to 1989. Courtesy of NET Archives.

3. Television interview with John Neihardt in his study in Bancroft, 1967. Courtesy of NET Archives.

4. On the interview set with Mari Sandoz, 1963. Courtesy
of NET Archives.

5. Interviewing Vivian Vance (Ethel Mertz on *I Love Lucy*),
1968. Courtesy of NET Archives.

6. Early staff of Nebraska Educational Television: Ron Hull with (from left) Hobe and Bonna Hays and Lee Rockwell, 1961. Courtesy of NET Archives.

7. Teaching English to Vietnamese TV production staff, 1966. Courtesy of NET Archives.

8. Saigon's street kids sold newspapers in the mornings and
shined shoes in the afternoons, 1967. Courtesy of NET Archives.

9. Nguyen Van Thieu, president of South Vietnam, 1966.
Courtesy of NET Archives.

10. Nguyen Cao Ky (far left), prime minister of South Vietnam, 1966. Courtesy of NET Archives.

11. On board *Blue Eagle II*, one of two flying broadcast platforms for Armed Forces television in Vietnam, 1966. Courtesy of NET Archives.

12. Ron Hull, 1976. Photo by Robert McMorris, *Omaha World-Herald*.

13. On the set of *Restoration Wits* with actor Cyril Ritchard, from the
Anyone for Tennyson? PBS series, 1976. Courtesy of NET Archives.

14. Ron Hull and Jack McBride raising money on an NET auction, 1975.
Courtesy of NET Archives.

15. Governors' reunion: Ron Hull with former Nebraska governors Robert Crosby, Charles Thone, Frank Morrison, Robert Kerrey, and J. James Exon, 1990. Courtesy of NET Archives.

16. Interviewing friend Dick Cavett, 2009. Courtesy of NET Archives.

17. The house that Jack built: the NET building
(completed in 1971), 2007. Courtesy of NET Archives.

15

Brief and
Memorable
Far East
Encounters

It was my good fortune to accompany the contingent of Vietnamese TV team members to Taipei to see that the training program was successfully launched at Taipei's Chengchi University's communications school. I was to observe their progress for a week or so and then return to Vietnam. My greatest fear was that I would lose a few people during our two-day stopover in Hong Kong.

These mostly young people had endured many hardships in their country, and the freedom to enjoy life outside Vietnam was enticing. When we gathered at Hong Kong's Kai Tak Airport for the trip on to Taipei, I was relieved to see there were no defectors. Twelve students and I arrived in Taiwan, and six months later twelve students returned to Saigon, the core of a professionally trained television production team.

LORETTA YOUNG

Ruth Roberts, an American woman who had spent many years in the film industry in Hollywood, was working at the communications school as a unpaid volunteer when I was there. She had dedicated a year of her life to assist the Jesuits, motivated out of her own Catholicism. In Hollywood she was a voice coach. She had given Loretta Young her Academy Award–winning Swedish accent for *The Farmer's Daughter* in 1947, and they became lifelong friends. While I was there, Young came to Taiwan to see Ruth as part of her round-the-world trip with longtime friend Pilar Wayne, John Wayne's wife. While at the school Loretta generously donated fifty thousand dollars to the Jesuits.

Ruth invited me to join Loretta and Pilar for dinner in Loretta's suite at the Grand Hotel. This magnificent hotel is one of the world's grandest examples of Chinese architecture. It was commissioned by Madame Chiang Kai-shek, who insisted on the finest wood interiors and embellished the great halls with priceless examples of Chinese art. At every turn, there are paintings and tapestries, sculpture, jade carvings, and calligraphy. In one lobby an exquisite golden dragon stands four or five feet high amidst miniature trees, streams, and pools. The entire hotel reflects the refinement and taste, not to mention the wealth, of Madame Chiang Kai-shek.

Ruth met me at the door, and as I came in, Loretta Young, a trim, classically beautiful fifty-three-year-old woman, glided into the room, coming straight toward me with her hands extended in welcome, a gracious smile on her face. It reminded me of her glamorous entrances (without stopping to twirl her billowing skirt) on television's *The Loretta Young Show*. We immediately fell into conversation, and after about two minutes Loretta said, "Wait a minute, young man. When it comes to talking, you've met your match." It was a lively, stimulating evening for me. We talked about old Hollywood, television, the war in Vietnam, and our children.

At that point Loretta, in a measured and thoughtful way, said, "We make choices, don't we?" Our animated conversation took a pause as Ruth Roberts, Pilar Wayne, and I turned toward her. She related that in 1948, when she had won the Academy Award for *The Farmer's Daughter*, Hollywood offered her the opportunity to continue her career, guaranteeing many more films, with a contract worth a fortune. It occurred to her that she could not only secure her own future but that of her children as well. Torn by the lure of continuing a spectacular career and wanting to be home with her young daughter, she had a choice to make.

She graced many more films with both beauty and talent, and followed those successes with her own dramatic television series. Her family's future was secured.

She found a wonderful woman to "be there" at home with the girl while she continued to work. I remember saying that she made the right decision and had the best of both worlds—success, fame, *and* a family. It was a good decision, she admitted—if, for example, you don't mind that when your daughter is about to get married, rather than coming to you, she asks the woman you hired to help her pick out her dress and plan the wedding. She smiled and the evening continued.

When it was time for me to leave, Loretta called down to the desk and asked that a Catholic priest be sent to her suite. She was concerned about my safety working in Vietnam. Soon I was kneeling in her doorway with the priest praying for a safe journey back to Vietnam, with his hands and those of Ruth Roberts, Loretta Young, and Pilar Wayne resting on my head.

Back in Saigon, I was having some second thoughts about the wisdom of making the Foreign Service my career. The Vietnamese nationals I worked with were candid with me when we spoke of the aspirations of the Vietnamese and America's role in the country. These conversations left me feeling uneasy about what we Americans were trying to accomplish, and I was beginning to doubt that we would be successful.

I respect the people who serve in our Foreign Service, but I was gaining a better perspective on the impact that living overseas has on the family. I had seen firsthand on a stopover in Manila an example of one of the schools overseas dependent kids attended. One Foreign Service wife told me that American parents were often forced to hire tutors for their children because the teachers held their students back. It wasn't that the children couldn't do the work, but that the teachers had found a way to extort money from the parents. But I was here to do a job, and these considerations did not have to be dealt with at the moment.

I was fortunate. My job every day was always interesting, often surprising, and sometimes disappointing. Besides the pleasure of interacting with the legions of talented Vietnamese musicians, actors, and artists, our days were brightened by the numbers of people stopping by to visit Vietnamese television. People in news, film, or anything related to "the business" nearly always came to see us.

GLENN FORD, JOHN WAYNE, AND SEAN FLYNN

While actor and movie star Glenn Ford spent two weeks in-country narrating a film for the navy, he came by nearly every day. This was a down-to-earth, affable man with no ego, whom we all enjoyed. He expected no privileges or special treatment and even joined us at a couple of our parties. He and Rita Hayworth were sensational in one of the most famous film noir classics of all time, the unforgettable *Gilda*. Rita Hayworth, he said, was one of the most generous people he had ever known. They lived near each other for a time, and as he put it, "She would literally give you the shirt off her back."

When John Wayne walked into the control room one afternoon, I started whistling the theme from *The High and the Mighty* (it was whistled in the picture), one of his films from the early 1950s. Hearing this, he looked over at me and said, "Best damn film I ever made." My opinion exactly, Mr. Wayne.

One morning during English class, a young American we didn't know stepped into the studio. I stopped working on pronunciation for a moment, and he asked if he could join us for a while. This unassuming blond-haired young man who looked like Adonis captured everyone's attention. Asians, particularly, are fascinated by blonds, and he was one of the best-looking men any of us had ever seen, in the movies or in real life.

He told us he was a writer, photographer, and reporter, in Vietnam to cover various aspects of the war. He introduced himself as Sean Flynn, and then we knew that this was movie hero Errol Flynn's son. Though he made a few movies himself, his life was one of a true adventurer. Later we were saddened to learn that Sean Flynn and a companion were ambushed and murdered in Cambodia.

THE REVEREND FRANK COURT

We even had visitors from Lincoln, Nebraska. An airmail letter brought the news from Dr. Frank Court, my family's minister in Lincoln, that he and his close friend, a physician, were planning a trip to Saigon. They hoped to stay with me, and they needed my help. Frank wanted to see firsthand how the war was going and discover for himself what the situation was in Vietnam. His letter told me that he wanted to meet Dr. Tom Dooley, a young physician accomplishing some fine work in Southeast Asia, particularly in Laos, General William Westmoreland, the military commander of American troops, and Ambassador Henry Cabot Lodge, our American ambassador to the government of South Vietnam. These were not people I hung out with in Saigon.

Frank Court's desire to meet personally with this trio represented high expectations. As a newly arrived Foreign Service officer, I had on one occasion been introduced to the ambassador, but Dr. Dooley and General Westmoreland were faces on *Time* magazine covers to me.

I responded to Dr. Court stating that to get beyond the embassy receptionist I would have to have a letter of introduction from some highly placed person in the U.S. government. About two weeks later, a letter from Washington arrived. It read: "To Staff members, United States Embassy, Saigon, Vietnam. Please accord my friend, Dr. Frank Court, every courtesy while he is in

Vietnam." It was signed by Hubert Humphrey, vice president of the United States.

I took the letter to the embassy, and appointments with Ambassador Lodge and General Westmoreland were promptly booked. Dr. Dooley was not in Southeast Asia at the time. Further, I noticed that my standing at the Joint United States Public Affairs Office, to whom I reported, was suddenly enhanced. That's how Washington, and in this case its Saigon extension, works.

My apartment mate, Fred, and I immediately began making plans for our two houseguests and to arrange their schedules. We could provide rooms for them easily, and since we had a combination cook-housekeeper, we knew we could handle their "board" as well.

Her name was Te Lan and she came to the apartment every morning in time to fix our breakfast. She stayed on during the day, prepared lunch, did the shopping, cleaned the apartment, and always prepared dinner for us. She would leave as soon as our dinner was served and return the next morning, five days a week, and we each paid her fifteen dollars a month.

Te Lan was an extremely quiet, shy, young Vietnamese woman. She was average-looking and seemed like she was always trying to get out of your way. Her head was often down, she looked at the floor a lot, and she backed away from you during conversations. We became fond of Te Lan—she was a good worker, a fine cook, and she had a sweetness we enjoyed.

Fred made arrangements to stay with his American girlfriend and soon-to-be wife when my guests arrived. I put Dr. Court in my bedroom at the back of the apartment and gave Fred's front bedroom overlooking Le Loi Street to Dr. Court's friend. To go from my bedroom to the living room meant walking past the kitchen, then through the hall past Fred's room, and into the spacious living room with French doors opening onto a balcony bedecked with plants and flowers. During this time I slept on the living-room couch.

Their first morning in Saigon was a lovely one. The sun was brilliant, and there was a scent of flower blossoms in the air. Te Lan arrived, anxious to make my guests welcome with a well-prepared breakfast. It was an invigorating kind of morning that raises everyone's spirits.

The soft, early calm of this new Saigon day was suddenly interrupted with loud, out-of-tune singing. The first few lines of Rodgers and Hammerstein's "Oh, What a Beautiful Mornin'" came bellowing from the untrained, off-key baritone of Dr. Court. "Oh, what a beautiful day. I've got a wonderful feeling, everything's going my way." Then, here came the great preacher himself, striding out of the bedroom into the hall, past the kitchen toward the living room, full of life and joy—and stark naked.

I couldn't believe my eyes. No pajamas, no shorts, no nothing. This was one of those situations when we try to avoid looking at what we can plainly see, and this view dramatically collided with my image of him holding forth with great dignity in the pulpit at Saint Paul church. My shock was nothing compared to poor little Te Lan, who couldn't come out of the kitchen all morning. We served ourselves breakfast.

BACH TUYET

Our first TV studio, before the new building was completed, was in the Film Center. We called it the MoPix building for short, at Muy Lam (15) Thi Sach Street. This old motion-picture production center was a typical two-story French-designed building. It had very broad overhanging eaves on the street side, with light bulbs at fifteen-foot intervals to light the area after dark.

This was a perfect spot for the homeless. They could set up makeshift quarters with some boards and cardboard, bring in small charcoal burners for cooking, and have lights until ten fifteen each night, when they were automatically turned off. Five or six homeless peasant families took advantage of these overhanging eaves with their electric lights and protection from the rain. One advantage of subtropical Saigon was that the poor were seldom cold.

One of these families was a single mother with three children, all under the age of seven. Her name, I discovered, was Bach Tuyet, which means "Snow White." Her two daughters were Kim Bao and Tan Ku, and the boy, the youngest, was Fuch Hai (Beautiful Sea). She was a young woman from a village south of Saigon whose husband had been killed during a skirmish in the delta region. She had gravitated to the city for work to support her three children.

Bach Tuyet's demeanor reflected a quiet refinement and a sure sense of perseverance and determination. She carried herself with a graceful dignity that belied her station. Her figure was slim and youthful, her eyes alert and intelligent, and her hair, like most young Vietnamese women's, was brilliantly black and reached to the middle of her back. This particular day she was diligently trying to make this space comfortable for her children. Seeing this, some of my coworkers and I procured some cinder blocks from a construction site nearby, and we found some large sheets of plywood in the studio. We also found some large sheets of cardboard that provided walls for privacy on two sides. Bringing these back to her location under the eaves, we built a floor nearly eight feet long by five feet wide. Using the blocks we were able to raise the floor two and a half feet off the ground. This was vital for when "the rains came"—during monsoon season—as there were no culverts, no efficient drainage, no pavement to speak of, and the street immediately filled with running water nearly two feet deep. Bach Tuyet's family, therefore, was happily "high and dry."

By day, Bach Tuyet worked as a cleaning woman in the large telephone building across the street. She would return every two or three hours to check on her children, who were left to play. The six year old was the primary caretaker looking after the younger ones. Each noon Bach Tuyet would return, bringing rice and tea, and the four of them had lunch together.

I walked past this scene every day, and over time got to know Bach Tuyet. Though we never had a true conversation, as I spoke very limited Vietnamese, I liked to stop and play with the children and converse with her as best I could. Gestures, expressions, smiles, taps on the shoulder—all these means of the "silent language" were used. Every now and then I would give her a little money, but not much, because the embassy emphasized that being too generous gave people false hopes. I admired this woman, and I was moved and impressed with the love and care and discipline she brought to the lives of Fuch Hai, Tan Ku, and Kim Bau.

This admiration took a quantum leap the afternoon of our first monsoon. I came out of the MoPix building and noticed that it was starting to rain. I knew that with the monsoon, once you saw the clouds, it was too late to outrun the sudden downpour—a warm, torrential, hard-driving sheet of rain. The street was filled with water in no time. While standing on the landing under a roof, I watched incredulously as the women, Bach Tuyet and her neighbors, rolled up their pant legs, took off their sandals, and with angry energy and determination briskly waded out into the street vigorously brandishing their weapons—sticks, boards, barrel slats—furiously attacking the rats as they came swimming from every direction in panic, searching for high ground.

The rats were crisscrossing each other's paths—huge, black, repulsive-looking rodents with desperation in their eyes. There, in water up to their knees, in the middle of this torrent was Bach Tuyet and her friends, women of Vietnam, valiantly facing down these filthy swimming menaces and killing them by hitting them over the head. Bam, bam, bam, and their bodies would stop moving, roll over, and float down the street. Rats would chew on the ears of their children at night and were the hosts for the lice that carry the bubonic plague. Awed by this brigade of mothers—and paralyzed by the moment, I am ashamed to say—I just stood there and watched.

In spite of the war and its privations, these same women also knew how to celebrate and enjoy their family and friends. This was most evident during the observance of Tet, the Vietnamese New Year. Tet is truly a wonderful, holy time, the Vietnamese equivalent of the Chinese New Year. It's a time for reconciliation. It is the time to go to your friends and apologize for past hurts and slights, to pay your debts, to clear your conscience, and to renew your friendships and tell people how important they are to you. The first visitor to a home on the Eve of Tet is thought to be symbolic of the year to come. The Vietnamese are very careful who they invite across the threshold. I was humbled to be asked to spend the night in Hoa's parents' home and enjoy with them the family reconciliations, the marvelous food prepared, and the joyful spirit of welcoming the new year.

That evening before I left for Hoa's house I stopped under the eaves and gave Bach Tuyet twenty U.S. dollars. This was probably as much as she made in a month. But her children could use some dental work, among other needs, and though I knew what the embassy said, I rationalized that this was okay because it was Tet—a special time that came only once a year.

The fireworks of Tet were a bit unnerving because you couldn't distinguish between the festival explosions and the occasional real ones. On Hoa's street the outside walls and rooflines of people's houses had been lined with firecrackers, that when lighted, suddenly etched the whole street against the sky in sparkling lights and with thunderous noise. We had a wonderful celebration, feasting on Vietnamese shrimp on sugarcane sticks, the most delicious, delicate spring rolls, as well as beef, pork, and chicken—four-star cuisine. When it was time to go to bed I was handed a grass mat to sleep on. Then Hoa, motioning to a smooth two-foot-long wooden log nearby, said, "You get the pillow." I had a stiff neck in the morning after sleeping with my head on that "pillow" at a ninety-degree angle. Though I didn't want to hurt my host's feelings, I should have insisted that he take the pillow and not make the sacrifice for me.

Two days later, as I was walking toward work, I saw a group of women up ahead, the families under the eaves, animatedly talking among themselves. The object of their attention was a statuesque young woman in a white ao dai, the Vietnamese national costume consisting of a tailored bodice with a long panel down the front and back, and with pants worn underneath. She looked beautiful, with her hair piled high above her forehead and dramatically pulled back from her face in great swirls. Her hair was accented by two sparkling devices that looked like chopsticks, which were outshone only by the sun hitting the lavishly lacquered coiffure. Standing in that dusty road, the young woman looked like a glamorous model, strangely out of place. Nearby, Fuch Hai and Kim Bao were beaming at this lovely vision, and it was then I realized they were looking at their mother.

I walked closer and saw a genuinely happy face, the strength of which is still with me. Bach Tuyet had gone to Tu Do Street to one of the fancy shops and spent the Tet gift of twenty dollars on a hairdo. The smiles of her children told me this was one of the best investments I had ever made.

For three weeks after that, Bach Tuyet's hair stood perfectly in place, thanks to all that lacquer, and each day as I walked by, the women on the street made a point of tipping their heads and bowing slightly from the waist, with closed eyes. "Cam on," they said. "Thank you."

THE MONTAGNARDS

Shortly after our celebration of Tet I was invited by a group of military people from Armed Forces Radio and Television Vietnam to join them on a trip to Kontum City in the Central Highlands. I eagerly accepted, as this was an opportunity to visit the area that is home to the Montagnards, or "mountain people." The Montagnards are a distinct people from the Vietnamese. The Vietnamese migrated down the peninsula from China in centuries past, and the Montagnards were people from islands of the

South Pacific who had made their way by boat to Vietnam and had made homes in the mountains. There are many great stories about these resourceful, tough people. During the war they were of great assistance to our Army Special Forces, the Green Berets.

Always hospitable, the Montagnard hosts invited us to take part in a ritual of friendship after the events of the day. I had heard stories of this, and was excited to have one of the Montagnard brass bracelets awarded each participant at the end of the ceremony. I had seen a few of these simple brass bracelets, which featured intricately cut designs, being worn with pride by American military friends. To me, the bracelets embodied a sense of mystery and valor. To own one symbolized an adventure with a mythic people and locale. The legend was that no matter how far you traveled away from these mountains, the bracelet would someday bring you back to the valley of Kontum.

There were six of us sitting around the campfire ready to be inducted, to become a "Montagnard brother," five military and one civilian—me. The ceremony was to begin by killing a sacrificial animal. I'm told that if this was being conducted for a person of high rank or a prestigious party, a large beast of some kind is killed. We were not a prestigious party by any means, and so in our case they killed a baby pig. They brought jugs of rice wine, placed them between our legs, and, using reeds out of the river for long straws, we were directed to begin drinking. The wine is necessarily potent.

While we were busy imbibing, they were draining the blood of the pig into a jug and then into a cup. This was brought to the campsite. Since I was closest, the cup of blood was first offered to me—to drink. I don't think we were expected to drink much, but even though my senses were already somewhat numbed by the rice wine, I knew that drinking pig's blood was not something I wanted to do. At the same time I recognized that I had agreed to take part in this, so I had to think fast.

I took the cup of blood in my right hand, and borrowing a

habit from the Vietnamese, I covered my mouth with my left. It interested me that my Vietnamese friends rarely threw their heads back with mouth wide open for hearty laughter in the manner of westerners. Rather, they were discreet and very conscious of their mouths and their teeth. They laughed alright, but they were careful to cover their mouth in the process. That's what I did. I put my left hand over my mouth, clenched my lips tightly shut, tipped the edge of the cup under my left hand and slowly let blood run out, over my lower lip, down my chin and neck, and some down inside my shirt. I faked it. When I took my hand away I could tell from the taut stares of my American partners that they were convinced I had actually swallowed some.

Dramatically wiping my mouth I turned to hand the cup to the soldier next to me. Staring at the blood, he took it with a shaky, trembling hand. With the cup to his mouth he tipped it up and swallowed and passed it on. He was more of a Montagnard brother than I was.

After everyone had their share, we quickly went back to seriously drinking the rice wine. At the end of the ceremony the brass bracelet was put on my wrist, and I wore it from 1966 until 1971. Hanh, one of my friends at the TV station and an excellent photographer, reminded me that, as the legend goes, the bracelet would someday take me back to the valley of Kontum. Back at home I used this legend as part of a bedtime story I made up for my children.

I worked in Vietnam on the television project for a year, from 1966 to 1967, and the State Department sent me back on TDY (temporary duty) for nearly two months in 1970 and twice during 1971 as part of an evaluation process of the television project for the U.S. Information Agency. In 1967 the U.S. Agency for International Development hired NBC-I (National Broadcasting Company–International) to serve as advisors to the project. I was fortunate because overall I spent about eighteen months in-country, but I knew my friends there over a five-year period.

In 1971, while waiting at the airport with my family for United Airlines to take me back once again to Vietnam, my nine-year-old son, Brandon, who knew about the legend of the bracelet and the valley of Kontum, said to me, "Dad, when you get back to that valley this time, leave the bracelet there."

16

Programming the Vietnamese Way

Just as it is in America, working each day in a public television station in Vietnam affords you a liberal arts education. Scholars, politicians, civic leaders, entertainers, and accomplished people from all ranks come across your threshold and in half an hour or so distill a lifetime of experience and knowledge for the sake of a television broadcast. Being with these people who come together to produce programs is the rewarding part of the work, and just like at home, I was endeavoring to help them produce programs worthy of people's time.

In Vietnam the largest share of programming was locally produced in the studio. We had one or two religious shows a month, produced predominantly by Buddhists and Catholics. We had children's programs featuring games, songs, education, and health tips designed just for them.

When a particularly popular program attracted a lot of viewers, it often caused serious shortages of power and blackouts in various parts of the city. Without question the most popular programs were *cai luong*, the ancient Vietnamese operas that told the stories of the land and the people. Vietnamese viewers wanted to know who they were as a people, where they came from, the adventures that happened before their time, stories about battles and victories—all the tales of their ancestors. Many of these stories dealt with the eternal struggle the Vietnamese have waged for hundreds of years with the Chinese. The valorous Truong Sisters, for example, who led the armies against the Chinese and preserved Vietnamese independence in 43 AD, was a great favorite. Though it seemed inscrutable to me, they particularly liked the American-produced crime and war programs offered to the GIs on Armed Forces Vietnam's television service, which the general public could also receive on Channel 7.

The Reformed Theater, or *cai luong*, productions were so lengthy that we broadcast them over two nights. If the opera was broadcast on the same night, parts 1 and 2 were often interrupted for news or public affairs programs like *The People Want to Know*, featuring a speech by some high-ranking government official or coverage of a current event, and then the opera would be resumed. You might say a bit of spoon-fed propaganda was sandwiched between popular programming.

The ancient Vietnamese operas were at least four hours long, and they used the myriad sounds of bells and gongs, the squeal of the traditional instruments, the slapping of sticks, and the high-pitched voices of the singers, all unfamiliar to westerners' ears. After three days of taping this cacophony of voices and sounds, the decibels were almost more than I could take. At times I went outside the studio just to hear the reassuring purr of motor scooters, bikes, and taxis with their bleating horns and the growl of the worn-out mufflers on the twenty-year-old Renaults still plying the streets of Saigon.

Some of our programs were produced by the military, others by various cultural groups, and still others by the education department. We had a weekly Thieu Nhi (Children's Show) called *Do Vui De Hoc* (Quiz to Learn By), which was so popular that parents would drive through the often hostile countryside to get to the studio in Saigon where their children could be "on television." There were news programs, interviews with politicians and community leaders, and programs giving the current leadership a platform from which to talk to the people.

These "nation-building" programs were a big challenge. For centuries the Vietnamese had a saying, "The emperor's influence ends at the village gate." This is how they saw their world. As long as things were okay in their particular hamlet, it did not matter what was going on in the world beyond. Most of them would never in their lives travel to Saigon or anyplace else.

The *New Talent Hour* was designed as a showcase for young, untried amateur singers, dancers, musicians, and other performing artists. There were many music programs, both classical and modern, featuring musicians from professional music groups and nightclubs.

Drama was an important staple, and the contemporary scripts were most susceptible to not-so-subtle propagandistic messages favorable to the government and the Nguyen Van Thieu regime. However, the anti-Communist themes were somewhat diluted between the scripting stage and the actual performance. The actors appearing in the television plays also toured the provinces. Many times in the field, actors were approached by members of the Vietcong and told that if they appeared on television with anti-Communist statements again, it could be their last performance. Naturally, these incidents inhibited many of the professional actors and the performances they were willing to give.

Almost all the drama, whether anti-Communist or not, usually accentuated love, love for each other, love for country, village life, and life in the countryside, and with a decidedly sentimental style.

Out in the countryside, our viewers not only had never seen television, but many of them had never been to the movies either. There were stories about people going behind the screen to see where the actors were, but of interest to me was that they had no knowledge of the language of film and television.

In America, film has been a part of our lives for more than one hundred years. We know that a fade-to-black means the end of that portion of the story. We know that a dissolve means either a change of time or a change of place or, in some instances, an attempt to draw a relationship between two ideas, for example, to dissolve from the face of a beautiful woman to a rose. But our rural audiences in the villages and hamlets didn't have the benefit of this familiarity. They took everything they saw on the screen at face value.

I would often go to one of these sites and sit near the TV set to observe the reactions of the crowd while they watched one of the programs we produced. How long was interest sustained? When did they get restive? What subjects or shows were popular? Our mission was to try to improve the lives of all who watched, so we mixed drama, music, and interviews with information about health care, raising children, where to go for vaccinations, what is happening in the country, and practical assistance in learning skills. The nature of our rural audience came to me vividly one night while I was visiting one of our TV reception sites in a village north of Saigon. This was an audience for whom both television and film were a new experience. They had no notion of the language of film or the use of close-ups, dissolves, or montage.

In this instance, we had produced a short, eight-minute film designed to show poultry farmers how to raise healthy chickens. We found a farmer who had followed, to the letter, all the advice from the USAID agricultural advisor. He had built the proper kind of chicken house and feeding trough, and had provided the chickens with a water supply. All this we recorded on film. His chickens truly were excellent specimens, and our hope was to help others achieve these results.

Sitting at the edge of the front row, I could watch our work on the set and also keep an eye on the reaction of the audience.

I was there when our film on how to raise healthy chickens came on. Everything was going well—the points were made clearly, I thought, and the audience was attentive and interested. At one point, we suddenly cut to a close-up of one of the beautiful eggs this chicken had produced.

As soon as the egg popped up on the twenty-seven-inch TV screen, half the audience stood up in agitation and excitement, marveling at the size of the egg. The egg filling the screen was the biggest egg they had ever seen! Puzzled, I stood up saying "*khong, khong*" (no, no) and cupping my hands to show the true size of the egg. They shook their heads, and with arms outstretched, insisted the egg was at least two feet long.

We learned to make our points step-by-step on film, to not spring anything unexpected on them, and to slowly teach some of the language of film. For later showings we shot that sequence over, leaving the egg in the farmer's hand and slowly moving in for a close-up, so the audience would have a point of reference and make no assumptions. Our job was to educate, not to startle.

One afternoon in the studio, while we looked over the eight-by-ten black-and-white photos we were going to use on the news program that day, I noticed a light, fine powdery substance on some of the prints, which created an unwanted dusty film on the pictures. Obviously, this detracted from the sharpness of the photos, and we had to wipe each one clean with a cloth. This was an unusual development that made me question what was going on downstairs in the photo lab.

Every morning for about three hours during our English and TV production class sessions, I had the luxury of an interpreter to assist me in communicating with the eighty-plus men and women with whom I worked. He was equally nonplussed and suggested we go down to the lab.

The last phase in the photo-developing process is the clear-water "bath" that washes the prints and removes the chemicals used. Our photo bath was a large, round crockery tub about five feet in diameter, containing two-and-a-half feet of water, and set on legs, which made it easy to work with the photos while standing. Here the prints received their final washing.

As we walked in I could see a number of photos draped over the edge of the tub. From where I was, it looked like one of the men, shirtless, was bending over, working with the prints. I thought he was standing on the back side of the tub until I noticed that I couldn't see his legs through the struts of the vat. No, he was sitting in the vat and taking a soapy bath.

Turning to my interpreter, I remarked, "Those photos aren't the only items getting a bath in that vat."

Without any change of expression, covering for his friend and "saving face," the interpreter said, "No, Mr. Ron, he's in there so that he can wash the vat."

I knew better than to point out that the man was naked and the white powdery substance on the pictures was soap. With some irritation I said, "Tell him he doesn't need to get into the water to clean the vat." Mystery solved, we left.

About a week later, I was just starting up a ladder to set some lights when the young man I had seen in the vat came over to the ladder. His comment, translated for me was, "Mr. Ron, I was taking a bath in the vat."

Nodding, I replied, "I know."

17

Goodbye, Saigon

Several months later, in February 1967, Bernard Fall, my teacher at the Foreign Service Institute in Washington DC, walked unannounced and alone into the office foyer where I was working.

"Has the magic of Vietnam captured you yet?" he asked, even before saying hello.

Pleased to see this man for whom I had much admiration, I shook his hand and looked him in the eye. "Yes, it has," I replied. My response surprised me a little, because I had experienced many conflicting feelings and emotions about Vietnam. I had wondered about what were we doing here, and about my place in all of this, but I was comfortable with the word *captured*.

He mentioned that he was inviting a number of people for dinner that night and would welcome my being there. This was immensely appreciated, as I was a junior member of the Foreign Service team and I knew that I would be seriously outranked at this party. This proved to be more true than I had anticipated, but the surprise of the evening was that the guest of honor that night was Mary McCarthy, the writer. Her heralded best-selling novel *The Group* was widely read and much discussed, but it wasn't her book we talked about that night.

Though I was at the far end of a table that seated nearly twenty people, her verbal energy, and the focus and persistency of her remarks, riveted my attention. She gave us a verbal assault, calling our situation in Vietnam a debacle and possibly the greatest foreign policy bungle of our nation's history. This opinion was articulated forcefully, dramatically, intelligently and, ultimately for me, convincingly.

I went to Vietnam knowing very little about the geopolitical history of that part of the world, specifically Vietnam and America's diplomatic relationships to it. It gives me no pride to admit that I naively assumed that since my country was involved and committed to this war, the cause must be just. When I was sworn in as a Foreign Service officer, I did not question America's role in Vietnam. I truly thought that for America to bring television to Vietnam was an opportunity and that I could accomplish some valuable work and serve my country in a manner I had never before been called upon to do.

As Mary McCarthy's words hurtled down to my end of the table, I could feel my heart sinking, my face and jaw becoming numb, my mind dizzily reeling, and my eyes blurring as I stared at the white tablecloth before me. She cited history, literature, foreign and domestic opinion, conversations with world leaders, interviews with the military, and quotations from presidents, mingling in her own vitriolic comments, in a two-hour tour de force. As I heard her reasoning and mixed that with my personal experiences in-country and the stories my Vietnamese friends had told about the historic struggles the people of Vietnam have been waging with their enemies for two thousand years, I felt instinctively, devastatingly, and sadly that she was right. My legs felt paralyzed. I wasn't sure I could stand up and walk out of the restaurant with the weight of these revelations pounding in my head. She was the catalyst that brought together all the discussions, questions, and doubts that had been lurking in my psyche these past months. These, coupled with my own experiences working with the Vietnamese, led me to the irrevocable conclusion that my country had made a tragic mistake.

It was after midnight when I stumbled out into the street. It had rained, and the brick streets were glistening with moisture. The warm air was heavy with fog hovering just above the trees, and Saigon was quiet. Mary McCarthy's words were reverberating through my mind and I was overtaken by the realization that we were wrong. She was right. We were wrong. Oh, God.

I walked back to my apartment at Passage Eden on Le Loi Street, at the intersection of Tu Do Street in the heart of Saigon. The reception level of this large apartment building contained a mini-mall and movie theater, and I particularly enjoyed riding in the graceful open French elevator that lifted us up very slowly to the third floor. At my bedroom window I looked down on the open-air corner bar of the Continental Palace Hotel, the spot where in 1952 Graham Greene wrote much of *The Quiet American*. As I stood there, I recalled that powerful scene when the young American, so full of energy, so eager to please, asks a venerable Vietnamese elder, "What can I do to help?" The elder in effect responds, "Go home."

That night my dream of having a career in the Foreign Service died. A Foreign Service officer has to publicly support the policies of the administration he serves, but I now knew that I couldn't always do that. As I fell asleep that night, I could hear the rumble of the trucks taking American materiel and supplies from the docks on the Saigon River out into the countryside to build runways, ports, housing, and fortifications. Can we liberate and build a nation for these people, I asked myself? No, I knew we could not. My last thought before falling asleep was, "It's their country and if they want a democratic society and the necessary infrastructure, they will have to do it themselves." The bombs falling not far from where I slept were shaking the building and making the cluster of my keys hanging in the lock of my bedroom door rhythmically bang against the wood like the sound of a drum over and over and over.

One morning a week later I came down from the apartment, and there, as usual, were the two spirited ten-year-old boys who took turns selling me the English-language *Saigon Post*. I was constantly amazed at their vitality and lust for life. If I happened to see one of them in the city later in the day, he would call out, "Ngày mai tôi," which means "Tomorrow it's me," indicating that it would be his turn to sell me the paper.

I bought the paper, opened it, and there on the front page was a three-column-wide black-bordered picture of Bernard Fall. He had been killed, Tuesday, February 21, just outside Hue. The world press reported that Dr. Fall had been riding in a jeep with a sergeant and they hit a land mine, killing them both not far from the route that gave its name to Fall's book *The Street without Joy*. *Time* magazine reported that Professor Fall was walking with a combat photographer when Fall's foot hit a land mine, killing him and the photographer in two minutes' time.

Later, my apartment mate shared a cable he had read that reported a slightly different version of Bernard Fall's death.

This report said that Professor Fall was with a small platoon in the hills outside Hue. He saw a claymore mine, one of those highly explosive bombs filled with plastic, embedded with nuts and bolts and pieces of glass and metal, set up just off the trail, and he went closer to photograph it. According to the report the lieutenant in charge ordered him back on the path, and when he didn't respond immediately the lieutenant told a sergeant to get Professor Fall back on the trail. The claymore was accidentally triggered and both men were killed.

During our dinner conversation with Mary McCarthy, one of the guests asked, "Dr. Fall, over the years how many times have you been back and forth between France and Vietnam?"

Dr. Fall replied, "This is my sixteenth trip." Then he added, smiling, "I'm not sure you can come to Saigon sixteen times," implying that to do so was pushing his luck.

A few months later, having made the decision that the Foreign

Service was not going to be my career, I prepared to leave Vietnam and go back to Nebraska and public broadcasting. My last night in Saigon I walked again down Tu Do Street to the Saigon River and sat on a wall looking out over the water.

Just across the river was a wide-open plain that, after dark, was controlled by the Vietcong. Many evenings while enjoying a glass of wine in the rooftop bar of the Caravelle Hotel, friends and I would look out over the landscape past the river and watch the flares being dropped to light up the area, and we would follow the red staccato spitting of the tracer bullets from the planes aimed at the ground.

I feel guilty when I think of being that person sitting there drinking Cabernet, safely removed from the battlefield just down the street and across the river. I was saddened that their "enemy," my country's military and civilians like me, was being used in a misguided foreign policy blunder of major proportions. Though I never experienced combat, the difficult hardships, great sacrifices, and challenges of the military, I know that all who served in Vietnam, military and civilian, have had the arduous mental and emotional task of dealing with having been a part of all that.

But tomorrow I was going home. This night, as the light was dimming at dusk, I stared intently across the river into the coming darkness, contemplating my future. I was thirty-seven years old. What was the second half of my life going to be? What did I want it to be? Then I sensed a curtain coming down and I saw thick, dense fog rolling up the Saigon River and quickly enveloping me. As I remained sitting there I was suspended in a kind of limbo of mist that yielded no answers. When the fog dissipated, revealing the outlines of the classical buildings and the traffic of the river once again, I realized that I didn't need answers right then. I walked up the street eager to find out what would happen next.

18

The House that Jack Built

Having given up the Foreign Service as a career, I knew I would be spending a good share of my life on this or some university campus. Therefore I decided to take advantage of the university's policy of offering classes to staff people for only one dollar per credit hour.

An advanced degree is directly related to pay scale at a university, and the prospect of broadening my career options and getting a larger paycheck were the major motivations. The price was right, and the early-morning and late-night classes allowed me to continue working my day job full-time. In three years I finished my doctorate degree.

In the fall of 1967 Congress passed the Public Broadcasting Act, thereby changing educational broadcasting to public broadcasting and providing major federal funding.

In the early 1950s the Congress had decided, wisely, that at least one channel of the powerful television spectrum would be reserved for education and the noncommercial presentation of the highest levels of art, culture, and public affairs programming available from throughout the world. The 1967 act meant the government would now help support it.

This was an exciting development, something worthy of one's time and energy, and though it didn't pay much, for my family it was the entrée into an exciting, diverse world inhabited by artists, teachers, actors, intellectuals, musicians, philosophers, poets, and writers. Being an active part of a great university gives one an upper-class lifestyle on a middle-class income. As Willa Cather wrote, "The end is nothing—the road is all," and this road, though bumpy at times, led to the life I wanted.

By 1968 eight additional transmitters were in construction or had been added, giving us a nine-station educational television network serving all of the homes between Iowa and Colorado, South Dakota and Kansas.

The next step was to use state-appropriated money to study the feasibility of building and financing a state-of-the-art telecommunications center. It took well over a year to bring the ETV commissioners in line and convince key city, state, and other political entities to support us in our need for a new building. Our operations were scattered across the campus in over fourteen separate locations, including an old grocery store, three decrepit frame houses, and space under the bleachers of Memorial Stadium. What used to be a cafeteria in the basement of the Temple Building served as our lone studio.

Our administrative offices were in one of the three old houses where everything creaked and groaned, the roofs leaked drastically, and floors and walls were sagging. These were truly minimal accommodations, surely violating every building standard by any measure and certainly hazardous to our health and well-being. Later, after we had vacated these premises, we were told the houses were going to be "pushed down." That seemed to be a strange way of stating it. Wouldn't they tear them down? When the day arrived, I went to that corner of city campus to say goodbye to those three old places. Excellent work by many gifted and industrious people had taken place within those creaky walls.

I watched as a Caterpillar bulldozer slowly crossed the gravel parking lot and approached the northwest corner of the first old house, then gently struck the corner of the building with one solid blow, just one. The entire edifice crumbled on the spot. I was awestruck. I knew the buildings were firetraps, but I had no idea they were so ready to collapse.

The assignment Jack McBride gave me after arriving back from Vietnam was to lobby the state legislature for the proposed new educational telecommunications building. I knew nothing about lobbying, had great fear I wouldn't be successful, and didn't know where to go for help.

That first day at the capitol building I encountered a seasoned statehouse reporter for the Lincoln newspaper and an acquaintance. He was sharp, and I knew he knew what I was getting into. So I posed him a simple question, "What should I do first?"

His response was, "You can't do it, Ron. It won't happen. You'll never get legislation for a new telecommunications center passed in these hard times. But if you're going to spend a lot of time trying, I'd find out what the governor thinks of the idea. Even if you got the bill through final reading, he could always veto it. He's got the red pen."

That sounded sensible to me, so I promptly went to the governor's secretary and asked for an appointment. There are real advantages living in a sparsely populated and unique place like the state of Nebraska. There are only 1.7 million people in Nebraska, and half of them are related to each other and the other half know each other. Nebraska governors are on a first-name basis with dozens of people in every county. Where else can you go to the governor's office and say, "I just have to see him for a few minutes. Can you work me in?"

"Sure," was the secretary's reply, "Wait by the newsstand. I'll send someone for you." The home of the only Unicameral in the nation means that if you can get twenty-five of the forty-nine senators to vote for your project, you can do almost anything. There is no two-house legislature to complicate or delay matters.

The late 1960s were bad years for farming, and in Nebraska if the economy is bad for the farmer, it's bad for everyone. I am as anxious as any farmer that Nebraska has bountiful annual rainfall and the crops are good.

I told Gov. Norbert Tiemann that we had in mind constructing a state-of-the-art telecommunications center for Nebraska at a cost of 3.2 million dollars. Before he could react, I said, "Governor, if we work our heads off for nine months to get this legislation passed, I'd like to know if you feel you can support this and not veto the bill?"

Governor Tiemann was surprised by the question, but it took him only a second to reply. "Ron, if you people can get that legislation through during this session, that will be a miracle—and if that unlikely event happens, which it won't, I will not veto it." That's all I needed. So this is what it's like to be a lobbyist, I thought.

Reporting to the legislature each morning was exciting, and Jack McBride prepared me well with his detailed strategic plans for handling any questions the sometimes difficult members of the legislature could ask.

Jack, a Nebraska son, founder of Nebraska Educational Telecommunications, was a man with an unerring moral compass. He knew right from wrong, and his infallible integrity permeated our organization and all his business dealings. He was a private man, even taciturn, and he rarely revealed his emotions. I often told new people joining our staff that if they had to have verbal acknowledgment from Jack for their personal accomplishments, they would be disappointed. It took a number of years for me to understand that he was a man whose feelings ran deep, who regarded his staff with genuine affection, but simply was so constructed that he was unable to express it.

Jack was a true visionary, always seeing what he wanted to make happen five years down the road. A favorite expression of his was "As we look to the future." Our staff, many of whom spent their entire career at NET, was loyal to him and worked hard for him because he engendered our respect. No one in the building could match him for the amount of work he could get done in eight hours. Boyishly handsome, with jet black hair throughout his life, he simply didn't age. He was my boss, my colleague, my lifelong friend. Over the years our relationship was a most successful one, because he let me manage television programming while he looked to the future for growth and financial support.

But at the moment it was a new production facility we needed in order to support our programming efforts, and he sent me to the legislature to shepherd that through.

Standing in the back of the legislative chamber one morning, I overheard a senator say to one of his colleagues, "I get tired of seeing all these university people and lobbyists with their fancy briefcases." A majority of the forty-nine senators were farmers and ranchers or business people from small towns, and most of them had never used one. I looked down at my own briefcase, recognized it as a negative, and never carried it into the chamber again. From that point on, I used manila folders. The papers would inevitably slip out in a disorganized array, but while I was straightening the papers I made sure the legislator could see the frayed cuffs of my shirt. No city slicker me. However, in truth, most of those agrarian legislators could, as we say in Nebraska, "buy and sell nearly everyone in Lincoln." But perception is still everything.

"Terrible Terry" had to be reckoned with in all legislative matters. State Senator Terry Carpenter was the most powerful man in the Nebraska Legislature at that time. A self-made millionaire, he had made his money from oil and business interests in western Nebraska, and he had served two years as a U.S. congressman. In 1956 he was a delegate to the Republican National Convention in San Francisco and is remembered as the man who nominated "Joe Smith" for vice president instead of Richard Nixon. He was smart, politically savvy, a clever strategist, and an intimidating figure in state government. "Terrytown," Nebraska, is a real place. "Terrible Terry's" was the name of his filling-station chain.

He and his wife, Hazeldean, lived amid mind-boggling European splendors of dazzling Venetian crystal chandeliers, vases, and paintings. These were the accoutrements of world travelers who bought one of everything that caught their eye and brought it home to the small city of Scottsbluff, Nebraska. Terry told me they had to enlarge the dining room to accommodate a table Hazeldean had to have.

Senator Carpenter didn't think much of educational television. I heard him say to Jack McBride, "You're not going to bring that educational crap to my end of the state." His attitude had nothing to do with our programming; he wanted to secure the available VHF channel 13 we were pursuing so that he could develop a commercial television station for the panhandle of Nebraska. We needed that channel as a vital link in our proposed nine-station statewide ETV network.

During the process of developing these interests, he had a heart attack, not a terribly damaging one but serious enough that his doctor advised against his entering the competitive world of television. Typical of him, Terry, not wanting any other commercial entrepreneur to upstage him and take that channel for themselves, suddenly became our friend in the legislature and significantly helped us develop the Nebraska Educational Television network. We got channel 13, and that was just the beginning of our relationship with "Terrible Terry."

By 1968 the nine-station ETV network was complete, and we turned our full attention to developing the new communications center building. Through Terry Carpenter's leadership, that legislation also passed, and by late 1970 our new building was nearly completed. Unhappily, our relationship with the senator was about to take a perilous turn.

In October 1970 I received a phone call from an agitated, irate Senator Carpenter. "Listen to me carefully," he said. Terry was exceedingly upset because he had just learned that the university's English department was initiating a new course of study dealing with homosexuality. This he was not going to allow.

"I'm going to have a public hearing to alert the people of this state about what the university is up to." If Terry had his way, no homosexual enlightenment was going to darken this university's doorway. "I want that TV remote truck in Omaha next Thursday for a live broadcast from the Omaha campus, and I want this broadcast during the afternoon for as many hours as it takes. This will be a major public hearing to be broadcast statewide, so set that up," he ordered.

My ears were ringing. So much for the government keeping its hands off broadcast programming, I noted to myself. This was a reality we've always had to be aware of and protect ourselves against. Jack was vigilant in maintaining editorial independence for public television, and so was I. However, I wanted to set this up, because with a hearing on the provocative subject of homosexuality led by Senator Carpenter, I knew that every person in Nebraska would be watching our stations and a good number of them for the very first time. Public television was made for just such communication with the people.

Taking a look at the schedule, I realized I couldn't honor his request. The hearing would interfere with a presentation we were planning in cooperation with the university's drama department. We had been working for over three weeks with them on an unusual presentation of *Julius Caesar*.

The play was being given a modern treatment using a Nazi Germany motif. At curtain time the audience would be forced to stand and in single file be led out of the theater by gruff Nazi-uniformed soldiers and marched across the street to the Sheldon Sculpture Garden, where the first act of the drama was to be presented. This was our version of the Roman Forum, travertine marble and all. We planned and extensively rehearsed all of this for a statewide broadcast of the play's opening night. The theater students were excited about it and had worked many hours to make it successful.

Thursday was the night this was going to happen. We couldn't be in Omaha with the truck in the afternoon and in Lincoln that night. It meant either acquiescing to the senator's wishes and letting the kids down, or incurring the wrath of Terry Carpenter. Because we had heavily promoted this live telecast of *Julius Caesar* and I didn't want to disappoint the students, and because I resisted the idea of a state senator making such a demand, I took a deep breath and chose the latter.

I suggested a possible date for the next week, and mentioned he might consider radio. After I repeated that the truck simply wasn't available that day, the long silence that followed was concluded by Mr. Carpenter saying, "You'll be sorry," as he slammed down the phone.

One of the first bills Senator Carpenter drafted in the next session of the Unicameral was legislation converting the nearly completed ETV building into a new College of Law. Architects figured the nonrecoverable costs related to such a move—the high ceiling of studio 1, for example, was to be given a second floor to become the law library. The senator was serious, and we were devastated. This development meant we had to go back to the legislature, manila folder in hand and frayed cuffs on display, to make our case for the new building one more time. Mr. Carpenter was a sophisticated, wily solon, and he could play the members of the legislature like a puppet master. He did favors for people and he never forgave a debt. If Terry wanted something from the body, he almost always got it.

Our colleagues in the law school were all too eager to cooperate with the senator and make the building their own. I knew that under the circumstances, they had little choice. Terry enjoyed that kind of omnipotence.

The legislative session lasted from January to September. We pressed our case and the law college pressed theirs. When the bill to convert the building came up on final reading, our side prevailed. As a result of the floor debates, we kept our new building and the College of Law had legislation, supported by a budget, to "plan" a new facility. It is possible that this whole scenario was a tactic employed by Senator Carpenter, who in order to have his way would sometimes sponsor legislation he didn't want but which gave him leverage to introduce something he did. We couldn't read his mind and we couldn't take the chance this was the case with our building, so every day we diligently fought to maintain the legislature's support. The pain and stress will go undescribed, but it was real.

The legislature voted to name the new building the Terry M. Carpenter Nebraska Educational Telecommunications Center. Though such a move was not unexpected, I am reminded of these conflicts every time I drive past the sign coming in to work. Since the completion of the building in 1971, I have harbored the deepseated feelings that this center is in reality "The House that Jack Built," and he deserves the recognition.

Every now and then something turns out right. The summer of 2010 I asked Senator John Harms, Forty-Eighth District, to submit a bill modifying the name of our building. Senator Harms submitted Legislative Bill 122 during the 102nd Legislature "to rename an educational telecommunications building," and the bill was passed almost unanimously by the state senators. Our building is now known as the Terry M. Carpenter and Jack G. McBride Nebraska Educational Telecommunications Center. My regret is that Jack did not live to see this day.

I was given the privilege of showing Senator Carpenter around the new building for the first time. When we stepped into our expansive new studio, he stopped, looked at the massive lighting grid and instruments, drapes, sets, cameras, audio booms, ladders, and said, "Jesus Christ, I had no idea you were building something like this." Later in the tour he saw a small "baby spotlight" he liked and commented that it would work very well in his backyard. We were quick to agree and he left with it in hand.

The new building was one of the preeminent facilities in all of public television, and we were now able to step into the public broadcasting "big time." We were respected for what we had developed in a sparsely populated state, and we now had the capability of producing television programs at a high level of artistic and technical sophistication. Further, we had also attracted a highly competent, skilled and talented cadre of producers, directors, engineers and technicians, editors and cinematographers. We were ready to show the world that they make television programs in Nebraska, too.

19

Back to Vietnam

My return to the University of Nebraska and educational television in 1967 did not sever my ties with the Vietnamese television project. The United States Information Agency invited me back to Saigon twice on temporary duty, once in 1970 and twice in 1971. Bringing television to Vietnam was a "turnkey" operation, which meant that we were planning to turn the entire operation over to the Vietnamese. I was asked to evaluate the television project and write a report of our assistance and contributions. I was eager to get back to see my friends in Vietnam.

It was during this assignment that I worked for a few weeks with the television project and simultaneously, with a borrowed Super 16 millimeter camera, began filming *Vietnam Beyond the Fury*, a documentary I was producing for broadcast on PBS. Jack Murphy, the USIA advisor to the project, invited me to accompany him to inspect the television site at Hue, the old imperial capital of Vietnam, just south of the demilitarized zone. This gave me the opportunity to visit and get some footage of the famous tombs of past Vietnamese emperors that lie in the highlands between Hue and the Laotian border. This area is at a point where Vietnam is only about sixty miles wide from the China Sea to Laos, and since it was adjacent to North Vietnam, this part of the landscape was always being contested. Just three years earlier, during the Tet Offensive of 1968, the military contingent of engineers operating our television transmitter in Hue was marched into the yard and killed by the Vietcong.

The day I visited was a clear, cool, beautiful day, and after our discussions at the transmitter site, I was anxious to be off to see those ancient tombs. Along with three colleagues, we set out in a government "carryall" for the foothills situated a few miles west on our way to find the monuments.

The grounds of the intricately designed, elaborately ornate tombs were silent testimony to an ancient past, and I secured some stunning footage for my film. Always alert to the dangers of the Vietnam countryside after sundown, we started our twenty-five-mile trek back to the safety of Hue about four thirty in the afternoon. The road—in some places more accurately a path—wound its way faintly etched through the natural grasses as we followed the wheel tracks where vehicles had gone before. The surrounding mountains were striking and vivid against the sky, and the air was pure and refreshing. The four of us were enthusiastically recounting this trip back into Vietnam's history when our conversation was interrupted by Bill, our driver. Slowing down, he said, "Take a look at what's up ahead."

A few hundred feet ahead we could see that our road was blocked by three large barrels with planks across the top, and guarded by four people. They had guns and were dressed in black—commonly referred to as "black pajamas"—usually worn by peasants and therefore often by the vc (Vietcong).

Sitting in front with Bill, in as calm a voice as I could muster, I asked what we were all thinking: "Who are these people? Why have they blocked the road?"

His tentative reply was, "Well, they are either home guard or Vietcong." There was silence in the carryall.

I knew that in many parts of Vietnam the people were loyal

to whichever side had the power at the time. Naturally, we were all fervently hoping this welcoming party considered themselves home guard.

We stopped. A man stuck his face in my window and said rather gruffly, "Where you go?"

I knew some of the most useful phrases in Vietnamese, so quickly I said, "Tôi về nhà," which means "I go home."

And he said, "Nhà?" (Home?)

I said, "Co, tôi về nhà vôi Mỹ" (Yes, I go home to America).

He said, "Bạn hay vaô Mỹ?"

"Yes," I said. "I go to America."

Then I said, "Tôi thích Việt Nam . . ." (I like Vietnam). "Tôi thích nguôi Việt Nam" (I like the Vietnamese).

And the man said, "Bạn về nhà? Bạn hay vaô Mỹ?" I nodded an emphatic yes.

Then he said again, more I think to impress his countrymen, "Bạn về nhà! Bạn hay vaô Mỹ!" (You go home! You go to America!) with gruffness and some anger in his voice.

With that, he had the barrels pushed to one side and motioned for us to move out.

In an instant Bill had that carryall gunning down the road. When we were at a safe distance I said to him, "Well, were they home guard or vc?"

Bill, not looking at me, but with his voice rising on the last word, replied, "We'll never know." The four of us collectively exhaled as we flew down the path toward the old imperial capital of Hue.

I spent much of that night lying in bed in the U.S. Army barracks "Ohio" building in Hue, looking up at the stars overhead through the shell-damaged roof and wondering whether or not the people we encountered on the road were the enemy Vietcong or simply peasants on home guard. My life seemed very insignificant. I knew that had they decided to do away with the four Americans that afternoon, it's possible that no one would ever have known what happened.

Every now and then while I was serving in Vietnam, I was reminded of the harsh reality that there are people out there who would like to see me dead. This sobering realization left me feeling vacant and of little worth. Though I didn't know my enemy personally, I suspect he felt the same way.

I fell asleep making connections with the stars shining through the shattered roof.

We flew back to Saigon the next morning with anticipation to take part in the dedication ceremony of the new production facility.

The dedication ceremony was held outside in the television compound we shared with the U.S. Armed Forces Radio and Television Service, though we were separated from them by a ten-foot wire mesh fence. The invitation list included all the people who worked in the television center and dignitaries from the Ministry of Information and related Vietnamese and American government agencies, including Ambassador Ellsworth T. Bunker, who had replaced Ambassador Henry Cabot Lodge, and General William Westmoreland.

Seeing General Westmoreland and Ambassador Bunker at the lemonade table after the formal remarks of dedication had been made, and hoping to catch a bit of their conversation, I stood respectfully apart from them and picked up the pitcher of lemonade to pour myself a glass. I edged as close to them as possible, and to create the impression I wasn't listening in, I nonchalantly turned my head to look the other way and began pouring. A finger touched me on the shoulder and the general's familiar voice said, "Young man, you're pouring that lemonade on your shoe."

Dedicating the new Saigon production center was a moment of culmination in my temporary duty for USIA. With my report written and submitted, I returned to Nebraska.

20

David and
Goliath

Our new telecommunications center lived up to its promise. We were producing local, regional, and national programs of recognized merit. But it was an unexpected incident that propelled our reputation and put our network in newspaper headlines and television broadcasts throughout America and Europe.

New Year's Day morning, January 1, 1976, I turned on the TV set to watch the Rose Bowl Parade from Pasadena. Turning to NBC I was puzzled to see our Nebraska ETV logo, a red stylized letter N. Thinking I had made a mistake, I switched channels, only to discover that I hadn't. NBC was using our logo and extolling it as their new corporate image! There goes our logo, I thought. They were, after all, bigger than we were, and I was surprised, dismayed, and disheartened.

The following Monday morning I went immediately to my weekly production meeting at eight o'clock. There were twenty-five people in the room, and all eyes were riveted on me. I took my seat, said good morning, and almost in one voice they responded, "That's our logo, and what are you going to do about it?" I told them I didn't know—but quickly the events of the morning dictated what I was going to do. I had no time to think about it—everything just happened.

The phone rang and it was the program director at NBC affiliate KHAS-TV in Hastings, Nebraska, a hundred miles west. The young man said, "Ron, we have all been watching over the weekend. They've got your logo. I called up NBC headquarters in New York and told those guys that their new logo is already in use." I knew then that the situation was not in my hands.

NBC was dropping its famous peacock logo for the stylized N, and they were hyping the introduction of this new logo into a major media event. Walls on NBC buildings in San Francisco, Houston, and dozens of other cities were painted overnight, eliminating the peacock in favor of a big red N. All their stationery was printed and shipped for use after January 1. Luggage tags and press cards were issued; mobile trucks and equipment across the land were transformed. NBC's identifying symbol was changed overnight and was introduced during the Rose Bowl Parade broadcast. It was reported that the design, production, and implementation of their new corporate identity represented an investment of 3 million dollars. Though they didn't realize it at first, they didn't own the now famous stylized N.

The next phone call I received was from a senior vice president at NBC. He opened with the comment that we had a rather unusual and interesting situation he wished to discuss. I agreed, and then he said he had a suggestion: "What does it matter? Why don't you go right on using your logo and we'll use ours." The implication was that we were so insignificant that no one would notice. It was then that the David in me recognizing the Goliath in them instantly bristled at this dismissal of Nebraska ETV.

I do not know where my next words came from, but I heard myself saying with authority, "Sir, it's our logo. We like it and we're going to keep it." The NBC vice president hung up.

Shortly thereafter, I received another phone call. This one was from NBC Radio News. The voice said, "Mr. Hull, what did you just say to our senior vice president?"

I replied, "It's our logo. We like it and we're going to keep it." At ten o'clock that morning, the programming staff and I gathered around the radio and heard me repeat that statement nationwide on NBC news. Needless to say, the staff was cheering.

A little later that morning, a former student now working as a director for NBC called and said, "Ron, the entire NBC production floor of the RCA Building is on your side."

Jack McBride told me to call our Washington legal counsel, Richard Marks. When he answered, I asked if he had watched television over the weekend and did he notice the big splash NBC was making introducing their new corporate logo?

He said that he had. I told him to take a look at our Nebraska ETV stationery because the new NBC logo is exactly like ours.

Richard said, "Exactly?"

There was a brief pause on the line and then I heard him say, "Noooo shiiiiiiiit!" The sound of glee in his voice told me that his little lawyer heart was thumping away and picking up speed.

He directed me to gather up all documentation of the use of our logo that I could possibly find, get on a plane, and bring it to him in Washington that day. I packed stationery, station identification artwork, slides, film, video, examples of the use of the logo on our programs (our PBS series *Anyone for Tennyson?*, for example, established the use of our logo in all fifty states), newspaper and magazine ads, posters and flyers, and even some T-shirts emblazoned with that stylized N.

We had even produced decals of our logo that we put on our car windows and bumpers to help promote Nebraska ETV. I scooped up one hundred of those, put all of this in a bag, and headed for Washington DC that afternoon. While changing planes at O'Hare, I passed a newsstand selling the *Chicago Tribune*. There, on the front page, *above* the masthead, was our story and two identical pictures of our logo and NBC's.

I walked into the lobby of the L'Enfant Plaza Hotel in Washington shortly after 10:00 p.m. At the front desk I gave my name, and immediately the people in the lobby, over a dozen, stood up and came forward, everyone speaking at once and all aimed at me.

They were from the *Philadelphia Enquirer*, the *New York Times*, the *Washington Post*, *Newsweek* magazine, *Time* magazine, and there were television and radio station reporters. They all crowded around wanting more of the story and asking if I had artwork with me of the Nebraska logo. That was easy—I answered questions and passed out Nebraska ETV decals for the next half hour. This was an exciting time—nothing quite like this had ever happened to me.

As this David and Goliath story evolved, it traveled far and wide. Friends and agencies sent me copies of the story from London and Paris and other cities of the world. Human nature does love the underdog. Since it had been reported that NBC spent nearly 3 million dollars developing a logo they didn't own, the question to me was, how much did Nebraska spend on developing ours? I went to Bill Korbus, our art director and the designer of the logo. After computing the time he spent and the original materials involved, he advised me that we had spent about thirty-five dollars of out-of-pocket cash on the design.

Early in the litigation we decided we would do everything in our power to make Nebraska look good and to make NBC look good as well. NBC dragged their feet at first, hoping we'd go away, but we made the decision to sue. We had a good case. We had been using our logo for over a year, and its use had been established on television and in the press in all fifty states. Further, we too were a network—as was NBC. Had we been a bakery, there would have been no case.

In time, thanks to Richard Marks at Dow, Lohnes, and Albertson and to Harold Mosher, Nebraska assistant attorney general, the situation was resolved happily for Nebraska and also for NBC. They established their new corporate logo far more dramatically and memorably than their Madison Avenue advisors had ever envisioned.

NBC gave Nebraska one of their remote mobile television vans, other sophisticated production equipment, and fifty thousand dollars in cash, for a total settlement of over seven hundred thousand dollars. NBC, of course, got the sole right to use the stylized *N* logo. The remote van served us well for a number of years and allowed us to bring high school football games, concerts, and public affairs debates and programs from every corner of Nebraska to all Nebraskans.

21

The Big Time

This unexpected episode exponentially helped establish Nebraska ETV's national image. Our place in the pantheon of public stations was enhanced overnight.

To create a successful public television and radio service requires significant participation in the life of the community. Our community is the state of Nebraska, and we have built a successful state network by remembering that all politics is local and that the grass roots must be consistently nurtured.

This philosophy has led to working with the Mari Sandoz, Willa Cather and John Neihardt literary centers, the YMCA, the Lincoln Community Playhouse, the Nebraska Repertory Theatre, the Omaha and Lincoln symphonies, the Sandhills Symphony Orchestra, Opera Omaha, and myriad other music, theater, and civic organizations throughout Nebraska. With personal friends on these boards from every corner of the state, we enjoy their financial support and when necessary the vocal support of real people in real places scattered across the landscape to make our case with the governor, the appropriations committee, and members of the legislature, not to forget the fiscal analysts. This is a never-ending process, and knowing people and working with them on a one-to-one basis is a constant reminder that our programs go into real homes and have impact on real families. Making our programs and services meaningful and useful to all Nebraskans has always been our goal.

To help ensure this local involvement statewide, I initiated a series of program advisory committees in eight towns and cities throughout the state. Each committee had twelve to fifteen people from the surrounding countryside who received regular mailings bringing them up to date on new programs, educational services available to parents, teachers, and the public, and successes we were enjoying with the legislature, the governor, and other sources of support.

Once a year I visited these eight communities and took each committee either to lunch or dinner, depending on my itinerary. I drove in a wide circle from east to west, north to south, bringing with me a videotape playback machine and a twenty-seven-inch television set so that I could give them previews of the new programming and make them feel they were "insiders," which they were.

We listened carefully to their advice.

There's one quality you can always depend on from Nebraskans, and that is, they will be candid, direct, and honest in voicing their opinions. Mary Jane "Pug" Gottschalk, editor and owner of the *Sheridan County Star* newspaper in Rushville, Nebraska, took her role as an "advisor" seriously. She watched the programs, took notes, came to the meetings prepared, and didn't mince words.

"You mean you spent our hard-earned tax dollars bringing that inane series to Nebraska?" (referring to a British comedy series) was one of her memorable opening lines. She said what she thought, and I knew she understood our value. I appreciated her vigor in encouraging us to present controversial material, offering wide-ranging views on crucial social subjects. Further, she knew that thanks to Nebraska public television, the kids in her small Sandhills town had the same access to great art, music, literature, and culture as those in urban areas. They could enjoy the sparsely populated land, the animals and wonders of nature, and still be active participants through this window to the world—the best of both worlds, in her view.

After you've lived in Nebraska for a few years, you begin to realize that almost everyone knows someone or is related to someone in the myriad towns and villages spread across the state like marbles randomly scattered. It is a unified family, aided largely by the early decision to develop one major university. With that one university came the singular loyalty to the beloved Cornhusker football team, "Big Red." This is without doubt the most unifying factor in the state, though it is widely acknowledged that the statewide educational television network has done its part in providing an electronic connection binding the state together intellectually, culturally, and socially.

With public television's ability to provide daily coverage of the Nebraska Legislature, people in the Panhandle are much more likely to turn their attention toward Lincoln rather than wishing they were a part of Wyoming (which has been threatened and where much of their commercial television originates). Our gavel-to-gavel coverage of the legislature speaks directly to the motto carved in stone over the main entrance of the state capitol building: The salvation of the state is watchfulness in the citizen.

That family concept came home to me one night in the 1960s during a live television interview with Frank Morrison, one of the great and most popular of all Nebraska governors. Frank was a big-boned, tall man with a broad-shouldered, heavy frame. During the telecast he was being interviewed by a journalist, and I was directing the program in the control room. We had a very small staff, and that night there was a three-person crew in the studio and one engineer and me in the control booth.

When the phone rang, which was just to the right of the

director's console, I answered it while continuing to direct the program. It was the governor's wife; the message was brief.

"Ron," she said sternly. "This is Maxine. Tell Frank to sit up."

Over the headset I told the floor manager to write a big sign and hold it up. It read, "Frank, sit up. Maxine." He was slouching quite far down into the chair, saw the sign, rolled his eyes just slightly, and dutifully sat up.

Though Nebraskans love their beloved Cornhusker football team and for decades have made Memorial Stadium the state's third-largest city every Saturday during the season, let it be said that Nebraskans also embrace the arts. The development of the Mari Sandoz Center on the campus of Chadron State College and the John G. Neihardt Center in Bancroft, and the restoration and maintenance of eight buildings related to the work of Willa Cather, including preservation of the Opera House in Red Cloud, are testimony to the importance Nebraskans bring to saving and advancing the art and culture of our state. Working on the boards of each of these literary centers and foundations has deepened my appreciation for literature and history, and has provided lifelong friendships with some fascinating individuals.

Mildred Bennett, the charismatic founder and longtime president of the Willa Cather Pioneer Memorial Foundation, could have literally stepped out of a Willa Cather novel. Like some of Cather's heroines, Mildred was a strong, fiercely independent, intelligent woman who loved the land and planted her roots deeply in the soil of Webster County, Nebraska.

One day, thirty-some years ago, she called and said, "Ron, let's get our heads together and plan something special for this year's conference." Our focus that year was Cather's novel *Lucy Gayheart*. At the beginning of the book, the young banker of the town watches, unnoticed, a lithe, thirteen-year-old Lucy run through the wet cement of the last square of the new sidewalk on the western edge of town, leaving three delicate footprints. Many years later these footprints play a significant role in the epilogue of the novel.

Mildred and I agreed, "That's it." We decided to add a square to the sidewalk at the western edge of town, and to bring authenticity to our work, we had a great-granddaughter of Annie Pavelka, the prototype for Ántonia in Cather's *My Ántonia*, run through the wet cement, leaving three delicate footprints. This, we thought, was a good way to commemorate the conference that year, and people enjoyed it.

Twenty years later I was in a school bus on the "Cather Country Tour" during the conference. We stopped at the western edge of town, everyone got off the bus, and we listened to our tour guide point out the three footprints preserved in the last panel of the sidewalk. "Here," she said, "are the original footprints that inspired Willa Cather to write *Lucy Gayheart*." I couldn't believe my ears. Everyone was oohing and aahing, and commenting on the poignancy of those tiny footsteps, totally immersed in the tragedy of *Lucy Gayheart*. I started to object, but then I couldn't. It didn't seem right for me to contradict the earnest young tour guide, nor did I feel I should disappoint the reverent, attentive people who were so moved by seeing "those very same footprints" in the sidewalk. I said nothing, and as the bus rolled on, my thoughts were about the effect of Cather's powerful story.

One role I enjoyed was serving as president of the Lincoln Symphony Orchestra Association. Symphonies, like nearly every other piece of the public sector, depend on the generosity of "people like you," foundations, and endowments. We were always looking for money. Just like public television.

Just before the concert broke for intermission, I would often go onstage and remind the audience that it is the season ticket sales that keep the orchestra playing and that we need their continued financial support and of new patrons they might bring on board. One night I made the appeal, and as I was walking through the backstage area, a young man stopped me. He was a member of the orchestra, holding a cello.

"Mr. Hull," he said, "I'm from Burwell" (a rural community

in western Nebraska) "and I just want you to know that about ten years ago when I was twelve years old, I turned on the television set and there was this large, buxom blond woman playing the cello. I didn't know it could sound so wonderful, and right then I decided I had to play the cello, too."

That *Master Class* with cellist Zara Nelsova had reached deep and productively into the remote Sandhills of Nebraska. Hearing anecdotes like this is the payoff for a life in public television.

One year, as a fund-raiser, the orchestra decided to perform Aaron Copland's *Lincoln Portrait*, and we at Nebraska public television planned to televise it. The first section of the work requires a narrator to read the words of Abraham Lincoln over the orchestral music. Seventy-five hundred dollars was a lot of money to us, but that's what we agreed to pay Walter Cronkite to narrate this piece. He was expensive, but with his fame, countenance, and gravitas, he was nearly as effective as Abe Lincoln himself might have been.

Not long before the concert, our executive director of the symphony, LaVon Crosby, called excitedly to tell me that Aaron Copland would be in Lincoln as a visiting artist at Nebraska Wesleyan University and would conduct his *Lincoln Portrait* for our concert.

Imagine how we felt, Cronkite and Copland, and the Lincoln Symphony. We will not only make splendid music, we will sell tickets!

We had a tremendously successful concert, followed by a lucrative postconcert party for those who could part with fifty dollars each. This was a "big ticket" for Lincoln, Nebraska.

Backstage, Walter Cronkite was telling everyone about *Annie*, the new Broadway show he had thoroughly enjoyed, and while waiting for things to begin, he was reading a novel. He said to Mr. Copland, "Aaron, you're mentioned in this paragraph."

"And I'll bet they misspelled my name," he responded.

"Well, it's printed here as C-o-p-e-l-a-n-d."

"I knew it," Mr. Copland said.

During the concert, as we looked at Mr. Cronkite sitting on-stage waiting for his part to begin, it seemed that he slowly began to look like Abraham Lincoln, and when he spoke he read the words with such intelligence and feeling that he became Mr. Lincoln.

Later at the party LaVon and I were congratulating ourselves on having put together such a great combination for the benefit of the orchestra. I asked her what we had to pay Mr. Copland for his participation.

"I didn't ask him about that," she said.

Uh-oh, our profits may be diminished significantly, I thought.

I called him the next morning and thanked him for helping us have such a tremendous success. Then I mentioned that he seemed to be having a wonderful time himself . . .

"A splendid time. That's a fine orchestra you have in Lincoln," he said.

Then I struggled with the hard part. "Mr. Copland . . . in discussing your conducting the symphony, we . . . uh . . . failed to talk about your compensation."

Silence. My heart sank.

"Compensation. You're right! We didn't discuss that, did we?"

Bracing myself, I thought "Here it comes."

"Mr. Hull, my next gig is in Denver, Colorado. Why doesn't the Lincoln Symphony buy me a one-way ticket from Lincoln to Denver."

We paid Aaron Copland's one-way fare to Denver and it cost us sixty-five bucks.

With the tools of the new building, we embarked on what was to be a series of PBS programs featuring the world's great poetry. Though it would come from the heartland, I felt having an eastern partner on the project would give us additional credibility with the PBS stations, foundations, and other possible underwriters.

William Perry, the series' creator and producer, and I went to one of the top arts and cultural producers at WNET, Channel 13, in New York. If we could partner with WNET, I felt sure we could sell the series idea to the entire PBS network of stations. Their support was essential. It was a short meeting. After carefully describing our ideas for *Anyone for Tennyson?*, the Channel 13 producer said, "Gentlemen, when we decide to do poetry, we'll do it."

Standing on the sidewalk at Fifty-ninth and Broadway, Bill and I almost at the same time said, "Looks like we have to do this ourselves."

Anyone for Tennyson? is remembered as a highly original, edifying, and entertaining public television series. Featuring a talented cast of two men and two women (The First Poetry Quartet) joined by a guest "star," the series brought poetry to the television screens of America each week—and often from the geographic location of the poems. Most of the programs were presentational in style, but at times we created mini-dramas in presenting the poetry.

Claire Bloom played the poet in our program *The World of Emily Dickinson*, produced in Hartford, Connecticut; Ruby Dee brought us *Voices from the South*, from Atlanta, Georgia; Massachusetts's Mystic Seaport served as the location for *Poems of the Sea*; England was the setting for *William Shakespeare: Poet for All Time*. From our studios in Lincoln, Henry Fonda brought us *The American Dream*; William Shatner, *Spoon River Anthology*; Valerie Harper, *Journey through Life: Edna St. Vincent Millay*; and Vincent Price, *A Poetic Feast: Poems about Art and Food*. Even Broadway actress Irene Worth came to Nebraska to appear in *William Butler Yeats: The Heart of Ireland*, and Jack Lemmon was wonderful in *Ogden and Dorothy, Phyllis and Yip*, produced in Los Angeles. Our budget for each program was a mere nine thousand dollars, and we could pay these headliners only a one-thousand-dollar honorarium plus expenses for two and a half days' work. Even so, we could get virtually any person we needed. They were available to us for one reason, and Claire Bloom said it best: "I'm rarely asked to read Emily Dickinson."

Our experience with William Shatner was particularly

memorable. Our lobby was filled for three days with Trekkies sitting, squatting, and waiting for just a glimpse of *Star Trek*'s Captain Kirk as he walked by. During the first read-through, he read his lines in a perfunctory, almost distracted fashion. Our expectations and hearts began to sink. During the second read-through he wasn't much better, and we left the studio that afternoon disappointed that we might not be able to capture the brilliance of Edgar Lee Masters's *Spoon River Anthology*. He was paying more attention to his beautiful female companion sitting not far away than he was to the business at hand.

When we convened the next morning Mr. Shatner began to go after the material with real energy. His line reading was becoming less routine, was taking on new life. His performance was gathering momentum and the spirit of Spoon River was beginning to live. Our hopes were stirring. That afternoon, he returned to the studio without his companion, and his interest in the words was heightened; there was humor and wisdom and drama coming through his interpretations. Recognizing the power of the poetry, he was beginning to bring his considerable gifts to the work.

On the third day, when taping commenced, William Shatner brought us a poignant, polished, moving performance—living up to the demands of the script and his own auspicious talent. It was fascinating to watch him slowly make that poetry a part of his own psyche.

The show was directed by one of the great names of the golden age of television, Marshall Jamison. Marshall had enjoyed a productive career at the highest levels of American theater and television. He had been enticed to Nebraska by Jack McBride to produce and direct a series of films about the Great Plains for use in college classrooms. He was a director, producer, and writer, particularly of poetry. The Great Plains series was completed, and when I offered him *Anyone for Tennyson?* and the work of Edna St. Vincent Millay, Whittier, Longfellow, and Shakespeare, he, like the actors, couldn't resist the opportunity.

In 1947, while Leland Hayward's *Mister Roberts* was in tryouts, Marshall was cast as one of the sailors. Playing the nurse and the only female role in the play was Eva Marie Saint in her first chance at Broadway. After a triumphant series of performances in Philadelphia, Mr. Hayward and the director, Josh Logan, called everyone backstage, congratulated the cast, and announced that they had a theater booked in New York and the show would be opening on Broadway. Then Mr. Logan called Eva Marie aside and told her that the decision had been made to recast her role. She could stay with the show as the standby, but she would not be opening with the others in New York.

Years later she told me that as devastating as that was—she remembered the late-night train trip back to New York afterward, thinking that her mother would have to take the star off her bedroom door and that life for her as an actress seemed in jeopardy—it was one of the best things that ever happened to her.

Marshall Jamison told me that as he looked at her standing on the stage contemplating her disappointment, he knew instinctively that she had a wonderful talent and there would be other parts. Eva Marie Saint's Academy Award for *On the Waterfront* was just up ahead.

Marshall left acting and joined Broadway producers Leland Hayward and Josh Logan as Mr. Logan's assistant. They produced plays together, including the musical *Wish You Were Here* and Henry Fonda's *Point of No Return*, and Marshall directed Shirley Booth in *By the Beautiful Sea*. He also directed the distinguished network drama series *The U.S. Steel Hour* and the comedy series *That Was the Week That Was*. Their *Ford Fiftieth Anniversary Special* (simulcast live by NBC *and* CBS) featuring Ethel Merman and Mary Martin is one of early television's greatest triumphs. Marshall was at the directing console the unforgettable night Ethel and Mary sang the "I" songs: "I Cried for You" and "I'm Forever Blowing Bubbles" and "I've Got a Feelin' You're Foolin'" and on and on for thirteen minutes.

While he worked at Nebraska public television, each of us aspired to meet, or at the very least come close to, the production standards and expectations of Marshall Jamison. He was professional, talented, experienced, compassionate, and always the gentleman. He knew how to calm things down in chaotic, time-driven situations, and he knew what we all needed in order to bring forth our best work. He was a daily reminder of how good something could get. And he did it with a persuasive, loving hand and a true hero's heart.

In the late 1930s, when he was a freshman student at the Yale School of Drama, he went into New York to see Maxwell Anderson's free-verse play *Winterset* starring Burgess Meredith. Marshall was so moved by this performance that during the intermission he sent a note with an usher backstage asking Mr. Meredith if a young Yale drama student could come to his dressing room after the curtain to tell him personally what this evening had meant to him. Mr. Meredith handed the usher his reply, "Sorry, kid, I don't have time."

Thirty years later Marshall was directing *The U.S. Steel Hour*, and Burgess Meredith came in to read for one of the leading roles. Everyone involved—Marshall, the unit manager, the sponsor—all agreed that Mr. Meredith was perfect for the part. In the discussion, the unit manager, who kept track of the budget, said that he would assign five thousand dollars for Mr. Meredith, which was the top amount paid at that time for a starring role. Everyone agreed, but Marshall said, "Hold on, let me negotiate the salary with Mr. Meredith personally." When Burgess Meredith agreed to do the part for thirty-five hundred dollars, he never knew that his "Sorry, kid" note written back in the 1930s had just cost him fifteen hundred dollars.

Broadway's much-honored Irene Worth came to Nebraska for the William Butler Yeats program on *Anyone for Tennyson?* Though born in Nebraska, she wouldn't give us permission to mention this in any publicity. She read the poetry superbly, but unaccustomed to seeing her face close up on a television monitor, she froze in horror. Abruptly stopping her performance, she declared she couldn't possibly look like that.

Unlike the theater, where audiences see the person on stage from twenty-five feet away, the camera and the lights, particularly in close-ups, can be harshly real and critical. Our lighting director quickly softened all the lighting, and Marshall showed her how he would use "medium" shots and not extreme close-ups. But her confidence was shaken. It was at this moment I saw a great director perform his magic on a fine but insecure actress.

Marshall asked everyone to leave the set for a few minutes, and he quietly asked her to begin her reading, at the same time showing her on the monitor how the shot would look. I was standing just out of range. I could hear him tell her how her interpretation was brilliant and that she had just the right intensity for the words. All the time he had his arm around her waist and his big right hand rested on her hip. As he talked he gently patted her butt while giving her these words of assurance. It was exactly what she needed.

He returned to the control room, and Irene Worth gave a beautiful interpretation of the spirit of Maud Gonne, the Irish revolutionary and the love of Yeats's life.

Many years later, when the undertakers at his burial asked me and Marshall's son, Josh, to help carry the casket from the hearse to the gravesite, I did so feeling supremely privileged.

22

Sandy, Jean, and Phil

My life has been enriched by knowing actors like Sandy Dennis, Jean Peters, and Philip Abbott.

SANDY DENNIS

A Lincoln friend of many decades who made her mark on the stage, on television, and in the movies was Sandy Dennis. Sandy and I met at the Lincoln Community Playhouse in the spring of 1956. She was a quiet, unassuming young woman who listened carefully to the director and the other actors. A natural blond, she had an adorable face with large expressive eyes, qualities of which she was totally unaware. She was judged the best actress of that season for her performance as Lizzie in N. Richard Nash's *The Rainmaker*, and I received the best actor award for my portrayal of Dignan in Jean Kerr's *King of Hearts*. Our friendship began that spring, and grew and flourished over the next four decades until her death in 1992. I was in the audience for most of her plays and in her dressing room afterward. She included me in cocktail and dinner parties in New York, and we spent many evenings with friends at dinners in Westport, Connecticut.

Sandy Dennis had it from the beginning—she interested audiences.

"Let me tell you about Sandy Dennis," critic Walter Kerr said, reviewing her 1964 Broadway hit *Any Wednesday* for the *New York Times*. "Every home should have one." As an actress she took implausible characters and breathed into her performances an originality and freshness that stunned audiences and critics alike.

Sandy attended Nebraska Wesleyan University for one semester, during which she electrified audiences as Emily in *Our Town*. For her second semester she transferred to the University of Nebraska, and it was here that a wise, dedicated man of the theater, Dallas Williams, recognized her talent and told her to go to New York immediately and try her luck. Early entry, he said, is one of the keys to success.

Success came easily. An off-Broadway performance her first summer there in *Riders to the Sea* brought her good notices, and she was cast in a CBS soap opera for a number of weeks. After that, parts in Broadway plays were beginning to open up. She was in the business for the right reasons. Fame, money, and materialism were never her primary motivations. When she was nominated for her first Tony Award in 1963 for *A Thousand Clowns*, she showed up at the event in a long, flowing, black, belted dress that her agent insisted she buy for the occasion. When she arrived, no one recognized her, and she, not knowing there was a special section for nominees, sat way in the back with the public. And she won.

The next year she was nominated for the Tony again for her work in *Any Wednesday*. That year she dug out the same black dress, and when she couldn't find the belt, she simply wore it without one. She won that Tony, too, but this time she sat closer to the stage.

She made the cover of *Time* magazine, and the caption under her picture read, "The star in the seven-dollar dress," which was true. True to midwestern frugality, and not being used to having any money, she shopped in Macy's basement and took a bus rather than taxis after performances to her apartment on West End Avenue.

Later, when she won the Academy Award for her performance as Honey in Mike Nichols's film *Who's Afraid of Virginia Woolf?*, she didn't bother to go to Hollywood but instead watched the ceremony on a TV set at Frankie and Johnnie's Restaurant in New York City.

One of her close friends was Geraldine Page. Page had toured the country in *Agnes of God* and later asked Sandy to appear with her in the play at the Westport Playhouse.

During the run of the play, Geraldine Page blew her lines and struggled to get back to the text. All the while Sandy, who had only rehearsed the play for a week, was of no help. Finally Miss Page turned to Sandy and said, "Sandy, go backstage to that nice little girl with the playbook and find out where we are." This, Sandy said, was one of the most humiliating moments of her life on stage.

She shuffled offstage in her nun's habit only to find the girl with the playbook, tears in her eyes, mumbling, "I don't know, I've lost the place, too." At that moment Miss Page's memory picked up the correct line and the play went on.

Sandy took her work seriously and once said to me that if she ever went up on her lines—the most unprofessional act of all—she knew that God would send a bolt of lightning and strike her down right then and there, just leaving a smudge on the boards. She felt a strong sense of responsibility to give the paying audience her best—always.

As Sandy said, "You know that horrible incident happened, but there was no bolt of lightning. I didn't die on the spot. In fact, people came backstage and said how happy they were to be in the audience when this happened."

Sandy and Geraldine Page starred together on Broadway in

Alan Ayckbourn's successful comedy *Absurd Person Singular*. Each of them had their own eccentricities which they brought to their professional work and their personal lives. Sandy's performances were often peppered with twitches, mannerisms, gulping, and starting some sentences two or three times, but like Miss Page she was capable of enormous emotional delivery that audiences believed and embraced.

I was in Sandy's dressing room before one of her performances in *Absurd Person Singular*. She was finishing her makeup when there was a knock on the door and she asked me to answer. There stood a woman, hair straggling out from a stocking cap, wearing layered, nondescript clothing and holding in each hand a large, overloaded shopping bag. Looking at Sandy, she said, "Good luck tonight, honey," and she left.

To me she could have been the bag lady of Third Avenue, but when I asked who it was, Sandy said, "That's Geraldine Page." Later that evening, when Miss Page made her entrance, she swept into the play's upscale East Side apartment in a shimmering gown, sparkling jewels, and a sophisticated upswept hairstyle and "grande dame" demeanor. The transformation was astonishing, but as Sandy said, "She's an actress."

Sandy was a person who knew who she was, and acted on that. Although she had remarkable talent, combined with some lucky breaks, she achieved success through her own will and determination. All she wanted was to do good work. I never saw her in a phony moment either in a play or in her life. She always delivered an honest performance and lived an honest life.

She loved men and had productive relationships. Actor Jerry O'Laughlin taught her volumes about pursuing a life in the theater, and they were together for seven years. After that she and jazz saxophonist Jerry Mulligan lived together for ten years. She never married because, she said, "If you're married and have children, I think you should be there—and I don't plan to be there." Eric Roberts played a role in her life for three years, but it was the two summers that his sister, Julia Roberts, then in high school, stayed with Sandy that were particularly rewarding for her. When Sandy was dying of cancer, I saw a check on her bedroom bureau in the amount of five thousand dollars, signed by Julia Roberts.

Sandy collected strays—people and animals. There were usually forty-five or more cats at her place. As you walked from one room to the next, there was a cat on each chair, end table, or flat surface, and those heads turned and those eyes followed you through the house. She couldn't resist taking care of homeless cats she would find when she traveled, playing various theaters throughout the country. In addition there were usually two or three dogs, and once I saw a raccoon in the kitchen. It probably wandered over from the next-door neighbor, actress June Havoc, who enjoyed wild animals at her place.

One evening I was sitting in Sandy's living room visiting with her and her mother during a dramatic, driving rainstorm, accompanied by great flashes of lightning and deafening thunder. The house, the many-gabled former summer home of Alice Roosevelt Longworth, was the perfect setting for a Charles Addams cartoon. We sat in the dimly lighted room with extraordinarily high ceilings as the storm outside created a foreboding, creepy atmosphere. Every few minutes the room was punctured by brilliant flashes of lightning, which revealed six or seven determined cats hanging on the screens outside every window, clawing to get in. It seemed the very walls were moving, like something out of an old horror movie.

Sandy had a housekeeper, Mary, and a young man who did the handyman work around the house and drove her to the train each day for her performances in New York. Her mother lived with her for years, and there was always someone staying there who needed help. Once it was a young woman with her new baby, and for some time it was an actor she had worked with who was now pursuing a degree at Yale, which was only a half-hour away.

She loved to read and was a serious reader of the classics and philosophy. One of her favorite authors was Nebraskan Loren Eiseley. She once mentioned that his work is "all I know about life." Next to reading, she liked to scrub floors and was completely content to get up at 4:00 a.m., have a cup of coffee, get her mop and brush, the book she was reading, and scrub and scrub and scrub.

When she died, her friend and executor of her will, Doug Taylor, called and asked me what to do with Sandy's ten thousand books. The University of Nebraska appraised them, and nearly every one was shipped to the library of the University at Nebraska–Kearney, near where Sandy was born.

Sandy and her father, Jack Dennis, suffered from cancer at the same time. Often I would stop by his house to visit and to read her letters to him. Religion was a subject I never explored with her, and I was moved when I read in one letter to Jack, "Dad, please keep the prayers coming. I believe that everything is heard somewhere."

We went out to dinner together in Westport four months before she died. Our conversation was lively. We talked about new plays I had seen and about the pictures I had brought with me that I had taken of her parent's home in Lincoln. She stared at the images and then clutched them close to her heart as she thanked me. When we drove back to her home, we sat in the car for a few minutes. Her face and profile, and her lovely golden hair, were silhouetted against the yard light when, looking at me, she said, "I'm fighting this. I'm giving this everything I've got. But if I don't win—I've had a wonderful life." She spent the last weeks of her life finding homes for every one of her cats.

JEAN PETERS

Movies, especially those produced during Hollywood's golden age, have been a life-long passion. I was naturally excited when friends asked us if a relative of theirs could stay with us for a week or so.

Jean Peters was a beautiful young actress who worked for Darryl Zanuck at Twentieth Century Fox in the late 1940s and early 1950s.

She won the Miss Ohio state beauty contest in 1946 and with it a trip to Hollywood, where she subsequently captured leading-lady roles in *Captain from Castile* opposite Tyrone Power, *Viva Zapata!* opposite Marlon Brando, and that lush and colorful visit to postwar Rome, *Three Coins in the Fountain*, opposite Louis Jourdan.

As her film career was beginning to diminish, she married Howard Hughes, and when his health and mental stability declined, they were divorced. She later married the brother of close friends of ours in Lincoln. She once said to me, "I've enjoyed a film career and all that excitement; I've been married to one of the wealthiest men in the world; but now being married to Stan Hough, I have a real home and family, and this is the best part of my life."

When Stan's brother, Bud, a distinguished and popular English professor at the university, died, Jean came to Lincoln to help his wife, June, and the family. Jean stayed at our house. At the same time, coincidentally, Howard Hughes's will was being contested, and Jean was being accosted by the media. Though she didn't say, I suspect she chose to stay at our house knowing the press would never find her in the anonymity of 3001 Jackson Drive, Lincoln, Nebraska.

When I came home after work the day she arrived, she was standing in our front yard watering our tulips. I stopped the car and said, "From living in the penthouse of the Sands Hotel in Las Vegas to watering our tulips in Lincoln, Nebraska, has got to be a long distance."

She laughed and replied, "You have no idea how far." Bud's family informed us not to ask any questions about Howard Hughes.

Listening to Jean talk about those early days at Twentieth

Century Fox was my cup of tea. As she put it, "I was just a contract player," and that meant that each morning she would report to work, often joined by her friend Jeanne Crain (*State Fair*, *Pinky*), where they sat over coffee in the commissary waiting "on call" for some director to summon them to test for a part.

When the call came, they were ordered to report to "makeup" and "hair" and costume fitting, then ushered on to a sound stage to test for a role. After that, they went back to the commissary for more coffee and more waiting. Often they didn't know the title of the film or what it was about, and they certainly didn't have anything to say about the script, the director, or the leading man. They were contract players who did as they were told.

"Jeanne and I," she said, "often wished that we were working over at MGM where the stars really shine." They looked up to Louis B. Mayer's MGM and down on Carl Laemmle's Universal Studios. There is always a pecking order.

Long after her film career was over, she was asked to play an aging, reclusive former movie star in an episode of *Murder, She Wrote* with Angela Lansbury. This experience was a revelation to her. She was used to working in feature films, which usually took approximately five weeks of shooting, completing perhaps three to five pages of script each day.

In this case, shooting *Murder, She Wrote*, the limousine picked her up at five o'clock in the morning and delivered her to Universal Studios in North Hollywood. She was immediately ushered in to makeup and hair and then costume and was on the set by 9:00 a.m. As she was the guest star playing the leading role in this one-hour production, she had many scenes to shoot. She worked all day, with barely time for lunch, and was back in her home in Beverly Hills by 7:00 p.m. Her comment was that Hollywood has always been a business, but it was never an assembly line of these proportions.

She was a delightful houseguest, made the best tacos we've ever had, and we honored her husband's request not to mention Howard Hughes.

Philip Abbott, a friend and former Lincolnite, had a successful career on Broadway, in the movies, and on television. For nine seasons he played the head of the FBI alongside Efrem Zimbalist Jr. in the popular TV series *The F.B.I.*

We asked Phil to host a public television series for us called *Hidden Places—Where History Lives.* His easygoing manner and ingratiating personality deftly guided viewers to some wonderful, little-known places in the mountains of the West that had played important roles in American history. During one of the film shoots, I shared with him my great disappointment that a program proposal I had spent extraordinary time and effort refining and polishing had just been turned down for funding by the National Endowment for the Humanities. I often felt vulnerable working in television, because like actors, we put so much of ourselves on the line, and some unknown evaluator or critic, in just a couple of paragraphs, can kill a project you've worked on for months. I'm reminded of a critic's brief review of the Broadway play *I Am a Camera* with Julie Harris: "No Leica."

Phil, with a knowing smile, nodded and told me that when he was just starting out as an actor in New York City, he was overjoyed when notified that he would get the job of Henry Fonda's understudy in his new Broadway vehicle *Two for the Seesaw.* All his friends pointed out that Henry Fonda never misses a performance and that Phil shouldn't get his hopes up. This was a two-character play in which Fonda played opposite the estimable Anne Bancroft.

Opening night for *Two for the Seesaw* was an immediate, resounding success, garnering lavish critical praise for the two stars. Then the unthinkable happened. Henry Fonda became ill and couldn't go on for the second performance. Phil Abbott was standing by to play opposite Miss Bancroft to an eager second-night audience.

As Phil stated it, "Stand backstage ready to go on and listen to the house manager announce on the PA system, 'Appearing in the role tonight usually played by Henry Fonda is Philip Abbott,' and then be overwhelmed and virtually suffocated by the unanimous groan from a packed-house audience, disappointed they would not see one of the icons of American theatre that night." But as he said, the curtain goes up and there you are, more vulnerable than if you were stark naked, but you go on. He played the role most successfully and was forever grateful for the support Anne Bancroft gave him that week Fonda was out of the show.

23

The Gang of Seven

The National Committee on United States–China Relations invited seven public television programming executives from around the country to visit China and tour their radio and television networks and stations for three weeks, from February 19 to March 11, 1981. Always sensitive to politics, they needed someone from the middle of the country. Since Nebraska is about as middle as you can get, not only geographically, I was invited to be one of the lucky ones.

Looking at the ground as we approached the Beijing airport, I felt as though I was stepping back in history, into the unknown and possibly into something mysterious and uncertain. My imagination dramatizes everything, and dancing across this stage came the Mongols, Sun Yat-sen, Mao Zedong, Madame Chiang Kai-shek, and images of Pearl Buck's *The Good Earth*.

Our interpreter in Beijing, Shangming Su, was the first person we encountered, and she welcomed us in flawless English and with a quiet and gracious presence. Shangming and I connected that first moment, and our friendship remains important to us. The sights, the sounds, the food, the language, the atmosphere—all may be strange and foreign, but these considerations quickly fade when human connections begin to grow.

Shangming was working for radio and television in Beijing in addition to serving as an interpreter for foreign guests. Shortly after we left China that March of 1981, she successfully secured an exit visa to work on a doctorate at the University of Hawaii. Though this separated her from her eight-year-old daughter, she eagerly embraced the opportunity to better herself and her family. After receiving the degree she was given a green card to work in the United States. She held a few positions in Hawaii and Washington DC and finally achieved a perfect professional fit at the U.S. State Department's Voice of America writing and broadcasting stories back to China.

I admire the steadfast determination, persistence, and focus the Chinese can bring to their lives. Shangming was separated from her daughter for ten years before she had the resources to bring her out of China and enroll her, at the age of eighteen, at Boston University. Her daughter shares her mother's intelligence, and her education eventually included MIT and the University of California–Berkley. Realizing that her daughter might forever resent those ten years of absence, Shangming nevertheless was willing to make this sacrifice. She faced the painful price of alienation stoically with no thought of self, concentrating only on her daughter's future.

When we met her that bitterly cold February day in 1981, she introduced us to Beijing. The Chinese have a saying, "There are only two things colder than December in Beijing, and that's January and February." It wasn't that we hadn't faced those temperatures before but rather that most of the buildings we were in were not heated and we suspected never had been. The Chinese couldn't afford it. We could see our breath in our hotel rooms and during all our meetings. Out of deference to their foreign guests, managers of the various hotels sometimes turned on the heat for one hour between 10:00 p.m. and 11:00 p.m. We couldn't wait to spend that hour sitting on the radiators.

During our meetings I would take the covered cup of tea offered, put it inside my ski jacket, shirt, and long underwear, as close to my heart as possible, in the hope that the tea would warm my blood and then spread throughout my body.

In Beijing we met Yu-Wei Geng, the deputy director of the Beijing Music Conservatory, who was our host and guide throughout our visit. She introduced us to some of her students in voice, piano, Western, and traditional instruments. These young performers gave us music that made our spirits soar. We heard flawless interpretations of Beethoven, Chopin, and Puccini. She told us how this conservatory had suffered mindless destruction during the Cultural Revolution. When the Red Guards, those youthful recruits of Chairman Mao who were galvanized to "purify" the country, came rampaging through the conservatory, they broke, mangled, and destroyed everything they could find of Western culture and much of the finest examples of their own. The pianos were vandalized, violins and other instruments were smashed, and even some of the fine ancient and priceless Chinese works of art and instruments were destroyed.

We were directed into the music library, a spacious room with countless shelves filled with hundreds and hundreds of orchestrations and compositions of the great musical literature of the world. This, she proudly related, was not destroyed. Lowering her voice, as if an enemy were still listening, she related how she saved this room by a clever act.

When the news arrived that the Red Guards were rushing wildly throughout the campus, Yu-Wei Geng knew instinctively that she had to save this irreplaceable collection. Her mind searched wildly for ideas, and then frantically, because the Guards were in the next building, she created big cardboard signs for either side of the entrance to the library that said, "Janitor's room. Throw trash in here."

When the Red Guards, stampeding down the halls while using rifle butts to break the windows and the glass on hanging pictures, came to the music library entrance, they slowed their pace, read the signs in great haste, then turned and hurried off to the hallway on the left intent on finding more pianos, instruments, artwork, carvings, and paintings to desecrate. She smiled and bowed slightly at our applause.

Back on the bus, Shangming reminded us that during the Cultural Revolution the universities were closed for nearly nine years, and the intellectuals were sent off into the hinterlands to get dirt under their fingernails and to personally empathize with how the common person lived. I was surprised when she said, "If that should ever happen to you, I have some useful advice." She said this in such a straightforward manner that we knew she didn't consider Americans immune. We listened attentively.

When Shangming was sent off to wash dishes in a school located in a remote region, she and all the women were ushered into a large dormitory building and the men into another. "When you get your bed assignment, look around," she said. "There are usually bunk beds stacked two or three high. Don't take the easy one on the bottom, but look for a top bunk situated under an overhead light."

This served her well, because over the next twenty-four months she could smuggle in books, hide them in her bed, and with that light overhead, discreetly read and read until the lights were shut off at 10:00 p.m. This was how she escaped her repressive life, snuggled under the covers and living through the histrionics of Scarlett O'Hara in *Gone with the Wind* and the adventures of *The Count of Monte Cristo*. They and other books were read at least three times.

She recounted that during the Cultural Revolution they were not allowed to listen to classical music. This was considered too bourgeois. In the city, the Russian film *Lenin in 1918* was shown frequently, and people flocked to this movie as often as possible to listen to a two-minute orchestral segment from the ballet *Swan Lake*. After people heard it, they left the theater.

Yu-Wei Geng told us that she was sent to a commune on the steppes of far western China, near Tibet, where she joined others in planting rice. "It looks so simple," she said, "but I was the exception." She told us how she carefully watched the others more experienced than her wade out into the water and one by one place the rice plants firmly down into the mud so they could take root. Everyone around her was doing this and leaving each plant with the green tops above the water. But inexplicably and frustratingly, no matter how hard she tried, her plants would not stick. After a few moments they would rise to the surface, roots and all, and start to float away. She was genuinely frightened because she knew she wasn't doing her job well.

One night in the dormitory, a group of women came to her and asked what her job had been in Beijing. She quickly assured the women that she would soon get the hang of planting rice and to please be patient. They said that wasn't important; they wanted to know what she could do really well.

"You don't need my skills out here" she said. "I'm a musician, a conductor. I work with orchestras."

The women looked at each other, murmuring and talking, and then asked, "Could you give lessons? "Could we have an orchestra?" Over a course of weeks, quite by magic, traditional and Western instruments began to show up. People would, one at a time, leave their jobs in the rice fields and secretly go to the dormitory for their lessons on various instruments. For over two years there was an orchestra performing traditional and classical music in that commune on the slopes of those far-distant mountains.

Living next door to us in Lincoln, Nebraska, was the Miguel Basoco family. He was a retired math professor from the University of Nebraska, and when he learned that I was going to Beijing he gave me the name of a Chinese friend of his and asked me to give him his regards if that was possible. This seemed like a long shot to me, but I said I would inquire.

Soon after our arrival in Beijing I asked our hosts if there was any possibility of locating a person in Beijing named Zho Pei Yuan. I was quick to request that they not go to any great trouble searching for him. My having seen the massive vastness of Beijing, I had no expectations and would not ask again.

On the fourth day of our visit our interpreter announced, "Today you will meet the highest-ranking person you will be introduced to in China. He is Mr. Zho Pei Yuan, president of the Chinese Science Academy and president of Beijing University, a highly respected scholar, teacher, and citizen of China. You have Ron Hull to thank."

Obviously, Zho Pei Yuan was an important man, and I soon learned he was a true patriot and had devoted his entire life to China. But what was his connection to Miguel Basoco back in Nebraska? We entered his office on the university campus, and all seven of us immediately gravitated to the small electric radiant heater nearby. This was the only warm room we encountered in Beijing.

I was escorted to his desk at the end of this long, narrow room. He was in his late seventies, lean and athletic-looking. He had a handsome countenance with high, chiseled cheekbones and a full head of steel-blue hair. Zho Pei Yuan was an imposing-looking man, but his manner was polite, modest, and quietly friendly.

He greeted me warmly and asked about his friend Miguel Basoco. He told me the two of them had been classmates at the University of Chicago and later at California Polytechnic Institute in the 1920s. Two friends: one a Mexican immigrant who distinguished himself as a professor at the University of Nebraska, and the other who went back to China and worked with a succession of leaders from Sun Yat-sen and Chiang Kai-shek to Chairman Mao. He too was a distinguished, respected scholar-teacher. He was eager to hear about Miguel and his family, the university, life in Nebraska, and he gave me a heartfelt message to carry back to Dr. Basoco.

In Shanghai our public television group was booked into an old, faded-but-elegant former British hotel in the Bund, the primary commercial center of the city, overlooking the river. We've all heard of the signs in the Bund, in the park along the river, that read "No Dogs or Chinese Allowed." That was in the 1930s and 1940s, when the Bund was controlled by the British. Now it was 1981, and as we entered the small nightclub off the lobby of the former Sassoon Palace, now known as the Peace Hotel, there was an echo of that same racism in the form of a sign that read "Overseas Chinese Only."

This respite from the busy Shanghai streets was a lively place, populated by foreigners and punctuated by an extraordinarily noisy five-piece band. They were blowing and banging out tunes my parents used to dance to in the 1930s. Conjuring up the past was "Amapola" ("my pretty little poppy") and "The Music Goes Round and Round," performed with the strictest rhythm and beat and incessantly loud volume. During a break I asked the leader where they got this popular American music.

The hotel, I was told, was closed and locked up in 1947 when Chairman Mao successfully took over the country. When the hotel reopened in 1979 the musicians had found this music stacked on the windowsills behind us, undisturbed for all those years. The band was playing the music at hand, and they hoped it pleased the foreign guests.

The Chinese government was in touch with its people all the time. Installed in every commune and apartment was a loudspeaker that could be turned down but not completely off. Outside, loudspeakers were placed in the trees and on light poles throughout the cities, and scratchy voices were often reminding the people of Chairman Mao's dictums and government pronouncements. Annoyingly, each morning in Shanghai at sunrise we were awakened by the noisy cacophony of martial music and "now hear this" informational announcements.

Looking out the window I saw streams of people coming from

all the apartment buildings, side streets, and alleys, quickly filling the entire area. Then, to the blaring recorded instructions piercing the early morning hour, everyone began their tai chi and other exercises. Some were moving while standing in place and others had one leg high on a light pole while slowly turning and twisting the rest of the body. Others seemed to be exercising only their fingers or their hands and arms. I gazed down astonished as hundreds of serious people of all ages labored intensely to improve their physical well-being. On every face was an expression of serious determination. The loudspeakers told them what to do, and there were signs everywhere giving them reminders about Chairman Mao's expectations: "One Couple, One Child" and "Healthy People, Healthy Country."

What would it take, I wondered, to get Americans out of bed and into the street at this hour for the good of a "healthy people and happy land"?

When we left Beijing to visit the other major broadcast centers, our interpreter, Shangming Su, was replaced by Mr. Ma, who brought excellent English skills to his work and was a patient font of information and our friend and traveling companion throughout the country. We were with him twenty-four hours a day, going from place to place primarily in a minibus but sometimes on planes and trains. Often in the train and minibus, particularly when the frost covered the windows and we couldn't see the sights, we took to group singing. We were soon competing with each other to identify songs that mentioned the people and places we were seeing. When we saw a bridge or a mountain, we'd launch into "San Francisco, Open Your Golden Gate" or "I'd Climb the Highest Mountain" or "Blue Skies" or "How High the Moon." We'd sing "School Days," "Mr. Five by Five," and "You Oughta Be in Pictures." These popular songs were appropriate reflections of our experiences.

"You Americans," Mr. Ma pointed out, "have a song for everything!"

On our last day in Guangzhou, he came to us with a challenge: "I have thought of a word that I think you do not have in a song."

Well, we doubted that. "What's the word?" we asked.

"Fantastic." he said.

We immediately thought of *The Fantastics*, but that was a musical, not a song, and it was a noun and plural. Fantastic? Hmmmm.

That night we went to our rooms thinking that one of us would have the word by morning. What song has the word fantastic in it? Morning came and not one of us had the answer. We had to tell Mr. Ma we would write him once we had thought of it. We knew there had to be a song with that word in it, but we had to admit that he had us stumped. We left China on the train bound for Hong Kong wracking our brains for the song.

Later that day while we were standing in line during the Hong Kong customs process, it came to me. I raised my arm, motioning to everyone, and said, "Listen, I've got it! It's in one of the first songs we ever learn in America." Quietly I began to sing, "East Side, West Side, all around the town," and with that our whole group, in loud unison, startling everyone else in the line, joined in singing, "tripped the light FANTASTIC on the sidewalks of New York." But it was a hollow victory, for Mr. Ma was back in China on his way to Beijing.

24

The Missed Opportunity

Washington DC, the Corporation for Public Broadcasting, and the important position of director of the Program Fund came to me—I had not even thought of going to them—but I'm happy they did, because the city and the job gave my life a new challenge and new dimensions. The Corporation for Public Broadcasting (CPB) is a quasi-governmental agency that receives the money Congress appropriates for public broadcasting and disburses it to the stations, PBS, and producers. It is a key player in the development of public broadcasting.

I received a call from an executive search firm to determine if I would be interested in applying for the position. I told the caller that I wasn't particularly interested but that I would forward a résumé if he wished. A few days later I was informed that the Corporation for Public Broadcasting hadn't hired an executive search firm, but that Ed Pfister, the president of CPB, had seen my résumé and wanted me to come in for an interview. I knew Ed Pfister, formerly the general manager of the Dallas public station, and I declined, saying that Ed didn't need to waste his time on a "courtesy interview," that I was very happy where I was. The personnel office insisted that Mr. Pfister was sincere in wanting the interview, so I agreed to one.

Some weeks later, in August, I was visiting my parents in Rapid City when Mr. Pfister himself called me. "Ron," he said, "I've forwarded your name with two others to the CPB board of directors for the director of the program fund position. You must be in Washington DC tomorrow morning by nine o'clock to be interviewed by the board."

I explained to him that it might be impossible. I was in Rapid City, South Dakota, and there weren't many planes in and out each day.

"Get here," he said.

I got there by connecting at midnight out of Denver on the red-eye flight, which deposited me at 8:00 a.m. at Washington National Airport via Atlanta, exhausted from sitting in airports and having stayed awake all night. Further, since I was on vacation and had taken no business clothes with me to South Dakota, I was barely presentable. At 10:00 a.m. I was ushered into the CPB boardroom wearing cowboy boots, jeans, and a denim jacket, the western costume, with everything looking tired and wrinkled, especially me.

The chairperson, Sharon Rockefeller, wife of Senator Jay Rockefeller, made the introductions of the CPB board of directors, all presidential appointees, which included actress Kathleen Nolan, Jeff Cowan, (his father was a former president of CBS), Gillian Sorensen (Ted Sorensen's wife), and other prominent Americans. It should be noted that the most recent members of the board were appointed by President Jimmy Carter, and therefore the Democrats had one more seat than the Republicans.

Mrs. Rockefeller told me to sit down and that the first half-hour was mine to tell the board anything I wanted them to know about me and my career thus far. The second half-hour was theirs to ask anything they wished. I agreed but said I would stay standing to avoid falling asleep.

A pivotal question was asked: "Mr. Hull, if you were given additional dollars, how would you invest them? In what area of programming are the people of America not being served?" That was easy for me.

From the beginning in 1955, when I produced a series called *Yesterday in Nebraska* and worked with poet John Neihardt, writer Mari Sandoz, the famous Butcher Collection of pioneer photos, and the letters and diaries of pioneers, these experiences led to my becoming enamored with telling people's stories—history. I told them I would start a series about the American people, where we came from, who came, why they came, and where we are now.

The director of the Program Fund, along with his staff, reviewed hundreds of program proposals each year from stations and independent producers. Daily they listened to testimony from producers about proposed series and single programs, and then after much deliberation, usually involving the opinions of peer panels, decided which projects would get the money. This position was central to the mission of public television, and the board was carefully analyzing me to determine whether my philosophy of programming was congruent with theirs.

When asked, I told the board that public television should never be judged by the number of people who watch. That's a competition we'll never win, but rather, the measure is the impact our programming has on the people who do watch. Our job is to provide viewers with programs in all the disciplines, backed by scholarship and accuracy and representative of the best the world has to offer in the arts, sciences, humanities, news, and public affairs. Our distinguishing feature is intellectual and artistic excellence—and audiences instinctively know when they are seeing the best. As someone once said, "You didn't have to tell the Italian peasant the *David* was beautiful." Though I didn't know how the board was judging me, through their questions I felt that a few of them shared my philosophy about public broadcasting, and I left the board room in good spirits.

At 11:00 a.m., the interview over, I was driven to the airport by Mr. Pfister's chauffer, and at 7:00 p.m. mountain time, I fell asleep as soon as I hit the bed in Rapid City. One hour later, Mr. Pfister called. "Congratulations, Mr. Director of the Corporation for Public Broadcasting Program Fund!" By this time I knew that I really wanted that job.

After that phone call, I lay in bed, exhausted, looking out the bedroom window of my parents' home. I could see the Big Dipper hovering in the night. In the Black Hills the night sky, especially in the summertime, with no metropolitan lights to dilute it, is awash with the bright, alive, vivid flashes of the starry nights. When I was young we called them "shooting stars," and I spent hours star-gazing, dreaming, wondering, and marveling at the vastness of the heavens. Looking at the stars gave me a sense of wonder. Years later when we were broadcasting a series of television programs featuring San Francisco's longshoreman-philosopher Eric Hoffer, every part of me responded to his statement that America's space program is in reality a "homing instinct": man's desire to get back to his origins. This fits neatly into my own Christian beliefs.

When the announcement of my appointment was made at a national public television meeting in Washington DC, David Liroff, WGBH Boston television executive, rose and said, "I'm happy Ron Hull finally got a job where he can drop his own name." And so began my Washington adventure. Each of us has to grab opportunities when they come. The timing may be imperfect, but if you are not willing to take chances, you limit your dreams.

I was able to accept this position because our daughter was finishing her last year in high school and the three boys were in college or had graduated. Positions in Washington can have uncertain futures, so Naomi and I decided that initially she would stay in Lincoln and I would commute to Washington. I soon learned that with cocktail parties, dinners, and so on, the proverbial "extended work day" was the reality of working in Washington DC, and so we continued to maintain our home in Lincoln and I commuted via United Airlines.

Working at the Corporation for Public Broadcasting opened a world of talented, creative, stimulating, hard-working, dedicated people and afforded the opportunity to travel every week or so to some interesting city in the country and often in the world. At least twice a year there were meetings in London or Paris, Copenhagen or Milan—I've never seen a trip or a place I didn't enjoy, and I've never met people I didn't like.

Serving as director of the Program Fund was similar to running a small foundation. Though the work was new to me, it drew from my experience as a producer and Nebraska ETV program manager every day. The people I met expanded my knowledge and forced me to stretch my imagination and creative thinking skills. These were producers and directors, artists and actors—all accomplished people with a common goal: to produce dramas, movies, documentaries, news programs, interviews—programs for television worth people's time. The most valuable asset of any life is the time we are given. Our job is to take that investment of our time and deliver back to the viewer programming of intellectual merit that edifies, educates, entertains, and inspires.

The CPB Program Fund was originally conceived by Robin Fleming, president of the corporation in 1980. It was designed to insulate federally appropriated dollars from politics. The program fund director was given sole authority over the fund, and was to keep the board of directors fully informed of program funding decisions, but the board was prohibited from discussing individual program decisions. Even the president of the corporation, who served at the pleasure of the board, was not a program decision maker. This model was in place the first two years of the fund under Lewis Freedman's creative direction.

In 1982, when I succeeded Lewis at the Program Fund, Ed Pfister was still on his honeymoon with the board as president. Shortly after Pfister's arrival, the board diminished the independence of the program fund director by taking away the unilateral authority in funding programs. From that point on, the program fund director reported directly to Mr. Pfister and not just to the board. This prompted the resignation of the highly gifted Lewis Freedman. When I entered the scene, I reported to the president, Ed Pfister, in all matters, including our funding decisions.

After I had been on board for seven months it became increasingly clear that problems arise when the money isn't managed from one central point or place. Ed, affable, competent man that he was, on occasion would tell producers that he could get them the money. Later we would discover that this much was promised to so and so and that much to this person or station. This made it difficult for us to manage the fund in a coherent, responsible manner, and it detracted from our goal of providing an equitable process for evaluating and funding programs fairly to that wide, diverse field of independent and station producers.

A good share of the Program Fund's independence might have been lost if CPB board member Kathleen Nolan, who had served during Lewis Freedman's tenure, hadn't approached me with some questions about how things were going. Her first comment to me on the situation was, "This isn't working is it?

I was reluctant to talk with her about it, and I told her that I would never initiate such a discussion with a member of the board. However, since she had asked a direct question, I had to respond honestly, so I replied, "No, it isn't."

A meeting with independent producers was scheduled in Los Angeles, and board member Jeff Cowan invited me to stay at their home overnight, as he was planning a small dinner party for the members of the CPB board living in LA. That evening Kathleen Nolan, Sonia Landau, Harry O'Connor, Jeff Cowan, and I sat down to dinner. Nolan and Cowan were the Democrats and O'Connor and Landau the Republicans.

They began by analyzing the former funding processes against the current policy giving the CPB president final authority over these decisions. I answered their questions, and after two hours of discussion, the participating members agreed that the board's role was to set broad programming priorities but that the individual program decisions should be made by the program fund director and his staff—thus reviving the original premise of the fund. It was to be an effective "heat shield" between those decisions and a board of directors appointed by the president of the United States. If the board were to agree, this was a productive step, going back to the original intent of taking politics out of television programming decisions and restoring the authority of the program fund director and the staff.

At the CPB board meeting in Washington two months later a resolution was drawn up and presented by this bipartisan group. The resolution passed unanimously, restoring the independence of the program decision making of the Program Fund. The staff and I, of course, were extremely gratified by this decision—one which is essential to a free and democratic broadcast service—and we felt this was an endorsement reflecting confidence in the program fund staff.

When I was being considered for the position of director of the Program Fund, the discussion I had with the CPB board about history programming was addressed, and with the assistance of a very able program fund staff, as well as cooperation and money from the public television stations of the country and the CPB, we were able to initiate the history series *American Experience.*

Over a two-year period the Program Fund invested 5 million dollars, which was matched at 6 million dollars by the stations. Producers at Boston's WGBH public station had proposed such a series earlier, but any endeavor with a heavy price tag takes planning, attention to political realities, and an alignment of a number of constituencies. Now with adequate funding and the stations' endorsement, the Program Fund was able to bring this about.

The series was an immediate success, and it defines the best in historical documentaries. The artistic and intellectual merit of the series is credited to the original producer, Judy Crichton, and her boss, Peter McGhee. With the help of my staff, I was the individual fortunate to control significant public television dollars, thus allowing me to make the decision that we would have a history series on public television. The talented people in Boston took it from there.

Of course not all producers and creative people are stimulating and pleasant companions. There were some I wish I could have avoided. The competition for our program fund dollars was fierce, and the diverse personalities combined with the tensions between the independent producers and the public television stations accounted for many moments of high anxiety. There were the obvious financial pressures and the inherent politics involved when fervent and great demands from a vast pool of talent with innumerable valid ideas are made on too small a financial pie. Half in jest, the staff and I joked about the level of funding some producers would kill for. We ultimately decided that the threshold wasn't all that high—about twenty-five thousand dollars. Being the gatekeeper of the fund led to many stressful days and many nights spent tossing and turning.

When you're "in the cauldron," as Bill Moyers once remarked, referring to the difficulties and tension inherent in making program grants, you need an old Washington hand to teach you the ropes, a strategist who understands the fiscal, social, and political consequences of every decision, someone who knows what makes an excellent television program. I had such a person in Gene Katt, my deputy at the Program Fund. An intellectual and a student with interests in a wide range of arts, humanities, and public affairs subjects, he advised me about money, content, and people. He was an irreplaceable member of the Program Fund.

There were times when some of the members of the CPB board of directors gave us anxious and dismaying moments, but fortunately I worked with a staff who supported me, inspired me, and made me laugh. We were a tightly knit, close group of friends who genuinely respected each other and knew that we had to hang together to survive. In this stressful environment, we believed that if we were not having a good time we were doing something wrong.

Each morning as I got out of bed and my left foot hit the floor, I took the time to say to myself, "It's the money they like." Once that was freshly established, I was ready to face the new day. There was a lot of money at stake and even more people lusting for it, and I knew that for my own psychological and physical health it was important for me to remember this. This realization gave me a glimpse into the lives of the very rich or very powerful concerning the question, "Do they like me or is it the money they like?" Which persons are true friends is a question that is often unanswered, but once the money or power is gone, you sometimes discover that your job had lots of friends.

To help in making funding decisions and ensure a fair and democratic process, the majority of projects submitted were judged by a "panel of peers" consisting of station people, independent producers, and other media professionals such as television critics and newspaper columnists. Chairing these panels and listening to the opinions of people who had been in the business for many years was the most rewarding part of the work. The panelists brought experience, insight, inspiration, and eloquence to these discussions and deliberations. At that time in our history, though there was tension among the various players—the stations, the bureaucrats, the independent producers—it was apparent to me that collectively we genuinely believed in the importance of a noncommercial, educational, cultural use of television. Bill Moyers said it best at a PBS national meeting: "Our job is to spark our people's imaginations to consider the noncommercial values of their lives." We believed that our programming was having a profound effect on the lives of children and families and that we were a significant part of American culture. We had a mission and the roads we followed were exhilarating.

Funding the best ideas is a tricky business, and with so many excellent proposals and never enough money to fund them adequately, we were usually able to be only a catalyst. Ours was the first money in, dollars to be used as leverage for the producer to acquire money from other sources. Aside from our significant underwriting of the major series such as *Nova* or *American Experience*, the majority of our funding to individual projects ranged from $20,000 to $250,000, and these grants represented only a fraction of the total program costs. This initial funding gave the projects the first signs of life, got them up and running, so to speak.

One president of CPB came to us from an important position dealing with the budgets of the U.S. Navy. His staff used to tell us that as he would analyze the CPB budget, they often heard him remind himself that at CPB it was "millions not billions, millions not billions." He was excellent with figures, and he kept a sharp eye on expenditures with an extremely pragmatic view of each CPB investment.

One time he came into my office saying that he noticed the Program Fund had given the Metropolitan Opera two hundred thousand dollars toward televising four operas, and it had been brought to his attention that later the decision had been made to present only three.

"Therefore," he said, "surely you'll ask for fifty thousand dollars back."

No, I explained, we're simply supporting, to a minimal extent, the necessary costs of bringing the operas to television. My comment that our two hundred thousand dollars doesn't even keep the curtain up for the first act of one opera didn't make sense to him. He was a bottom-line guy. In his mind it was logical that if four operas were $200,000, three operas were $150,000. I never succeeded in getting him away from the idea that we were buying into "units" of a "product," and I bristled every time he used the terms.

The group dynamics at play during the funding panel discussions sizzled with promise and disaster. The panels consisted of professionals and experts in the fields of proposed programs, station programmers, and independent producers. It was amazing to me how, in some cases, one persuasive person articulately making his or her points could influence the entire panel and lead them into some mighty strange directions. This is a highly subjective process, and the staff and I, whose responsibility it was to remain neutral during the discussions, sometimes sat there with arteries bursting when a project we didn't like was rising to the top. More often, because most professionals can smell a good program miles away, the excellent ideas quickly ascend, and during those years we created a body of television programs of value to all who watched.

The panels were designed to be polemical: rousing verbal confrontations, arguments, and discussion sessions, which for me were some of the most instructive, insightful continuing education experiences of my life.

Our days were filled discussing these ideas with seasoned, interesting, and talented people like Bob Drew (father of cinema verité), Ken Burns (creator of the Civil War series), Nancy Dickerson (one of the great television reporters), historian David McCullough (*Smithsonian World* and *American Experience* host), Henry Hampton (*Eyes on the Prize* series), Fred Wiseman (*Titicut Follies*, *The Store*, and others), Martin Carr (producer of *Smithsonian World*), Bill Moyers, Joan Konner (Moyers's producer and later head of the Columbia School of Journalism), and numerous others who recognized that public television afforded them the environment where they could produce their best work—unencumbered by advertising concerns and the tyranny of ratings. We didn't worry about the people who missed the program but rather the quality we provided over the free airwaves to all who wanted it.

We put the first twenty-five thousand dollars into the project that became *The Civil War* by Ken Burns, and we funded a number of his projects. Henry Hampton's *Eyes on the Prize* and Stanley Karnow's *Vietnam: A Television History* came to life in part through our funding. The fund created the major series that are the staples of the national schedule today. Under the tutelage of my predecessor Lewis Freedman, *Frontline*, *Nova*, and the *MacNeil/Lehrer Newshour* (now PBS *Newshour*) were created in cooperation with the producing stations. My staff and I added *American Experience* and many other series and specials. The programs were the point, but the people we worked with—the producers, directors, and writers filling our office hours, lunchtime, cocktail hour, and late-night dinners—made it all worthwhile. We lived a fourteen-hour workday that everyone who has ever worked in Washington understands.

A good share of the worthy and provocative programs offered on public television is produced by independents. These producers are not motivated by seeing their names on the screen and making lucrative deals. These are people who believe in the power of filmmaking, have stories they want—no, *have*—to tell, and they do it with skill, imagination, perseverance, and talent. Nothing ensures the success of a program more than a talented producer who has a burning desire to tell a particular story. My philosophy was to recognize these individuals, give them the money, and get out of the way—an attitude difficult for the business office to accept. Of course accountability is important, but I was interested in what showed up on the screen and not how every penny was spent. Remember, CPB was seldom the primary funder on any individual program.

The pool of ideas and producers always overwhelmed the funding available. The producers would use every psychological trick they could think of to persuade us to give them a program grant. The most overworked argument was that we had to support this program because the subject of the piece—a writer, an artist, a scientist—is "getting up in years and won't be with us long."

People wanting to make films came from myriad unexpected places and ranged from producers with Academy Award nominations to people just beginning their careers. While riding with a colleague in a taxi from National Airport, I was mentioning some of the proposals that I thought we should fund. About half an hour after getting back into my office, I was told there was a man at the front desk who had to see me. He came in, and to my surprise it was the cab driver who had just delivered us to 1111 Sixteenth Street Northwest. He had his script and treatment in hand. Knowing that the majority of Washington cab drivers were newly arrived from some third-world country, I had to point out that the money we had could be granted only to U.S. citizens.

There's a saying in the theater that if you work three times— you know everybody. Public television is that kind of small world. With fewer than two hundred stations it's like a fraternity, and over the years you know the universe. I learned quickly that the best ideas come from the producers. This means that you fund people. There are thousands of wonderful program ideas, but it's the talented producer who can keep us fascinated by bringing one of these ideas to life. The public television documentary filmmaker is often consumed by his or her passion for their latest idea. They would come to us for money and they were also willing to mortgage their cars and sometimes even their homes to get their story on the screen. Public television is a major platform, and a prime-time slot can give a producer the opportunity to gain the serious attention of an audience numbering in the millions. They infuse their reputation, their pride, and their heart and soul into their work, and this almost always results in a program worthy of other people's time.

Shakespeare said it best: "The play's the thing!" And in our world it's the programs and the people we worked with who brought them to the screen. Significant among these was Bill Moyers's *Joseph Campbell and the Power of Myth*. In the mid-1980s, Moyers, one of America's finest journalists, was woefully underutilized, doing brief commentaries on CBS two or three times a week. The staff and I fervently believed the country needed Bill Moyers on a weekly basis. Suzanne Weil, programming head at PBS, agreed, and she and I headed to New York to talk with him about what part we could play to bring him back to public television. His goal was to put together a ten-million-dollar package to fund television projects, and if he was successful he would leave CBS and join public television in Washington DC. When we arrived he had raised most of the money, and in a joint decision between Sue at PBS and me at CPB, we offered him the last 2.2 million dollars he needed to reach his goal.

The central theme Joseph Campbell emphasized in *The Power of Myth* was that people are yearning to find meaning in their lives. This made such an impact on me that I knew it would be powerful for countless others.

When, at the PBS annual meeting in Columbus, Ohio, Sue and I announced that Bill Moyers was coming back to PBS and that we had committed major dollars to this project, we were met with derision and downright hostility from many of the station program managers from throughout the country.

"Talking heads, talking heads, that's all you're giving us with this series" was the lament. But when the *Power of Myth* was broadcast it became the most popular, the most talked-about series we broadcast that year. Suddenly, the "talking heads" were vast numbers of Americans who had viewed the programs. The station program managers were of course delighted to respond to their happy audiences, and as Bill Moyers reminded us, you can accomplish anything if you don't care who takes the credit.

Sue Weil and I worked well together. She was deeply committed to the arts, she was feisty and witty, and as a catalyst she brought producers and ideas together in highly original ways. Though her staff described her style as "management by bombast"—sometimes she did enter the room and explode—they respected her and admired the energy and spark she brought to the PBS schedule.

It was her quick-witted humor that kept me laughing. She claimed she was the only Jewish lady who ever took a bus from Beverly Hills to downtown LA. At a dinner party one night we were discussing the advantages of power, and she summed it up and stunned all of us with the statement, "Well, what's the use of being Frank Sinatra if you can't fuck everybody?" Sue Weil cared deeply about providing quality programs to home screens and gave PBS programming and our friendship an exciting edge.

Of course, there were many other extraordinary people behind the extraordinary programs we were funding. The producers of the *Mostly Mozart* series for Lincoln Center in New York City came down to meet with funders from the National Endowment for the Arts, the Corporation for Public Broadcasting, and the Public Broadcasting Service. There were three tables of eight in our party in one of the small, well-appointed dining rooms of the Watergate Hotel. I was seated next to an elderly, diminutive black woman, Antoinette Handy, who served as a program officer for the National Endowment for the Arts. As we visited I was pleased to tell her that our program fund had just given a significant amount of money to producer Henry Hampton for his civil rights series *Eyes on the Prize*. (This was one of our best decisions made in those years, and the series should be repeated on PBS at least every five years.) Mr. Hampton was a gifted producer of important, relevant documentaries and provided some of public television's finest work.

Miss Handy, pleased at the prospects of this series, said that she used to teach at the all-black Tuskegee Institute in Alabama. She recalled that in the early sixties, one of her best students, having just completed freshman year, stopped by to thank her and tell her that college would be interrupted for now. This student was determined to quit school and personally work in the civil rights movement. Miss Handy replied to the student, "You can't do that. You're one of our finest. Others can do the sit-ins; you must finish your education." That was the last she saw of her prize student. "That was nearly twenty years ago," she reminisced, "and I've always wondered what happened to that gifted, brilliant young woman."

I glanced up, and sitting across the table from us was Jennifer Lawson, our drama and arts person at the Program Fund, and she had been listening. Rising, she said, "Are you Antoinette Handy?"

Miss Handy stared back. "Are you Jennifer?"

The two women rose and came into each other's arms and hugged and hugged and laughed and laughed. And there were tears. I touched Antoinette Handy on the arm and said, "I saw this happen."

Jennifer Lawson is a singularly impressive woman. Sophisticated, elegant in demeanor and appearance, she brought an uncommon level of insight, discernment, and intelligence to the decisions we made in funding programs. Even when she told producers they weren't going to get the money, they came away grateful to have had time with her.

By this time the Program Fund had 42 million dollars to be expended each year. Our programming decisions could not be countermanded by the board or the CPB president. We were an independent unit, and I reported directly to the board. Over time, if the board was not happy with my decisions, then of course I would have to go. And later, naturally, that happened.

There were times in this program funding game that we had to discontinue our support. A source of discomfort for me was a series called *The Lawmakers* that was produced by WETA, the Washington DC station. This public television series was burdened with the responsibility to "cover Congress." The program featured Paul Duke, Cokie Roberts, and Linda Wertheimer, journalists of the first order.

The staff and I felt that Congress should be covered and that these were eminently qualified reporters. The problem was that we were giving the series over 2 million dollars per year and less than half the stations were carrying it. The reporting was excellent, but it was a studio-bound show. It needed the reality of Capitol Hill. This was, in my view, not a good use of taxpayer dollars. So I reluctantly wrote to Ward Chamberlin, president of WETA, that in spite of the fine work being accomplished the funding for the series would end that season. That of course meant that the series would die and the station and talent involved would lose significant income.

I mailed the letter late Friday afternoon because I knew this would be shocking news to Ward, and I didn't want to have to deal with it until Monday morning when we could talk. Also, I was hoping for a pleasant, uninterrupted weekend.

That following Sunday morning Sue Weil hosted a small luncheon party in her apartment for departing PBS president Larry Grossman, who was going off to New York to become president of NBC News. His departure was a significant loss for public broadcasting.

At the party I was seated next to Jack Carmody, the renowned and highly respected television columnist at the *Washington Post*. Though he could be abrupt with people at times, I had a good relationship with him during my years in Washington, and we were grateful for his attentiveness to our work at the Program Fund. Always probing, pointing out weaknesses and misjudgments, he nevertheless was a solid friend of pubic television and wrote about our programs regularly.

He liked me, I think, because of an incident that happened the first time he called my office. Since I wasn't there, he left a message. I returned the call as quickly as I could, but I, too, had to leave a message. Later, he called, "Mr. Hull, this is Jack Carmody," he said with a bit of sharpness in his voice.

"Yes, Mr. Carmody. I assume you got the message that I returned your call."

"I have no record of that," he replied.

At that moment someone came into his office and handed him my message.

"Oh, yes, I see that you did."

His tone changed and it was smooth sailing with him after that. Sometimes that unexpected moment of exquisite timing can make all the difference.

He turned to me at Larry's party and said, "Ron, that was quite a letter you wrote to Ward Chamberlin."

After two or three beats, I said, "Hang on."

I went over to Ward Chamberlin's table and asked him if, by some chance, he had received a letter from me on Saturday. His reply was negative. "What's it about?" he asked.

"We'll talk about that Monday."

The *Washington Post* was directly across the alley from the Corporation for Public Broadcasting. I returned to my seat next to Jack Carmody.

"I have a mole, haven't I?" He just smiled. Another facet, I learned, of how Washington sometimes works.

As chairperson of the CPB board of directors, Sharon Rockefeller was my boss the first few years. This is a woman completely dedicated to the premise and promise of public television. Sharon is a hard-working executive, with a bountiful personality, warm, persuasive communications skills, and a knockout smile. We worked well together, and philosophically, I felt we were completely congruent regarding the potential of public broadcasting and the value of its programming. I was even able to forget that Mrs. Rockefeller's own personal "program fund" far exceeded CPB's.

Sharon sometimes had a driver but most often drove herself. One day she called and said that we had to have a private talk and that she would be stopping by to pick me up. As we headed around the corner at Sixteenth and L, she asked, "Where can we go that's truly private?"

Before I could answer, she said, "I have it," and she swung the Cadillac off L Street into the alley and into the parking garage deep beneath the CPB. It was dimly lighted down there, and there wasn't a soul around. We had found a private place, and simultaneously we started laughing, for we each had the same thought. Here we were in a parking garage two levels underground, our very own version of Deep Throat.

Granted, our discussion was not as momentous as Watergate and presidential politics. We were simply trying to figure out how best to work with the CPB board and the CPB president. But similar to Watergate, even in our part of the Washington spectrum, the political dynamics were both fascinating and excruciatingly frustrating. At CPB, we were often caught in the crossfire of competing entities, and it was almost always centered on money. There was never enough of it to satisfy the stations, the independents, or PBS. Even pressure from Congress was a constant, stressful reality as we tried to allocate the funds fairly in the most deserving projects.

Neither Sharon nor I anticipated the fireworks that were just ahead for CPB and the stations.

By now, 1985, the Reagan appointees were in the majority, and the power of the board was in the hands of the Republicans. Sonia Landau, former campaign chair of Women for Reagan and Bush, and close friend of the president's daughter Maureen, replaced Sharon as chairman of the CPB board.

Sonia, with her thin frame, chalk-white skin, and white-blonde hair, was a nervous but formidable presence and a most insecure person. She had power, having been raised in a wealthy family, she had a powerful husband, John Corry, the *New York Times* television critic, and she had powerful friends. From where I stood none of these attributes gave her emotional stability or peace of mind. Often she was stern or distraught; she seemed to live an emotional, hectic, seesaw life, with sadness hovering not far away. Still, we had work to do together, and much of the time any compassion I felt got lost in her wake.

The CPB board meeting in May 1985 at the St. Francis Hotel in San Francisco was one of public broadcasting's most public disasters. In this case it wasn't Mame but rather Sonia who "started to shimmy and shake, and brought on the Frisco quake." The meeting began with Sonia making introductions: "Please welcome my husband, John Corry of the *New York Times*, and sitting next to him is my ex-husband, Mr. Landau of Los Angeles." Sue turned to me and said, "Very California."

Everyone knew that Sonia wasn't fond of Ed Pfister, and when he announced that he was going to lead a delegation of public broadcasters to visit Moscow, this was all she needed to pit some of the board against him. The Cold War was still being fought, and a majority of the board felt this might compromise public television in some way. I never could see how communication, especially with those with whom you are in disagreement, is harmful, but the board's opinion prevailed.

I tried to stay out of board politics and spent as little social time with members of the board as possible. That evening after dinner I was cornered by one of the board members I barely knew who said he wanted to buy me a drink. Trapped, we went to the sky bar at the St. Francis where he suddenly, slurringly announced, "Tomorrow, we're gonna fire Ed's ass outta here." This was not information I wanted to be privy to, and I tried not to reply to his expectant stare. Finally I reminded him that I was staff, and that kind of action was the sole territory of the board of directors.

The sun did come up the next morning and the board secured Ed's resignation. Immediately thereafter, he gave an inspired, rousing speech about the journalistic integrity that must prevail in public broadcasting. Referring to the cancelled trip to Russia, he said his departure was "a matter of principle," and he knew that every manager in the room, given the same situation, "would do the same thing." The entire PBS body of station managers stood and vigorously applauded as the president of CPB made his way to the door and out of public broadcasting.

Sonia was right behind him. I was sitting next to her until she sprang to her feet, literally chasing him out the door and calling him, I am sure I heard correctly, "You schmuck. You schmuck." It got worse. Later, in the St. Francis lobby, six-foot-plus John Corry confronted five-foot-seven Ed Pfister and gave him a verbal shakedown in defense of his wife's honor. This was one of public broadcasting's less classy moments. Sonja was quoted in the newspaper as insisting she followed Mr. Pfister out the door calling, "You snook, you snook"—whatever that means. Taken aback by all of this, Ed's comment, pointing after Landau, was "That's not unusual."

Martin Rubenstein replaced Ed Pfister as president of the Corporation for Public Broadcasting. He had been president of the Mutual Broadcasting System, which was impressive, but I wasn't encouraged when my friend Marty Carr, who had known him, said, "Ron, he's a thug." As I got to know him I thought of him as Sammy Glick from Budd Schulberg's novel of Hollywood in the 1930s and '40s, *What Makes Sammy Run?* Life under him was not productive or pleasant. We labored on with difficulty, and fortunately Mr. Rubenstein's tenure at CPB lasted only nine months before he was fired. That worked in my favor, because he and I saw public broadcasting through different prisms.

That year the annual PBS meeting was in Washington, and the staff and I decided to enhance each of our major series with grants of an additional two hundred thousand each. The producers of *Nova, American Experience, MacNeil/Lehrer Newshour,* and *Great Performances* were overjoyed when we made this announcement during one of the general sessions.

Mr. Rubenstein, who never did understand the structure of the Program Fund, was furious that he was not asked to make the announcement. When I was called into his office, he began with, "Young man, who do you work for?"

I told him that I was not being facetious when I say that I work for myself, I report to the board. They hired me and they can fire me, and I report to him for various administrative matters. This was accurate.

"Well, buster," he said. "Your job can be had."

If I had learned anything by that time working in Washington DC, it was that boards and bosses can't stand it when an employee isn't afraid for his job. I had been in my position for nearly four years. I looked him in the eye and said, "Yes, Mr. Rubenstein, my job can be had. You always have to have one more board member for you than you have against you. If not, you're out."

Though my tenure was shaky with some members of the board, I knew I had a majority. This is something the staff and I monitored weekly. He was livid. But he knew I spoke the truth.

A few days later the monthly board meeting was convened in the seventh-floor boardroom. I happened to be just outside the door when Marty Rubenstein came out, humming a little tune, almost skipping along, in a very good humor. He was holding his fine china cup and saucer on his way for more coffee. The paper cups the rest of us used were not his style. I and the other senior staff were consigned to our offices during these marathon meetings in case the board wanted to call any of us in. Often we had to wait until they adjourned at 10:00 or 11:00 p.m., without ever hearing if we were likely to be called.

This particular night, Mara Mayer, head of the Annenberg Project, came down to my office with sandwiches and some coffee. It was 11:00 p.m. but no one had told us we could go home, and we didn't have the courage to go upstairs and ask, so we served CPB by sitting and waiting. Finally, at 11:30 p.m., the word came down that they didn't need to see any of us. Fine. We went home.

Every president of CPB has a private chauffeur to bring him to work, cart him to the airport and around town, and take him home. All of us in the Program Fund had a good relationship with his chauffeur, a long-time CPB staffer. To the "important people" in the backseat, he was of course merely the silent nonentity in the front seat, driving the car and listening intelligently to his passengers discuss the events of the day.

At one thirty in the morning, awakened by the telephone, I

heard Pat Hunter, our business manager of the program fund, with great joy in her voice telling me that Marty Rubenstein had been fired, Spode china cup and all. I wasn't surprised that Pat Hunter knew—nor did I wonder how she found out.

This news confirmed for me that every now and then something turns out right.

25

Exciting Times, Stimulating People

I enjoyed being the director of the Program Fund for the Corporation for Public Broadcasting. I enjoyed the autonomy we had within the organization and the power we had in making program funding decisions for public television, and most particularly for the opportunity to know the creative people working in the field.

Washington DC abounds with theaters, concerts, and cultural happenings. These, combined with the reality of being at the center of world events, makes living there exciting. And when you're in public broadcasting, there were even opportunities to visit 1600 Pennsylvania Avenue. During the Reagan years, I had four or five invitations for lunch or receptions at the White House which I gratefully accepted. It's quite sobering to stand in the doorway of the White House and look up Sixteenth Street, imagining how, across the years, people and previous presidents and their wives stood in that exact spot and looked out upon the Federal City.

In Performance at the White House was a staple of performance programming on PBS, and it gave audiences an intimate look at the first family and other leaders of our country enjoying music and dance usually performed in the East Room of the White House.

It was decided to stage one of these performances on a Sunday afternoon in the Rose Garden, behind the White House, and a special stage was constructed and folding chairs put in place for an audience of one hundred guests. Since the Program Fund was an investor in the series, I was one of the lucky invitees, and doubly fortunate because this particular program presented music from Broadway, featuring the talents of John Raitt and Mary Martin.

We were seated, the cue was given to begin taping, the president and first lady were announced, and from the door of the White House the smiling, stunningly handsome couple, Mr. and Mrs. Ronald Reagan, entered and walked through the audience toward the stage and took their places in the front row.

Nancy Reagan went on stage and told us how, early in her career, before her move to Hollywood and MGM, she was working in a Broadway show and every night it was her privilege and pleasure to watch one of the greatest musical stars of our time come on stage and captivate the audience with the music and story of *Lute Song*. She then welcomed Mary Martin.

"Mary, won't you sing, 'Mountain High, Valley Low' from that wonderful show?"

And with that, Mary Martin took Nancy Reagan's face in her hands and began singing a personal, emotional interpretation of the song. This was moving to the audience and obviously moving to Nancy Reagan, whose tears we could plainly see on the monitors near our seats. We were in heaven when, without warning, the heavens spoke. Wind, thunder, and lightning all began playing at once, and in no time it began to rain.

Assistants rushed to the Reagans with umbrellas, and most graciously, Mrs. Reagan called out, "Everyone go into the house." The taping of course had to stop and we all ran for the elegant "cover" of the first floor of the White House. Miraculously, it seemed to me, food and drinks appeared, and the opportunity to explore the Green Room and the Red Room, and to collect a few White House matchbooks from the men's room.

I had flown in that morning and had just learned that fellow Lincolnite and acquaintance Gordon MacRae, singing star of the film versions of *Oklahoma!* and *Carousel,* was dying of throat cancer. Gordon MacRae had a remarkably beautiful voice, and for years he opened each Cornhusker football game with a soaring rendition of "The Star-Spangled Banner."

In the foyer of the mansion was an elaborate grand piano, and a young marine musician was playing it. I walked over to him and asked if he could play something in Gordon's honor. In just a few minutes the lilting melody of "The Surrey with the Fringe on Top" was flowing throughout the room.

The rain date for completing the taping of this *In Performance at the White House* was scheduled for the following Tuesday afternoon. On that day, we all filed back into the White House, through security into the Rose Garden, to pick the show up where we had left off.

Once again, Mary Martin gently held Nancy Reagan's face in her hands as she sang "Mountain High, Valley Low," and once again, right on cue, the tears started coming down Nancy's cheeks. As we've learned, acting is good training for politics.

At the Program Fund we were always on the lookout for that program idea with a special, provocative twist. Don Marbury, one of my colleagues, called these ideas "lightning in a bottle" or "bottled fire." These ideas, of course, came from the myriad producers we worked with, spread throughout the land, from every walk of life. This was my opportunity to cross paths with, work with, or simply stand on the sidelines with exciting, creative, energetic people. These were people who loved the arts and had dedicated their lives to them, and these were journalists who were called to the fourth estate just as surely as the actors, singers, and dancers were called to their world. Each was doing his or her best to create excellent television.

The essence of every rewarding experience is always an individual with whom you make a connection.

MARTIN CARR AND DAVID MCCULLOUGH

At the top end of the scale was producer-director Martin Carr who was busily creating *Smithsonian World* for public television. The recipient of numerous Emmys for his consistently riveting and thoughtful documentaries on the commercial networks, he brought ability, experience, and intelligence to each of his projects. Though he often produced cutting-edge social-issue films, he was equally comfortable in the arts. He knew and loved opera, and he could expound on every American musical from Gershwin to Sondheim. He was an original and he was attracted to originality. Once, when he realized at the last minute that he had to have a costume for a New Year's Eve party, he bought some theatrical paint, stripped nude, painted his entire body gold, and went to the party as an Academy Award.

He brought an original "slant" to every program he produced. *Smithsonian World* was an example of public television's promise to bring fascinating content, well researched and presented, in this case, by the preeminent historian and host of the program, David McCullough. When *Smithsonian World* ended, David moved over to host the *American Experience* series. We brought him to Nebraska one year to keynote our Willa Cather conference in Red Cloud. The book was Cather's *My Mortal Enemy*, a novel I had read more than once without ever fully understanding it—that is, until after I had heard David's take on it. He mentioned that the protagonist's mortal enemy was time. Of course. I should have figured that out. Later he generously served as a guest on the Nebraska documentary *Willa Cather: The Road Is All*.

NANCY DICKERSON

With thanks to Martin Carr I became acquainted with Nancy Dickerson, first female reporter for CBS News. She was soon recognized as an important, prominent journalist and an excellent writer and on-air talent. Nancy also knew how to entertain. Sometimes when she needed an extra man, she included me in her dinner parties. Guests included Larry King, Roger Mudd, and other television luminaries. She was living in "Merrywood on the Potomac," the former home of Jacqueline Bouvier Kennedy, and one evening I admired the number of John Singer Sargent paintings lining the dining room walls.

At a later party, after her divorce and her move to a townhouse in Kalorama Square in downtown Washington DC, I remarked, "I see you got the Sargents."

"Half of them," she replied.

I mentioned that in Nebraska when people divorce they fight over the football tickets.

"I got 'em," she smiled.

Nancy was an excellent panelist for us at the Program Fund. Her experience, knowledge, and energy enlivened our work and provided a substantive mentoring experience for the young producers sharing the panel assignment. She came to my "farewell to Washington" party, and I still treasure the note she sent me on the death of my father: "It's tough to lose your dad. I know."

KEN BURNS

The CPB Program Fund was one of the first programming entities to recognize the brilliant storytelling abilities of Ken Burns. His gifts as a producer-director embrace a wide understanding of both the intellectual and technical aspects of film production. His sense of taste, of using minimalist moments to let his work speak, and his thorough scholarship inform every second of his programs. We had nurtured his talent with funding for *Brooklyn Bridge*, *Huey Long*, and others, and then he sent me a paperback book, *The Killer Angels*. This was to be his next project, a documentary tracing the events during the five-day Battle of Gettysburg. Based on his proposal referencing that fine book, the Program Fund gave him the first money toward the project.

Ken was one of the first producers to understand the value of including with his proposals seven or eight minutes of film showing the approach and style he intended to bring to the project. This idea grew from his original conception of the five-day battle into his magnificent series *The Civil War*, which brought to public television the largest audience ever achieved.

The man behind that talent and that zeal for hard work is a man worth knowing. He can talk faster and make more sense than almost anyone. He is generous, giving days and weeks of his time and energy at dinners, speeches, and fund-raisers in behalf of the individual public television stations in the country. I was equally impressed by the thoughtful care and attention he gave his two small daughters, who in their early years seemed to accompany him everywhere.

KATHLEEN NOLAN

A special person on the CPB board, a redhead, instrumental in restoring the independence of the program fund director, was actress Kathleen Nolan. Kathleen's show business roots went back to her childhood, when she performed with her parents on a Mississippi showboat in St. Louis. She was well known for her ongoing role opposite Richard Crenna in TV's *The Real McCoys* series. She distinguished herself as a crusader for women's rights and was elected the first female president of a major U.S. labor union, the Screen Actors Guild.

She was active in theater in New York, and I made every effort to see her performances. She opened at the Kennedy Center in Washington, along with Colleen Dewhurst in Chekhov's *The Seagull* directed by Peter Sellars. This was, in my opinion, the unsuccessful experiment of a brilliant director tampering with a classic. One addition to the proceedings included a neck-wrenching laser light show projected on the ceiling of the hall. Nancy Dickerson accompanied me that night, and after the performance we planned to go backstage to invite Kathleen out for drinks.

After sitting through this muddled mess, I kept wondering what do you say to an actor when something is so bad you don't know what to say? As we walked backstage, actress Zoe Caldwell was just in front of us. She approached Colleen Dewhurst's dressing room, opened the door, and said, "Colleen, thank you for tonight."

Oh, that's good, I thought. That's what you say: "Thank you for tonight."

About a year later I was having dinner with an independent producer and Miss Dewhurst, who was the current president of Actors' Equity. She was wrestling with the sticky issue of determining how long English actors appearing in a play coming from the West End to Broadway could stay in the part during the U.S. run. The case in point was the musical *Miss Saigon*. Naturally, the conversation that evening centered on the theater, and I was halfway through my story on how I discovered what to say to an actor when you're at a loss for words when I remembered I had learned it outside Colleen's dressing-room door. I mumbled something about wonderful performances emerging even in disastrous productions, and I heard my voice weakly trail off, saying that "Thank you for tonight" works. Miss Dewhurst looked at me quizzically for a second or two and then mercifully changed the subject.

CHRISTOPHER SERGEL

Chief Black Elk led me to Christopher Sergel, owner of the Dramatic Publishing Company of Westport and Chicago. We met in the early 1980s when the Folger Theatre in Washington DC was producing his dramatic version of John Neihardt's celebrated book *Black Elk Speaks*. My goal was to bring this powerful drama to PBS. Though this was never accomplished, we became friends and I spent many happy weekends with him and his wife, Kit, in their home in Wilton, Connecticut. Those weekends were filled with dinner parties, Broadway shows, and energized conversation with people who loved the arts. Sandy Dennis's home was just minutes away in Westport, and she often joined us.

Theater wasn't the only focus of Chris Sergel's life. He was also a big-game hunter and world traveler. One night Chris invited me to join them at the exclusive Explorers Club dinner. A falcon flying over our heads in the Waldorf-Astoria Hotel ballroom determined the winner of the door prize, a trip for two to Cambodia. The falcon was sent soaring to the table at the end of the room, laden with our ticket stubs. Fresh gold paint had been applied to the falcon's talons, so that he marked the winning tickets when he landed. I felt it was one of those times that if you brought someone from a third world country directly to this ballroom, he would believe everything he had ever heard about America.

KATHARINE, FRANK, AND COMPANY

Unforgettable is that magic night on Broadway when producers Joan Kramer and David Heeley ultimately convinced Katharine Hepburn to host a documentary on the life of Spencer Tracy. The premier of this major public television event was March 3, 1986, at the Majestic Theatre on Forty-fourth Street. Like all such affairs, there was an A-list and a B-list of invitees. Prior to the screening, the A-list people, at one thousand dollars per person, had the privilege of joining Miss Hepburn for dinner at the Marriott Hotel. The B-list people, at five hundred dollars per person (of which I was one), were invited to enjoy hors d'oeuvres and wine at Sardi's just down the street.

A group of us from CPB were chatting away when all the sudden Miss Hepburn walked in, dressed in a black pantsuit, black sweater, and a brilliant red scarf that reached the floor on both sides. We stopped talking and stared at her. She said, "Isn't this where I'm supposed to be?" Someone who knew more than we did said, "Oh no, Miss Hepburn, you are to join the A-list for dinner at the Marriott."

"The Marriott?" she replied. "Naturally I assumed that Sardi's was the A-list," and off she went.

On stage at the Majestic Theatre, Spencer Tracy's friends, at podiums on each side of the proscenium, reminisced about this great American film actor. Robert Wagner recounted how Tracy was his surrogate father after they had bonded while making the film *Broken Lance*. Stanley Kramer spoke with heartfelt affection about Hepburn and Tracy making *Guess Who's Coming to Dinner*. Frank Sinatra said that during World War II he was on the train from Los Angeles back to New Jersey to report to his draft board. Tracy was on the same train, and when Mr. Sinatra said he might be drafted, Tracy remarked, "Well, there goes the war."

Sinatra continued with a story about being invited to dinner at Tracy's house with Katharine. During the meal the lights went out, and it was total darkness. Starting to get up, Mr. Sinatra said, "I have a family—just tell me where the fuse box is." He felt Spencer Tracy's hand on his arm when Tracy's voice said, "Sit down. She does that sort of thing around here."

Frank Sinatra introduced Katharine Hepburn, and when she made her entrance from upstage center in that black outfit with the red scarf, everyone in the theater rose to their feet almost as if we were each pulled up by a rope fastened to our sternum. It was an immediate, spontaneous, unified, tumultuous tribute.

Her affection for Spencer Tracy was evident even as she "roasted" him. Spencer, she said, had been separated from his wife for more than two years before they had met. There were four places in his life: the Beverly Hills Hotel where he was living, Metro-Goldwyn-Mayer, just down Motor Avenue in Culver City where he worked, his favorite restaurant, Chasen's, and the Mocambo nightclub on Sunset Boulevard. Spencer knew how to drive to any one of these places from the hotel.

Director George Cukor had divided his property and built a nice house next door to his. Spencer liked it and rented it. But this was in a slightly different part of town from the hotel, and Spencer Tracy had no sense of direction whatsoever. Therefore, each morning to get to work he would drive back to the Beverly

Hills Hotel and find his way to Culver City and MGM from there. When he wanted to go to the Mocambo nightclub or Chasen's, he would first find the Beverly Hills Hotel and then proceed to his destination. Miss Hepburn estimated that every time he went to Chasen's restaurant he went twelve miles out of his way.

The poignant moment of the evening came after all the stories had been told, when Spencer Tracy's daughter, Susie, walked on from stage right, put her arm around Katharine Hepburn's waist, and gave her a kiss on the cheek. The documentary *The Spencer Tracy Legacy: A Tribute by Katharine Hepburn* captures the essence of both stars and is a superb example of filmmaking partially funded by the CPB Program Fund.

LEONARD BERNSTEIN

Great Performances presents the finest music and dance programming on American television and is one of the major series the Program Fund supported annually. Because of this support I was invited to New York to sit in the recording studio and witness Kiri Te Kanawa and José Carreras recording the album *West Side Story* under the baton of Leonard Bernstein.

I did not take for granted this exhilarating opportunity to observe firsthand these artists at work, and the afternoon was unforgettable. During the rehearsal of "Tonight," Mr. Bernstein stopped the proceedings, and turning to the cellists, said, "Celli, you're coming in a measure too soon. Try it again." They tried it again, and once again he halted the orchestra. "Celli, too soon."

One of the cellists, holding up the score and pointing, said, "No, Maestro, we are coming in here just as the music says."

Bernstein looked at it and replied, "I wrote it. You erase it."

These moments—witnessing artists in the creative process, screening rough cuts of new work, listening to talented people articulate the style and feel of a proposed project—were the true rewards of the job and the high points of my working life in Washington DC.

26

Feeling the "Old Washington Squeeze"

In Washington, if you get five or six years in a top position, that's major success. In time, the natural evolution of the political process takes over and the new crowd comes in to have their say . . . for a while.

I had to go when in 1988 the Corporation for Public Broadcasting board of directors was now dominated by Ronald Reagan appointees. Like all good Republicans, they preferred the hierarchal business model of hiring a president for the corporation and giving him complete authority over the workings of the company. They did not understand that individual program decisions to provide substantive, creative television programming cannot be accomplished by committee. Ultimately, these decisions should be made, and for eight years were made, by one person—the program fund director, after listening to thoughtful advice from staff and many other sources and after getting to knowing the quality of the producers.

Further, the board was uncomfortable with a program fund director who controlled over 40 million dollars per year, and therefore had more power than they did. Programming was back on the front burner for board discussion and consideration. This brought to an end Robin Fleming's creative idea to give a program fund director sole authority over program funding decisions, and it diminished the protective "heat shield" between those independent decisions and the opinions of a politicized board. From that moment on, the integrity of the funding decisions of the Corporation for Public Broadcasting was compromised, and the effectiveness of program funding at CPB was, in my opinion, seriously damaged. During those eight years from 1980 to 1988, the Program Fund was a major player and catalyst in creating much of public broadcasting's most enduring work.

I knew it was time to say goodbye to this patriotic theme park on the Potomac and think about the next chapter. I was on my way out, and I had no regrets. Washington, CPB, the independents, and PBS had all been good to me and given me six exciting years of professional and personal growth, which in Washington DC is a pretty good run.

Those of us who were there at the beginning of this idea of "education via television" in the early 1950s have to admit that the dream called public television has been only partially fulfilled. We were on our way in the 1970s and 1980s when we had adventurous producers giving us innovative work such as *The Great American Dream Machine*, program managers who weren't afraid to broadcast *Steambath*, when a regular staple of PBS offerings were dramas in *American Playhouse*, *Hollywood TV Theatre*, and *American Short Story*. Importantly, because financing of public television is always central, we were embraced by sophisticated audiences, public service–minded foundations who were interested in funding more than their own specific agendas, and, in large measure, a sympathetic Congress. But then, our nation was less conservative, less polarized, and far less divided than we were later to become, and we weren't in the process of replacing our distinct American culture with a lesser one.

The necessary autonomy from politics and stable, adequate

funding are still the major challenges for public broadcasting. After fifty years we find ourselves in the twenty-first century, and we have yet to create a comparable broadcasting service funded by the people as exemplified by the BBC in Britain and the NHK in Japan, and our citizens are not as well served as theirs.

We have endured congressional and administration leadership, including some in key positions at the Corporation for Public Broadcasting, who have hidden behind smokescreens calling for "balance" and "fairness," and for an end to "liberal press bias." These individuals have endeavored to deprive public broadcasting of adequate, and in some instances, all federal funds, thus helping, with some hoping, to ensure its demise.

And a major part of this missed opportunity lies with the White House. The first board of directors of CPB, appointed by President Lyndon Johnson, was a truly distinguished, bipartisan group of Americans representing business, science, education, and the arts. Had this initial level of appointees been sustained by subsequent presidents, we would have a more effective, important, and distinctive public broadcasting service in America today.

In too many cases partisan political appointees have taken their seats at the board table of the Corporation for Public Broadcasting determined to serve "their" president or party. Many appointees had no knowledge of broadcasting or education, and more detrimentally, had little understanding or acquaintance with the concept of a noncommercial public broadcasting service. These appointments over the years have not served America's public broadcasting interests nor our citizens.

Even so, public broadcasting in America is today more important to the country than it ever was. Look at the TV listings in the newspaper, and a judicious eye will quickly note that the public broadcasting schedule continues to offer, night after night, more substance, greater intellectual and artistic diversity, and better viewing pleasure than any other broadcasting service in America.

The major series on public television remain today the standard for high-quality viewing. These singular national series—*Nova* (science), *American Experience* (history), *Frontline* (investigative documentary), *Great Performances* (the arts), *American Masters* (biography), and PBS *NewsHour*—combined with the talents of America's independent producers, represent the heart of the national public television service. It is essential, excellent programming, week in and week out.

There will always be a need for the people who do this work, who aim high. They will provide programs driven not by the profit motive but by the merit and importance of the subject matter. These will be talented producers who measure success by the impact their programs have on people and not solely by the number of people who watched at some given moment.

A few years from now, with all communications accessible through the computer and the Internet, there may be no need for PBS or NBC or CNN, although history shows us that when new technologies bring about change, they do not necessarily erase the old. There will always be a need for excellent, thoughtful, accurate news coverage and for programs that nurture the minds and sensibilities of the people—and which are available at whatever moment the individual wants it. Public media is just on the cusp of a new and promising future. The men and women who step up to do this work have limitless opportunities to make life better for people throughout the world.

27

The Peace Tree

After the Washington DC adventure I returned to Lincoln, the Nebraska ETV network, and the University of Nebraska, where again, thanks to Jack McBride, I assumed the position of station manager of KUON-TV and associate general manager of the network and professor of broadcasting in the College of Journalism. I taught "Government and the Media" and "International Broadcasting," both graduate-level courses. The government course was informed by the firsthand experience of living and working in Washington and the daily lessons I received about "how Washington works."

Students and others often ask me if I was discouraged by the push-pull tensions, the inside deals, or the rough hardball played in the offices and agencies of our government. My answer is a quick, spontaneous "absolutely not." The tireless, experienced, energetic, ambitious people, young and old, working in these vineyards are the hardest-working people I know. It is those tensions, from every side of the spectrum in politics and philosophy, that result in the compromises so necessary to the flourishing of our democracy and the life we enjoy in the United States.

As Mark Twain said, "Pick an age you like and stick with it," and I've followed his advice to the letter. I seldom tell anyone my age, not out of vanity but because I'm still working. I have only two assets to sell in the marketplace: my experience and knowledge, and my level of energy. I don't want to be put in the box people reserved for people my age.

The reality of aging began dawning on me in my role as a professor of broadcasting. Over the years I would use examples of great reporters like Edward R. Murrow and Eric Sevareid. In recent years the mention of the name Murrow was often met with unknowing stares from the students. This led me, during the first day of class in a new semester, to ask students what year they were born. When the responses were 1992 or 1993, I realize that, though just yesterday to me, this is when their world began and, like most people, students believe that everything important happened after they were born.

References to Edward R. Murrow, Fred Friendly, Dave Garroway, Carol Burnett, and Milton Berle were no longer useful. Keeping your teaching fresh, relevant, exciting, and useful is the primary challenge for every professor. When you get tired of reworking every lecture to bring it into the twenty-first century, or you discover you do not have the same enthusiasm for the material or for beginning again with that new crop of students, your instincts tell you that it is time to step aside. Still, in the fall, a part of me aches just a little to see the robust new crop of students overflowing the campus, and to know they are going to move energetically and successfully forward—without me.

When Jack McBride retired in 1996, I decided to get out of the way of Rod Bates, the new general manager, a position I had no desire to assume (and it should be noted that no one asked me to). I accepted a half-time position at Nebraska Educational Telecommunications and a half-time position in the programming department of PBS in Washington DC.

That looks fine on paper. The reality is that in this day of computers, e-mail, cell phones, iPods, and faxes, if you work half-time for two entities you end up working full-time for both. It's all about access, and this access to you is instantaneous regardless of location or distance. Daily, you're doing Nebraska work in Washington and Washington work in Nebraska. They both need you, whatever you're doing, *right now*.

This meant that I worked for Nebraska on Saturday (preparing for class), Monday, and Tuesday, and I worked for PBS Wednesday, Thursday, and Friday. I flew out of Lincoln Tuesday evening and back from Washington Friday evening. I enjoyed that commute, getting to know the United Airlines personnel along the way and piling up thousands of free miles.

I was amazed by the number of people who were commuting to their work in Washington from Chicago, and it made sense. Positions in Washington are often short-term, families need stability, and as I discovered during these flights, these Washington workers have homes, wives, husbands, children, and grandparents in Chicago, and often the commute is a successful solution.

More surprisingly, I regularly saw one couple at Chicago O'Hare when she was leaving for work in New York City and he was flying to his job in Washington. But they told me that each Wednesday night, one or the other of them would take the shuttle from either LaGuardia or Washington National so they could be together for dinner.

The Public Broadcasting Service hired me to research the television programming archives with a view toward showcasing the best of vintage PBS programs—treasures from the archives. This was a journey into the past as I read descriptions, made notes, and screened programs produced from the advent of PBS in 1971 and after. I enjoyed every minute, because these programs were all old friends.

Hidden in the vaults are great dramas, documentaries, and music and dance programs featuring the finest artists of the twentieth century. Judith Anderson is incomparable in *Medea*; William

Shatner and others are captivating in *The Andersonville Trial*. Leonard Bernstein, Mikhail Baryshnikov, and Liza Minnelli are worth a return visit in *Celebrating Gershwin*. Bill Moyers with Joseph Campbell in *The Power of Myth* and Henry Hampton's *Eyes on the Prize* are among the most important television programs ever produced.

Lamentably, today on PBS there isn't a single ongoing American drama series on the air. From 1971 to the early 1990s we regularly presented myriad dramas from NET *Playhouse, Hollywood TV Theatre,* or *American Playhouse,* and each season brought us independently produced plays like *The Belle of Amherst* with Julie Harris, *The Lathe of Heaven* with Bruce Davison, and Meryl Streep in Wendy Wasserstein's *Uncommon Women and Others*.

One of the singularly most popular dramas in the early days was Bruce Jay Friedman's *Steambath* with Valerie Perrine and Bill Bixby. Even in conservative Nebraska this play was by far the most talked about and viewed drama we broadcast in 1971. Today, sadly, PBS, or at least most of the stations, probably would not broadcast it at all. There are large factions of people in America who would protest a drama in which a Puerto Rican towel boy in a steam bath is ultimately revealed as "God," not to mention when a naked Valerie Perrine casually showers before the glazed eyeballs of Bill Bixby. This was a pungent, satirical comedy perfectly suited to the times. It was hilarious, insightful television for adults.

When this walk down public television's memory lane was concluded I turned in a report recommending the programs and series I felt would be welcome additions to the public station's program schedules. I envisioned a series from the past hosted by Lauren Bacall or some other icon from the stage or screen.

The afternoon mail in late 1998 brought a postcard with the invitation to apply for a Fulbright fellowship to teach overseas. After successfully completing that process, I left my half-time position at PBS while retaining my half-time position at NET and prepared to teach international television at National Chengchi University in Taipei, Taiwan. The University of Nebraska granted me a semester leave of absence, and I was eager to get on that plane and back to Asia.

The students in Taipei lived up to the clichés you've heard about Chinese culture. They were serious young people, never taking their eyes off me while listening intently to the lectures. They were never late or absent, and when the bell rang they did not leap for the door until I gave the signal. Assignments were completed on time, the quality of work accomplished was high, and they generously kept me well supplied with hot tea during the afternoon classes.

Near the end of the semester I mentioned that I knew they revered age and education, and I thanked them, because apparently I was sufficient enough in both to warrant the most respectful courtesy. They were sharp, intelligent, energetic, ambitious, eager men and women. It was a joy to be with them. These students brought a sense of purpose, determination, and discipline to their educational pursuits, which made teaching a daily pleasure. I've heard it said that the twenty-first century belongs to the Chinese. Based on these young people, if that happens, I understand why. They are bringing the same high level of energy, willingness to work, and discipline to their lives that we in an earlier time brought to the growth of America.

The Fulbright fellowship gave me the opportunity after twenty-seven years to return to Vietnam. The American embassy in Hanoi, working with our consulate in Ho Chi Minh City, had made all the arrangements for me. As the plane was circling Tan Son Nhut airport I was excited to see the streets and trees of Saigon after all these years. I remembered the admonition given me by friends who, after having been in the Peace Corps, returned years later to where they had been assigned. They said not to be disappointed if there were no signs you had ever been there. A number of friends had recounted how they had returned to their Peace Corps country, and the village where they'd lived was gone, the well they had dug was no longer there. Everything was erased except the memories.

I wondered if the TV station was still there. The early experiences and memories came rushing forward, and I was both eager and apprehensive to contemplate stepping back into this place that had so changed and enhanced my life.

When I stood up in the aisle to leave the plane, my legs gave out for an instant and the man next to me took my arm. I thanked him, replying that my problem was more emotional than physical, and I walked into the bright, ripe air of old Saigon which was now Ho Chi Minh City.

Number 9 Hung Thap Tu, the address of the station we started in 1966, was now Number 9 Minh Thi Khai Street, and although a fire in 1986 had virtually destroyed the original building, the Vietnamese rebuilt it on the exact same floor plan and in the same space. In fact, when I was in the manager's office with the two large windows overlooking the studios, it was precisely as I remembered it from the 1970s.

My appointment with the general manager of Channel 9, Mr. Pham Khac, was set for three o'clock. I was escorted into the large conference room on second floor, given a cup of hot tea, and left alone to absorb my surroundings. The walls were a vivid yellow, and looking down on me was a large, almost handsome, smiling portrait of Ho Chi Minh. I looked at that picture and said to myself, not with disrespect, "You old son-of-a-bitch, you won."

Mr. Khac was escorted in by Ms. Truong Kieu Nga, the interpreter, from the Foreign Relations Department. Mr. Khac, in a khaki uniform without insignia, was polite, extremely reserved, and formal. He answered my questions about what happened at the station when the Liberation Army took over Saigon, what programs they acquire from Europe, and how are they are supported financially. He did all of this, but perfunctorily, with brief, almost curt, responses. It was obvious that he was meeting with me because someone in his government told him he had to.

I learned that the station was off the air only one night after liberation, that most of the outside program acquisitions came from Europe and consisted primarily of music, nature, and science programs, and that there was never enough money to adequately support what they wanted to do. Still, I was not getting through to him in the personal way I had hoped. He was doing his duty, and we were both having a rather dull time of it.

After half an hour of this frustration, I said to him that in 1970 I was working right here in this same building trying to teach the THVN staff how to run a TV station, and I asked what he was doing in 1970. He was somewhat younger than I, but not much. Looking directly at me for the first time, he said, "Mr. Hull, in 1970 I was a soldier in the People's Revolutionary Army stationed in Tay Ninh Province just twenty miles from here." He made the point that the Americans believed the enemy were troops coming down to the South from North Vietnam, but the People's Revolutionary Army were all southerners, like himself, who were fighting with the north for their country.

"In 1970, Mr. Hull, you and I were on opposite sides."

So that's it, I thought. I responded in all sincerity by saying, "Mr. Khac, that's right. But I knew even then that what you and your countrymen wanted was to have one Vietnam with the north and south united. You now have one Vietnam, and I am happy for you."

The ice melted, the man relaxed, took me by the arm, and gave me the seventy-five-cent tour of the premises. With joy I watched part of a drama being produced—the old *cai luong*, the traditional singing theater, was as popular as ever. In another studio, students were learning aerobics and would be clearing the studio in a few minutes for the second English-language news cast of the day. In addition, he informed me, there are two newscasts in French, two in Vietnamese, and two in Chinese each day. I was impressed by how well they were attempting to serve their audiences.

Later, one of the producers agreed to meet me over coffee at my hotel, and through him I learned that the newscasts were heavily censored to reflect the government's official position and that all news people practice "self-censorship" every day. They were cautious broadcasters. They had to be.

Mr. Khac explained to me that many television programs, particularly those imported from the West, simply did not work in Vietnam. This comment was congruent with my earlier experiences working there. Unless material is given an understandable context, the cultural differences are sometimes simply too great to allow some foreign material to effectively communicate. Back in 1966 my Vietnamese coworkers and students watching American programs broadcast on Armed Forces Radio and Television would remark, "Here in Vietnam we leave the whole front of the house open all day long. Anyone can walk in or out anytime, that's the Vietnamese way. You Americans always go inside and close the door, keeping everyone out, even locking the door in the daytime. Why is that?"

Also, they found our food very complicated. Almost incredulously they wondered how we could go through that ritual of sitting at a long table with everyone eating food off just their own plate. As they said, "This is very alien to Vietnamese." The programs that translated best to Vietnamese culture were most often music and performance programs, particularly from France, and those documentaries with single-voice narration. Foreign dramas are often not successful because too much of the way of life has to be explained.

But this day, and I resist feelings of pride, I felt gratified that I had played a role in initiating a television broadcasting station on this remarkable Asian peninsula that was alive, growing, and of significant service to the people of Vietnam.

As we were walking across the compound to the gate, I noticed the old guard post was still standing. Back in the 1970s, this round concrete mini-tower held two military men each commanding a machine gun, one looking up the street and one looking down. In any insurgency the broadcasting stations are often the first places to be captured.

But there was more. Growing out of this structure, which was now serving as a huge flowerpot, was a magnificent "flambeau rouge" tree. The flame tree. In the spring it bursts into bright red colors, and it's sentimentally called "the students' tree" because it flowers just as students are leaving to go back to their homes in the spring. I was admiring it when Mr. Khac, in a quiet, measured way, said, "That's my peace tree. I planted it when I took over here at the station in 1975."

I thanked him and walked away with a happy heart.

Often, after working late hours, which is the rule in television, I walk into studio number 1 at the Nebraska public broadcasting building and think back on the people who have come here to be on a program. I hear the voices of Henry Fonda, Walter Cronkite, Dick Cavett, Irene Worth, George McGovern, Mari Sandoz, Helen Stauffer, John Neihardt, Ernie Chambers, Frank and Maxine Morrison, Audun Ravnan, Margaret Mead, Ruby Dee, Bill Moyers, Cyril Ritchard, Bob Devaney, Tom Osborne, Yehudi Menuhin, Robert Knoll, and countless musicians, politicians, teachers, and other accomplished people. They danced across our stage, said their words, sang their songs, taught their classes, played their compositions, and without question, inspired and encouraged countless people to do better, to try harder, to live more fully, and to enjoy it. While working with these people and realizing these faces and voices should be saved for future generations, I created the "Nebraska Videotape Heritage Library." We now have over fifty years' worth of Nebraska people and history preserved in the NET Archives.

If you find work that you eagerly run to every day—that is happiness. And that has been my fortune since that first day I set foot in the studio of KSWO-TV, Lawton, Oklahoma, and introduced Fort Sill's *Front and Center* television program in 1953.

When leaving Saigon in 1967, I remember wondering what I wanted the last half of my life to be. Now, in 2011, after recently attending an international television conference, I settled into a familiar chair in the bar of the Peninsula Hotel in Hong Kong and contemplated, over a fine French pinot noir, my feelings about this last portion of my life. Only one thought came to mind:

I wish I had fifty more years.